PLAYING TO WIN

PLAYING TO WIN

THE DEFINITIVE BIOGRAPHY OF JOHN FARNHAM

JEFF APTER

NERO

Published by Nero,
an imprint of Schwartz Publishing Pty Ltd
Level 1, 221 Drummond Street
Carlton VIC 3053, Australia
enquiries@blackincbooks.com
www.nerobooks.com

Copyright © Jeff Apter 2016
Jeff Apter asserts his right to be known as the author of this work.

ALL RIGHTS RESERVED.
No part of this publication may be reproduced, stored in a retrieval system,
or transmitted in any form by any means electronic, mechanical, photocopying,
recording or otherwise without the prior consent of the publishers.

National Library of Australia Cataloguing-in-Publication entry:
Apter, Jeff, author.
Playing to win: the definitive biography of John Farnham /
Jeff Apter.
9781863958806 (hardback)
9781925435269 (ebook)
Farnham, John, 1949 –
Rock musicians — Australia — Biography.
Singers — Australia — Biography.
781.66092

Jacket design by Peter Long
Text design and typesetting by Tristan Main
Cover photograph: Robert Cianflone / Staff / Getty Images
Endpapers: Melinda Nagy/Dreamstime

Printed in Australia by McPherson's Printing Group.

CONTENTS

Introduction: 'If You're Not Standing, You Have No Soul' ... 1

1. Blue-Collar Balladeer ... 7
2. When Darryl Met Johnny ... 23
3. The Loneliest Number ... 39
4. The Prince of Panto ... 47
5. Wedding Bell Blues ... 61
6. A Fading Star ... 73
7. Help Is on Its Way ... 87
8. Uncovered and Reborn ... 97
9. Playing to Win ... 105
10. Reined In ... 117
11. Whispering Jack Phantom ... 139
12. Back on Top ... 159
13. Aussie of the Year ... 175
14. Spokesman for the Common Man ... 185

15. Burn for You ... 201

16. Riding the Rails ... 217

17. Facing Fifty ... 227

18. How Many Last Times? ... 247

19. Warm Undies and Shameless Nostalgia ... 259

20. Good Deeds and Close Ties ... 271

Epilogue: Jack's Back ... 281

Discography ... 285
Acknowledgements ... 297
Bibliography ... 301

For Diana, who found her own voice

INTRODUCTION

'If You're Not Standing, You Have No Soul'

ARIA Music Awards
21 October 2003
Sydney Super Dome

John Farnham has never had much time for cool. It's fair to say that the closest he's come was during his mid-1980s *Whispering Jack*–era resurrection, when he sported hair even bigger than his voice, and dressed like a rock-and-roll stormtrooper, with a shinbone-length Driza-Bone and upturned collar on full and bold display. Yet even that look was more yuppie than trailblazer. Nope, throughout the bulk of his six-decade-long career, Farnham's kept cool at a reasonable distance. He's always been family-friendly, G-rated, likeable. Daggy. And hugely successful, at least most of the time.

By 2003, deep into his fifties, he was part of the old guard, the music biz establishment. A survivor, an ageing sex symbol your gran would welcome in for tea and biscuits. But he was an uneasy fit at a time when every charting act seemed to boast awkward, multi-syllabic names like Powderfinger, Regurgitator or Silverchair and promote themselves as so damned ethical they'd rather live in a

INTRODUCTION

garret and focus on their art than 'sell out' by going commercial. These acts treated success on Farnham's scale – millions of records sold, many arenas filled, Australia's favourite middle-aged son – with extreme caution. They were in it for the music, man. Or at least that's what they liked the public to think.

And I have to take some blame for perpetuating that narrow mindset. As a reporter for *Rolling Stone*, I was swept up in the cult of cool, even though my taste (at least behind closed doors) ran to the more commercial. I bandied about the words 'credibility' and 'art' as if they were sacred cows – sacred vows, even. I found as much joy in a Savage Garden melody as I did in a You Am I rock-and-roll onslaught, but I wasn't being paid to celebrate my dagginess. So I wrote about the hip and the edgy. The alternative. The anti-everything. Bores, some of them, truth be told.

Yet I never missed the chance to attend the ARIAs. Sure, the next day I'd moan about how cheesy it all was, how the deserving acts went unrewarded, how the obvious won out, once again – blame the industry, so commercial and glitzy, blah, blah, blah. It was still fun, though. I guess I'd never quite shaken off my uncool suburban roots. I was always quietly thrilled to be surrounded by pop stars and rock heroes, household names – some of whom even knew me. Fancy that!

But I didn't anticipate what would happen at the 2003 awards. It might have been the night of nights for siren Delta Goodrem, but it would be remembered for something else altogether.

Towards the business end of proceedings, Rove McManus, the night's MC, a perennial nice guy – TV's very own Farnham – stepped forward.

INTRODUCTION

'When it comes to our next performer,' he gushed, 'they don't come bigger than this.' He listed Farnham's ARIA stats – 20 wins to date – before gushing some more. 'The name "legend" gets thrown around quite a bit, but this man is certainly deserving of the title.' Earlier that night Farnham had been inducted into the ARIA Hall of Fame. He was a lifetime achiever and he'd just been handed pop's equivalent of a retiree's gold watch.

The stage lights dimmed and the crowd started to make some noise, clearly excited, but not entirely sure what to expect. There stood Farnham, in a sharp black shirt and strides, his fair hair swept back, looking good. Conservative, a tad paunchy, but still pretty damned good. Brett Garsed was to his right, strumming an acoustic guitar. Together they began Farnham's signature song, 'You're the Voice', but in unplugged mode, low-key.

'We're all someone's daughter,' Farnham sang, gently urging the crowd to get involved, 'we're all someone's son.'

It was hardly a show-stopping start – but everyone in the room got the sense that the singer had something up his sleeve. Like a volcano starting to rumble, the band kicked in: drums, bass, keys, electric guitar, strings. Farnham sang more strongly, passionately, and the audience started to push towards the front of the stage. It was a rare sight: ARIA crowds, or at least the industry part of the audience, never got too engaged. Uncool. Not a good look. But tonight was different.

Two bagpipers, kilts and all, appeared on stage, blowing their lungs raw as 'The Voice' built and built and built. (They were actually jamming the bagpipe riff from AC/DC's 'It's A Long Way to the Top (If You Wanna Rock 'n' Roll)'.) The crowd was really in the moment

INTRODUCTION

now; even all the jaded industry hipsters in the pricey seats were on their feet. Farnham's long-time manager, friend and true believer, Glenn Wheatley, beamed a smile at his star. Behind Wheatley, Ian 'Dicko' Dickson, flavour of the month thanks to his role as head prefect on *Australian Idol*, danced a crazy jig, lost in the song.

On stage, Farnham powered on. 'Woah-ohh, oh-ohh, oh-oh-oh-oh,' he bellowed, and the audience roared right back at him. Then even more pipers, perhaps a dozen in all, invaded the stage, kilts and pipes everywhere you looked, and the audience lifted the roof right off the building. It was pandemonium. Blissful chaos.

In the crowd, the evening's winners and grinners were up and singing, forgetting all about the pointy statuettes and high-end booze on their table. Right now, everybody – from the men of Powderfinger to the indie trio of Something for Kate, from afro-ed pop star Guy Sebastian to Best Male Artist Alex Lloyd and golden girl Goodrem – was a Farnham fan. They stood, awestruck, gazing at Farnesy. Smiles lit up the faces of the crowd, which had formed a mini moshpit at the foot of the stage. They knew it was a special moment. Farnham responded with a signature microphone-stand twirl, throwing it high into the air and catching it with the ease of an Aussie slips fieldsman. He cracked a broad smile – *Shit, glad I didn't drop it* – and brought the song home.

As the band crashed and clanged to a thunderous close behind him, the crowd went berserk. Everyone in the room – and there were many thousands squeezed into the Super Dome – was screaming, yelling, clapping, stomping. The applause, the sheer noise, was deafening, and continued for what seemed, at least from the floor, to be longer than the song itself. Farnham beamed, saluting the crowd, before waving his arm and mouthing 'the band', generously bringing them into the celebrations.

Finally, McManus strode out onto the stage and vigorously pumped Farnham's hand. 'If you're not standing – in this room, or at home,' McManus shouted above the din of the audience, who didn't plan to stop cheering anytime soon, 'you have no soul.'

In just a few minutes, Farnham had finally bridged the credibility gap, turning even the most image-conscious muso into a gushing fan. He may not have been the coolest guy in the room, but John Farnham sure knew how to bring the house down.

1

BLUE-COLLAR BALLADEER

As birthplaces of Oz pop icons go, nowhere seems a less likely origin than Dagenham, East London. This Dickensian slice of blue-collar England might be capable of producing a captain of industry, perhaps even a sporting great, but an Australian pop star? Not bloody likely. Only 15 kilometres separate Dagenham from the City of London, but in 1949 Australia was another planet altogether.

Yet John Peter Farnham – whose surname means 'the ferny place where the river bends', probably referring to the town of Farnham in Surrey – came to be one of Dagenham's more famous sons – and an Aussie icon. His British-born father (also named John) was one of many thousands employed at the Ford motor plant, the most imposing sight in this very working-class town. John Sr was a pipe fitter. At its peak, the Ford plant, spread over 55 acres, consumed four million square feet of factory space, employed 40,000 workers and, during seven decades of operation, churned out some 11 million vehicles. And in postwar England, you lived where the work was to be found.

While this all sounds very grim – even the town's name smacks of grittiness – Dagenham was something of a boomtown around the time of Farnham's birth on 1 July 1949. It was the epicentre of England's industrial south-east. As well as the thriving Ford plant, the local docks were home to many then-thriving companies: Union Cable, Briggs Motor, Solvent Productions, Pritchett and Gold, Kelsey-Hayes Wheels Co. The nearby Barking Power Station employed another 1800 workers. If there was a golden age for Dagenham, this was it.

The area would produce some successful entertainers: Brian Poole, who, with his band The Tremeloes, hit big in 1963 with 'Do You Love Me', and Sandie 'Puppet on a String' Shaw, who, with Lulu, Dusty Springfield and Cilla Black, led the vanguard of successful female pop singers in the mid to late 1960s. All these acts first made it big in the UK, but John Farnham Jr's future lay elsewhere.

He may have been a Dagenham local, residing at 69 Waldergrave Road, but John was a Cockney by birth. He was born 'within the sound of Bow Bells', the bells of St Mary-le-Bow in the Cheapside district of the city of London. John's mother, Rose (née Rose Lilian Pemberton), a dark-haired, slender woman, quiet and reserved, who was attractive in an understated way, was forced to give birth to her first child at Mile End Hospital in Stepney: there simply weren't enough beds in the hospital at Dagenham, which says something about this fertile postwar period. Rose took one look at her five-pound one-ounce son and declared him a 'gorgeous baby'. John inherited his soft, almost feminine features from his mother – and his hefty ears from his robust, solidly built dad. Over time, John, whose blond hair grew out wildly as a baby, was joined by sisters Jean and Jaquiline (Jackie). His brother, Steven, was born in Australia.

John's early days were the stuff of a typical working-class Londoner: Dagenham provided his first object of desire ('a girl with beautiful red hair', as the adult John would recall), his first rejection (same girl) and his first whiff of danger – he and a mate would sometimes play under a railway bridge, dangerously close to the tracks. John was a lively kid, well mannered but with a worrying smoking habit, which he picked up at the age of five. John cut a hole in one of his books to hide his ciggies and matches from his parents.

During a childhood bout of pneumonia, John was given a record player by his Uncle Alf to stave off boredom. 'Here, take this,' said Alf, handing John a 78 record of American Jim Reeves' treacly ballad 'He'll Have to Go', a huge global hit in 1960. Bedridden and bored, John played the record over and over, eventually wearing it out. Alf also taught John a few basic guitar chords on a cheap plastic four-string, John's first guitar. As musical tuition went, this was pretty much it for the sandy-haired, jug-eared John Jr.

One day he heard Paul Anka's hit ballad 'Diana' on the radio. 'That's it,' John said to himself while strumming his guitar. 'That's a song I can play.' He learnt the basics of Anka's 'Diana' and other popular songs of the day from Tommy Steele and The Everly Brothers. Over time, they'd all become big influences on John. He'd sing them at family get-togethers, but wouldn't dream of performing at school. Once, invited by a teacher to sing, he ran out of the school hall and scarpered all the way home. Stage fright hit him hard.

Alf wasn't the only musically inclined Farnham. John's grandfather blew a mean penny whistle and was also a dab hand with the squeezebox. At family gatherings he'd sprinkle some sawdust on the floor and improvise a lively soft-shoe shuffle. John looked on, seriously impressed. A song-and-dance man!

There seemed no reason that the Farnham family wouldn't follow in the footsteps of their fellow hardworking East Londoners: find a job, have some kids, settle into the neighbourhood and stay there until retirement. Get buried nearby. Next. As one dock worker for Samuel Williams & Sons said of the time, 'Life was a bowl of cherries in them days. I never ever thought I'd leave. Started at 14, retired at 65.'

But one day at the Ford plant, John Sr had a chance conversation with two expat Aussies. 'You should go to Australia,' they told him. 'The sun shines every day.'

The Australian government, in its desire to bump up the postwar population and supply labour for the country's various booming industries, had introduced what was known on bureaucratic paperwork as the Assisted Passage Migration Scheme. (No wonder it was colloquially shortened to the 'ten-pound Pom' scheme.) It was open to all British subjects. The price of entry was, funnily enough, 10 quid, which subsidised the cost of travel by sea. As an added bonus, all kids travelled free.

About one million immigrants took full advantage of this and similar schemes, including the Gibb brothers (better known as the Bee Gees), one Redmond Symons (guitarist of shock-rockers Skyhooks) and the families of businessman Alan Bond, Hollywood hunk Hugh Jackman, pop star Kylie Minogue and prime ministers Julia Gillard and Tony Abbott.

A number of John's uncles and aunts had already signed on for the scheme, planning to leave grey and drizzly Dagenham for this enticing faraway place. Duly encouraged, John Sr, Rose and the kids booked passage on the ocean liner SS *Orsova*, bound for Melbourne via the Suez Canal, with pit stops in Bombay, Colombo, Penang, Singapore, Fremantle and Adelaide (the *Orsova* usually then continued all the way to the US west coast and, eventually, to Madeira).

John Jr was 10 years old when he and his clan and their 1500 fellow passengers boarded the ship at Southampton docks. Everything his family owned was contained in a few tea chests.

Young John got up to some hijinks on board the 220-metre-long ship, including one terrifying stunt that would stay with him for the rest of his life. He'd befriended another kid, and they'd been given rubber tomahawks with which they ran amok and caused mayhem. John had left his in the ship's play area, which was closed for the day; to retrieve it he needed to walk the ship's rail, the sea churning beneath him. At one point he slipped and nearly fell, just managing to hang on to the rail. 'I thought I was dead,' John recalled. When he retrieved the tomahawk he threw it into the ocean – too many bad memories.

Upon their arrival in 1959, the Farnhams learnt why Australia was called the Lucky Country. They were fortunate to avoid the migrant camps set up for the so-called New Australians, the many immigrants flooding into the country from eastern and central Europe and the UK. John's Aunt Mary was already settled in Joan Court in Noble Park, a humble slice of Victorian suburbia, and the newly arrived Farnhams moved in with her. Flinders Street and the bustling metropolis of Melbourne, the site of the Olympic Games just three years earlier, lay only an hour away on the train from Noble Park. Melbourne's population was growing fast, soon to top the two million mark. Its cultural mix was also rapidly expanding.

The Farnhams couldn't have picked a better city in which to settle.

John Sr got work at the recently opened Ford plant in Campbellfield, and soon progressed to a better job at a local plastic works. John Jr, however, had some trouble acclimatising.

'The first thing I remember [about Australia],' he once said in an interview, 'was wondering about all the sayings.' John was accustomed to terms like 'smashing', but what the hell did 'grouse' mean? And why did the local kids tell him to go to 'nicky woop'? Where was that? What happened when you got there? John was just as stunned when his aunt instructed him not to flush the toilet each time he used it – 'number twos only, please' – in order to save paying for the water. *Pay for water?*

Avoiding the migrant hostel was one stroke of luck, but something even more substantial was about to happen to the Farnhams. John was lying on the couch, sick, when the phone rang. His mother ran over to him, a huge smile lighting up her face. 'We've won the lottery!' she cried. Rose and an aunt had bought tickets in the state lottery, which paid the winner a hefty 10,000 quid – $200,000-plus in today's money. John tried to get his head around the news, but the numbers were simply too huge for him to comprehend. Ten thousand pounds? Seriously?

'Can you take me to the bank?' he asked his mum. 'I'd love to see all that money.'

Ever the pragmatists, the Farnhams used their windfall sensibly, buying two lots and building adjoining brick-veneer three-bedders, one for John Sr, Rose and their kids, the other for the grandparents. Noble Park – or Australia, for that matter – had never looked so good.

School, however, was another thing altogether for John Jr. He didn't last long at the local primary school, colliding head on with a headmaster by the name of Knight. 'He was deadly nightshade, a real ratbag,' John said. 'I think he had something against English kids.'

On his first day at school, which he'd recall as 'the worst of my life', John Jr broke a major Knight rule by speaking out of turn. John was only responding to another student, who'd farted and then snorted, 'I've shit myself!' But Knight had his target.

'You,' Knight said to John, the token Pom, 'come out here.'

As John timidly made his way to the front of the class, Knight produced a rubber strap. Three lashes on his hand later, John slunk back to his chair, his hand throbbing, his spirit broken. He was humiliated. School in Dagenham was nothing like this.

John went home, reported what had happened and was shifted to the recently opened Lyndale Primary School. The biggest problem there was confronting the heavy traffic while crossing busy Dandenong Road.

In the mid to late 1950s, Australia, at least in matters of entertainment, was undergoing a rowdy revolution. A wild-eyed Sydney black sheep by the name of Johnny O'Keefe – tagged the 'Wild One', in reference to both his onstage manner and his hit single of the same name – had been raising rock-and-roll hell with his band the Dee Jays in an old tin shed called the Sydney Stadium, blowing such international stars as Bobby Darin and Ricky Nelson right off the stage, and winning the admiration of Bill Haley and Little Richard. He'd even scored a record deal with local label Festival Records, a massive achievement. The mild-mannered Col Joye, a lanky, Brylcreemed nice-guy from Sydney's western suburbs, was also winning over the masses, cutting such hits as 1959's '(Rockin' Rollin') Clementine' and 'Oh Yeah Uh Huh', both chart-toppers in Melbourne and Sydney at a time when the pop charts were not a national event. TV shows *Bandstand* (which featured Joye prominently) and *Six O'Clock Rock* (hosted by O'Keefe) were doing for Australian music what *Countdown* would achieve in the 1970s: gaining recognition for local acts on the rise and building new audiences all over the country. Joye and O'Keefe were quickly becoming our first true homegrown rock-and-roll stars. In time they'd both play their part in John's own musical journey.

Getting locally produced music heard on the radio, though, was another matter. When an Australian record finally found its way into the hands of massively influential DJs such as Melbourne's Stan Rofe or Sydney's Bob Rogers and John Laws, it still had to compete with the best of the rest of the world: American hip-swiveller Elvis Presley, harmonising siblings The Everly Brothers, Britain's bachelor boy Cliff Richard. The persistent O'Keefe did manage to break through with 'She's My Baby', a number-one hit in February 1960, but that and Joye's two hits were rare Australian exceptions. Coincidentally, cardigan-wearing Jim Reeves, John Farnham's favourite from his days in Dagenham, usurped O'Keefe only a few weeks later, with – you guessed it – 'He'll Have to Go', a hit here some time after its initial release.

John watched and listened to Joye and O'Keefe and the rest with what could best be called a dabbler's interest: the idea of a career in music wasn't something he'd considered. To John, at least for the moment, singing was a lark, a hobby, a bit of fun. He did, however, find two like-minded kids at Lyndale High School, Steven and

Phil; between the three of them they knew enough guitar chords to strum their way through Elvis's 'Wooden Heart' and the old chestnut 'He's Got the Whole World in His Hands'. Usually they'd play by themselves in the classroom during lunch, although they sometimes performed at school assemblies, a big step for John. Perhaps having his two mates nearby helped a bit with his stage fright.

John was moving into an awkward teenage phase. He was prone to chubbiness, and the kids at Lyndale High didn't hold back, calling him 'Fatty Farnham'. John would go home, close the door to his bedroom and stare in the mirror. 'Maybe they're right,' he'd think to himself. After all, he was no Charles Atlas. He had prominent features – lips and ears, especially – and an oval-shaped face. At school, unwilling to expose his legs, John would try and talk his way out of any sport that required wearing shorts. His lack of self-confidence bordered on the chronic. Amazing to think that within a few years he would be the biggest pop idol in Australia, rendering thousands of young women weak-kneed.

At the time of John's musical debut, however, the fastest rising star in Australia was a sharp-looking Melburnian by the name of Normie Rowe, who'd been championed by DJ Stan 'The Man' Rofe. In 1965 Rowe, still in his late teens, had blitzed the local charts with a rockin' reworking of 'It Ain't Necessarily So', the old Gershwin show tune. Rowe had a rebellious streak, too: he'd been holding down a day job training as a technician, while singing after hours in and around Melbourne. When his boss told him to get a 'respectable' haircut, Rowe scoffed and headed for the door. So much for regular employment. His pop-rebel reputation was further entrenched when Sydney radio station 2SM – owned by the

Catholic Church – slapped a ban on 'Necessarily So' for its supposedly sacrilegious lyrics. Bingo. A hit. Five hundred screaming girls were treated for hysteria during one particularly wild Rowe show.

An end-of-year fundraiser was coming up at Lyndale High and the organisers of the event decorated the school with banners proclaiming: 'He is coming.' In Melbourne at the time, the only person this could relate to, John and his fellow students concluded, was Normie Rowe, pop star and accidental iconoclast. John was as excited as his classmates: Normie was playing at Lyndale! Imagine that. This was about the biggest coup any teenager could hope for in the 1960s.

As the big day grew nearer, John spoke with the girls who were arranging the event.

'How'd you get Normie Rowe?' he asked. 'That's amazing.'

They looked at John quizzically. 'Normie Rowe? What are you talking about?'

John was confused. 'So who is coming?' he asked.

'You are,' they told him. 'You can sing; we've seen you do it.'

John was mortified. For one thing, he was dead keen to see Rowe sing – with his latest massive hit, 'Que Sera Sera', Rowe had given Doris Day the same treatment he had Gershwin. And John knew there was no way he could live up to the hype. What chance did he stand? He was no Normie Rowe. 'He is coming?' *Really?*

'I can't even tune a guitar,' John pleaded with them. 'I just can't do it.' He hid in the art storeroom until the organisers found him and dragged him to the stage.

The curtains parted to reveal a fearful Farnham. What ensued was one of John's shorter performances; the booing began even before he started to sing, and he slunk off stage.

'That really hurt me,' John admitted. 'It was a big letdown for me, for everybody.'

Although they're not likely to be admitted to the ARIA Hall of Fame anytime soon, a group known as The Mavericks played an important part in Oz pop history. Made up entirely by Lyndale High students – known simply as the two Mikes and the two Johns – the band provided John Farnham with a musical apprenticeship when they recruited him as their lead singer towards the end of 1964, his final year at school.

On weekends The Mavericks (also known as the MJs, a nod to their Christian names) played at local dances, school socials and pretty much anywhere they could swing a gig. John's audition for the band took place at the Lyndale shopping centre, about a mile from his home. There were two songs they all knew – that old faithful 'Wooden Heart', and 'Love Potion Number 9', a Lieber and Stoller song turned into a hit by The Clovers, then The Searchers – so they played those two a few times. In the crowd that day was Hans Poulsen, an expat Dane. Poulsen was a multi-instrumentalist, a dab hand with the balalaika and the bouzouki, and a member of Melbourne act the 18th Century Quartet. Poulsen, who harboured ambitions as a songwriter, was impressed by Farnham. It wouldn't be long before he would re-enter the singer's life.

The Mavericks spent much of their time in the Farnham family lounge room, which they used as a rehearsal space. As they played, Rose would sneak a peek at the local kids gathered out the front, watching The Mavericks through the window. John, now performing as Johnny, looked sharp in his winklepicker shoes. And no-one seemed to mind that he was forced to use a broomstick as his microphone stand: Noble Park had never had a neighbourhood rock band before.

Rose was bursting with pride for her eldest son. Johnny Farnham had his first true believer.

Johnny did have one thing in common with Normie Rowe: both were from solid working-class stock. While Rowe pursued a trade, at least until the infamous haircut incident, Johnny, fresh out of school, was apprenticed as a plumber to a family friend, Stan Foster, who ran a company named Caulfield Heating. Despite the family connection, Johnny still needed a streak of good fortune to get his apprenticeship papers. His maths results were poor; he only managed 49% in his final exam – and he needed a pass mark in maths to get the job. Johnny rode the train into the city to the Apprenticeship Commission, and found a sympathetic staffer, who changed his 49 to 59, winked, nodded towards the door and told Johnny, 'Go on, go.' The next day Foster collected Johnny in his Holden ute at the crack of dawn, ready for work.

Johnny worked hard. Being the apprentice, he was given most of the crap work (pun intended): anything toilet-related. 'When it came to toilets,' Johnny laughed, 'the apprentice was the one who always had to roll his sleeves up.' Literally. Johnny might have been one of Oz pop's earliest singing tradies, but he certainly wasn't the last: Ted Mulry, John Paul Young, Graeme 'Shirley' Strachan and Daryl Braithwaite, among others, all got a little dirt on their hands before becoming pop stars.

To Johnny, an apprenticeship seemed a logical starting point in life. Learn a trade, maybe meet a girl, buy a quarter-acre block with a mortgage, settle down, get a dog, have a brood of kids – Johnny had bought into the Great Australian Dream.

Yet music continued to hover on the fringes of his straight-arrow suburban life. Johnny was a big fan of highly rated Melbourne band Strings Unlimited – 'I idolised this group,' he would admit. If The Mavericks weren't working he'd usually head out to see Strings play. What he didn't know was that Hans Poulsen had mentioned him to the guys from Strings Unlimited. One night Johnny spotted Nick Foenander, the gun organist from Strings, in the audience of a Mavericks gig. They were playing a 21st party, for the princely sum of five quid – and free drinks. During a break, Foenander approached a starstruck Johnny. 'We'd love you to audition for the group. What do you reckon?'

Johnny was stunned – and torn. Loyalty was his default setting, and he didn't want to bail on The Mavericks, who'd given him his first real chance. But he was also a huge Strings Unlimited fan, and this was a massive opportunity.

'That's great,' Johnny finally replied, 'but I don't know what to do about the group I'm in.' Foenander told him to think it through and stay in touch.

Johnny ran home to speak with his parents. He ran so hard and was so puffed when he arrived that he staggered on entering the family kitchen. John Sr and Rose thought he was drunk – they'd caught him out a few weeks earlier after a rowdy party.

'Have you been drinking again?' they asked him. 'What's going on?'

'No, no, I'm sober,' Johnny insisted. 'But you won't believe what's happened. I've been asked to try out for Strings Unlimited.'

Johnny's parents knew this was more than just swapping one band of hopefuls for another. Strings Unlimited was a semi-professional outfit, performing several nights a week and drawing good crowds. What would happen if Strings had a hit of their own – how would that affect Johnny's day job? What might he have to sacrifice? After all, he was only 16.

Johnny's parents told him to do what he thought was best. But first Johnny needed to actually audition for Foenander and the rest of the group, drummer Peter Foggie, Joe Cincotta on bass and guitarists Stewart Male and Barry Roy. The required song was the blues standard 'House of the Rising Sun', which Farnham sang – 'pretty badly', as he recalls, his voice still shot from another Mavericks gig the night before – but convincingly enough to be invited to join the band. He accepted their offer. The big time.

Their first gig with Johnny, at a local pub, comprised 'Wooden Heart', 'Love Potion Number 9' *and* 'House of the Rising Sun', sung repeatedly until closing time. Clearly, he was moving up in the world – a three-song repertoire!

Unlike The Mavericks, Strings Unlimited had regular work, in and around the local suburban dance-hall circuit. Johnny would sing with the band for a thirty-minute bracket, then the band would do their instrumental thing for another half hour. As loyal as ever and figuring he didn't have to work as hard as them, Johnny agreed to pocket just $5 a night, while the others made $10.

One of their recurring gigs was at a venue in Mitcham, to the east of the city. The owner, a lively character named Leo, also ran a pastry business. His money-maker was a flaky delight known as Leo's sausage roll, which he shared with the band. Then he'd join Johnny on stage to belt out the Righteous Brothers' 'Unchained Melody'. It was one of Johnny's favourite gigs: he got to sing *and* he got fed.

Meanwhile, the band's manager, Bob McConnell, was talking a pretty big game.

'I've got you on *Kommotion*,' he promised the guys.

Kommotion, hosted by DJ Ken Sparkes from 3UZ, was something of a pop institution in Melbourne; it was the homegrown answer to America's *Shindig!* and the UK's *Top of the Pops*. The weekly program, screened on ATV0, featured local acts – it had boosted the careers of everyone from The Easybeats to Normie Rowe and The Masters Apprentices – as well as a handpicked troupe of 'groovers' who would mime to the hits of the day. Among *Kommotion*'s regulars was one Ian Meldrum – well before he became known as Molly, the mumbler in the hat. Strings, however, appeared on the show only once. They also made a single appearance on Kevin Dennis's *New Faces*, covering Nat King Cole's 'Pretend' and running second. One of the judges was less than impressed with Johnny: 'The singer needs lessons.'

Strings Unlimited had a residency at the Hampton Hotel on Port Phillip Bay. There, Johnny began to sing for the band's entire set, his confidence growing with each gig. His childhood pudginess long gone, Johnny now had the shining hair, plump lips and easy smile of a true pop idol. Any female fan with functioning eyes (and raging hormones) could see that.

The group also held down a weekly spot at the George Hotel in St Kilda. In its storied past the George, a striking edifice of Italian-influenced architecture, had been among the most opulent and popular hotels in the city, a favourite for wedding parties and other big social 'dos'. But by the mid-1960s the George was rougher and rowdier, more down at heel, with a clientele to match. Johnny sometimes had to fight his way off the stage. No-one had warned him about this. Johnny described the George as a 'blur of crazy people', quite the sight for an apprentice plumber from the 'burbs. When he wasn't defending himself, Johnny was making new female friends; he groped his first breast after a gig at the George. Yes, he was still a virgin.

Johnny was living life at full speed – working by day, singing by night, sleeping and eating somewhere in between, encountering the occasional friendly female. In 1966 he and the band made the state final of Hoadley's Battle of the Sounds, a hugely competitive national event that drew up to 500 hopefuls and offered the winners passage to the UK and a chance to perform there. Afterwards, Strings made a demo, and they also cut versions of The Beatles' 'I Feel Fine' and 'I'm Down' at the Rambler recording studio; some 45 rpm vinyls were pressed of the two tracks as a 'Rambler limited release'. The label read: 'Johnny Farnham Strings Unlimited'. Everyone in the band was very excited. A real record!

The Strings had an upcoming gig at a pub in rural Cohuna. Little did Johnny know he was set to meet a genuine kingmaker – and his life was about to be turned upside down.

2

WHEN DARRYL MET JOHNNY

Darryl Sambell was unlike any other manager doing the rounds of the Australian entertainment biz in the mid-1960s. For one thing, at twenty-two he was the youngest. Sambell was opinionated, colourful and driven; he craved success and lived as large as the stars he managed. As one client, future TV presenter Richard Wilkins, would admit, 'Darryl knew how to get you publicity, but he also knew how to send you broke in the process.'

Sambell was notoriously highly strung. Once — allegedly — he pulled a pistol on an unwelcome scribe. It was the type of stunt you might expect from such international music-biz heavyweights as British strongman Don Arden or American deal-maker Allen Klein, not some Aussie up-and-comer. Clearly, Sambell meant business.

Though something of a snappy dresser — Sambell had a taste for bling before the word even existed — his comb-over, black beard, hooked nose and sharp features made it clear he'd never be a pin-up himself. Sambell, a native of Gawler in South Australia, was searching for someone to turn into a star.

In early 1967 Johnny and Strings Unlimited arrived for their show in Cohuna, a township 275 kilometres north of Melbourne. Heading the bill was Bev Harrell, a petite blonde with a slyly sexy gap between her front teeth. Cut from the Little Patti mould, a sort of pop ingenue, she'd recently shifted from Adelaide to Melbourne and had been crowned Best Australian Female Vocal at the 1966 Australian Record Awards. Harrell was managed by Sambell. They were also engaged, although Sambell's sexuality was ambiguous, at best. Almost every article about Sambell mentioned his 'flamboyance', a 1960s euphemism for gay.

Johnny was seated at the drum kit when Sambell and Harrell entered the venue. One thing struck Sambell immediately: Johnny was way too good-looking to hide behind a kit, lost up the back of the stage.

'You aren't the drummer, are you?' Sambell asked him.

'No,' Johnny replied, a little startled.

'Thank goodness for that,' Sambell replied, as he and Harrell headed in search of the dressing room.

Later that night, when Johnny came off stage after finishing his set with the Strings, Sambell pulled him aside to share some advice.

'Next time you go on,' he half suggested, half directed, 'could you sing a fast song and then do a couple of slow songs?'

'Sure,' the ever-agreeable singer replied. He didn't realise Sambell was sizing up his ability as a performer. This was a surrogate audition.

After the show, Johnny shared a drink with Sambell and Harrell. It seemed to be nothing more than a friendly post-show get-together, fellow travellers hanging out. But Darryl had an agenda. He took Johnny's parents' phone number and promised to get in touch. Soon.

In his management of Harrell, Sambell showed true entrepreneurial flair. Soon after the release of Harrell's 1968 hit 'One in a Million', Sambell secured the singer her first TV spot, advertising Hills Hoists, of all things. ('It's a dream, this new easy wind-up action,' she recited through a plastered-on smile in the ad, a condescending 60 seconds that wouldn't stand the PC test today.) It was hardly the edgiest gig, but the exposure was priceless – pretty much every Aussie suburbanite craved a Hills Hoist, and people from Devonport to Darwin soon knew the name Bev Harrell. This was just the type of salesmanship Johnny could use.

By July 1967 there were big changes in Johnny's world: two of the guys in Strings Unlimited announced they'd had enough, and the band folded. Sambell, who was now sharing a Melbourne office with Ian Meldrum, heard the news and acted quickly, setting up a meeting with Johnny and his parents. It was time for Sambell to make his big pitch.

Sambell understood the zeitgeist: the late '60s in Australia was a golden age for attractive male pop stars. Pretty boy-next-door Ronnie Burns – a former window-dresser at Melbourne's Myer department store – had left his band The Flies and broken out as a solo act. In August he would be voted Top Male Singer in the *Go-Set* pop poll. Billy Thorpe, having struck gold with the big ballad 'Over the Rainbow', was numero uno, having recently hosted his own TV show, *It's All*

Happening!, a rare opportunity this side of the helter-skelter days of Johnny O'Keefe and *Six O'Clock Rock*. Normie Rowe was still dropping hit singles, although in late 1967 he would be called up for National Service (not so much a case of 'he is coming' as 'hope he's coming back'). Golden-haired Russell Morris was poised to leave his band Somebody's Image in pursuit of a solo career: timeless hits 'The Real Thing' and 'Sweet Sweet Love' would soon follow. Former DJ Johnny Young had scored major success with the singles 'Step Back' and 'Cara-Lyn', both as catchy as Asian flu. And good-looking duo Bobby (Bright) & Laurie (Allen) had a run of hits between 1965 and 1969.

Darryl Sambell knew that Johnny Farnham was prettier than all of them – and could sing, too. Sambell had big plans for Johnny: he sensed that Farnham could become an all-round entertainer, a sort of super-pop-star. He had the kind of easy good looks and natural, boyish charm that could break teenagers' hearts *and* win over their parents. That was rare. Sambell envisaged Johnny branching out into television, theatre, maybe even films. Anything was possible.

Not long after the demise of Strings, the Farnhams met with Sambell.

'I can make your son a star,' Sambell told John Sr and Rose. 'He'll be the biggest entertainer Australia's ever seen.'

It was a clash of cultures – Johnny's caring, solidly working-class parents, and livewire Sambell, decked out in a turtleneck and denim, talking a huge game. Johnny's father wasn't convinced by Sambell's pitch. His son was barely 18 and only two years into his apprenticeship. John Sr had a classic (and perfectly understandable) blue-collar mindset: what would happen if Johnny failed? What would he have to fall back on?

'I'd suggest you stick with your plumbing,' John Sr told his son when Sambell had left. 'But it's your decision.'

'Well,' replied Johnny, clearly divided, 'if I don't try, I'll never know.'

They struck a deal: if his musical career didn't work out, he'd return to the building site.

They spoke with Stan Foster, who said he could release Johnny from his apprenticeship but they'd first have to meet with the State Apprenticeship Board and get their approval. The committee examined Johnny's tech results, which were strong, and recommended a two-year period of leave. But Johnny's plumbing days were well and truly over.

If Johnny Farnham needed proof of Sambell's belief in his talent, it could be measured in miles. At the beginning of their working relationship, Sambell still had business in Adelaide, so every weekend he'd drive all the way to Melbourne, collect his new charge and then drive back to Adelaide for Johnny's gigs. Then he'd return Farnham to Melbourne, having covered a few thousand miles in the process.

During these early days with Sambell, while playing an Adelaide venue called St Clair, Johnny had a strange new experience: young girls screamed at him. Loudly.

'What was that about?' he asked Sambell on the long drive back to Melbourne. Sambell said nothing; he didn't have to. Things were working out nicely.

Sambell had scored Johnny an ad for the airline TAA. The jingle that Johnny recorded, a chirpy tune called 'Susan Jones', was pressed as a single and given out free to customers. Farnham received $40 for his work, but got no formal recognition – the song was credited to the Susan Jones Rock Five. The tune was cheesier than Kraft, but the record's producer, David Mackay, was impressed by Farnham. 'He's a pro,' Mackay told Cliff Baxter, the Victorian manager of EMI Records. 'And he can sing really well.' It didn't hurt, either, that he looked so damned good.

Cliff Baxter was in the market for a pop star. He'd missed the boat with Normie Rowe, who'd signed to Festival Records and duly become a solid-gold idol, and he had no intention of striking out again.

Sure enough, Johnny Farnham was signed to EMI in September 1967. And so the search began for the perfect song, the track that would introduce Johnny Farnham to the whole country.

Over the years, many people have laid claim to 'discovering' 'Sadie (The Cleaning Lady)', the song that would become both blessing and curse for Farnham. Darryl Sambell claimed he'd found it, as did Cliff Baxter. DJ Rofe, who invited Johnny to appear regularly on *Uptight*, the TV show Rofe hosted, insisted he was the man who found the chirpy ditty.

'Sadie' was written by a team of three Americans: Ray Gilmore, Dave White and Johnny Madara. White and Madara had a big hit in 1957 with another novelty tune, 'At the Hop', an American number one for Danny & the Juniors (later dusted off by Sha Na Na during their legendary 1969 Woodstock appearance). White and Madara had also composed the big ballad 'You Don't Own Me', a huge hit in 1963 for the 17-year-old Lesley Gore. They had real form penning pop hits for the teen market.

Not everyone was sold on 'Sadie' on first listen. Johnny's dad, for one, wasn't mad for it when Johnny played it down the phone to him from the studio where he was recording with Mackay. Anyone with functional ears could tell it was corny, lightweight. But it was also incredibly sweet and catchy.

Once the recording was ready in late 1967, salesman Sambell engaged overdrive. Not the kind of guy to neglect a cross-promotional opportunity, he reached out to vacuum-cleaner retailer Godfreys to have their popular mascot, Mr Jolly, on hand whenever Farnham was promoting 'Sadie'. There was even a credit on the record that read: 'Vacuum cleaner solo – Mr Jolly'. It seemed that everywhere Farnham sang the song – especially on TV – a troupe of dancing cleaning ladies was nearby, ready to spring into choreographed action.

A Fairfax newspaper report from December 1967 earmarked 'Sadie' as a hit and Johnny as 'the big pop singing sensation of 1968'. The hype was kicking in.

Sambell convinced the ABC's *This Day Tonight* to produce a short piece on his new charge. They tailed Farnham with a film crew as he encountered screaming female fans at a rural show. The narrative of the segment was typical of the time – the 'serious' media trying to make sense of the world of pop, zeroing in on this smiling, slightly awkward teenager who seemed to be on the verge of stardom. The journo's tone was smug and more than a little starchy.

'The current number-one pop idol is a Johnny named Farnham. We caught him in the middle of a country tour with Col Joye.'

Images of giddy fans flashed on the screen; then the camera cut to an interview with Johnny.

'This evening I have in the studio with me Johnny Farnham, the 'Sadie (The Cleaning Lady)' Man, who's in town tonight with the Bandstand of Stars show.'

Johnny mumbled a polite hello as the host asked about his new-found audience.

'My fans are wonderful,' Johnny managed to say, clearly nervous. 'Last night at Tamworth I had the sleeve of my shirt ripped out. But that's okay. The fans made me. I haven't been mobbed very often, I've only been in the business for a while, but confidentially I love it.'

And what about the girls?

'I was a plumber, you see, before this,' Johnny revealed, looking a bit bewildered, 'and still don't have the nerve to ask a girl to go out with me. There were four girls in my hotel room the other night – I nearly dropped when I walked in. I don't know how they got there.'

The pop life, in all its many guises, was opening Johnny's eyes wide. Plumbing was never like this.

By 31 January 1968, with the heavyweight support of DJ Rofe and Meldrum, who was working as a reporter on the pop scene for *Go-Set*, 'Sadie' topped the *Go-Set* national singles chart and stayed there for several weeks, in some impressive company. Also in the top 10 were The Beatles' 'Hello Goodbye', backed with 'I Am the Walrus' (not a bad double A-side single), The Monkees' 'Daydream Believer' and the Bee Gees' 'World'. Great pop songs. But 'Sadie', an ode to a humble washerwoman with 'red detergent hands' and little time for love, cleaned up.

It was a sweet victory for Cliff Baxter and EMI, and a whirlwind beginning to the solo career of Johnny Farnham. 'Sadie' was the label's fastest-selling single since Slim Dusty's laconic 'Pub with No Beer', and it would go on to sell 180,000 copies, eclipsing Rowe's 'Que Sera Sera' as the biggest Oz single of the '60s. It would hold the record of biggest-selling Australian single until 1979.

When 'Sadie' reached gold record status, a reception was held at Hosies Hotel, not far from Melbourne's Flinders Street station. In attendance was Arthur Major, the national chairman of EMI Records; his presence said a lot about the impact of this shining new star. When Johnny received his gold record, he broke down in tears. Within a few fast months, he'd gone from humble plumber's apprentice, knee-deep in crap, to – in the words of The Beatles – 'the toppermost of the poppermost'. Johnny was speechless.

'This week I had my first taste of money,' Johnny told a reporter soon after the event at Hosies. 'I went out and spent $50 – just like that!'

Johnny splashed out on a gift for Sambell and some jewellery for himself.

'It was beaut,' he stated, thrilled by his windfall.

As for Darryl Sambell, he continued to dote on Johnny, even washing and ironing his clothes when they were on the road, which was most of the time. This earned him a new nickname: from now on, *he* was 'Sadie'.

Johnny Farnham's wasn't the first career to be based upon the shaky foundations of a novelty song. It was a curse that stuck like mud to groups such as Herman's Hermits (for 'Mrs Brown, You've Got a Lovely Daughter') or solo acts like Bobby 'Boris' Pickett, who sang about the 'Monster Mash' in 1962. The Monkees tried, over time, to escape the teen market straitjacket by writing their own songs, but their popularity quickly faded.

As for Farnham, credibility was hard to come by when your success was based upon something as lightweight as 'Sadie'. His easy-on-the-eye looks didn't help. Like The Monkees' Davy Jones, Johnny was your typical 1960s pop idol: saccharine-sweet, family-friendly, unthreatening. But he had a voice that deserved respect, if only middle Australia took the time to see beyond his pretty face and ever-present smile.

'The scarring for Farnham perhaps came from having begun his career with a novelty song and for that single to have then become the biggest-selling Australian record of the '60s,' Robert Forster observed in a 2010 article. 'He couldn't escape it.'

But Johnny had heard a new song that he thought would be the perfect follow-up to 'Sadie', an ever-so-slightly psychedelic pop confection called 'Friday Kind of Monday'. Like 'Sadie', it was the handiwork of some stellar American composers: in this instance, husband-and-wife team Jeff Barry and Ellie Greenwich, Brill Building stalwarts. Most songs with their imprimatur meant 'hit'; they'd written chart-toppers for The Ronettes ('Be My Baby') and The Shangri-Las ('Leader of the Pack'). Along with uber-producer Phil Spector, they'd also crafted the epic 'River Deep – Mountain High', which became a signature song for Tina Turner.

'Please let this be my next single,' Johnny pleaded with producer David Mackay, as soon as he heard the 1967 original of 'Friday', cut by Americans The Meantime.

This seemingly straightforward request revealed a lot about Johnny Farnham's situation: the key decisions about his career were being made by others further up the line, Sambell and EMI particularly.

'I knew very little about the business,' Johnny admitted.

This was something he'd come to regret.

'Friday' was a strong song, contemporary and catchy, but it was agreed that it would connect even more strongly if it was teamed with another novelty song. It would be one part of a double A-side single, giving radio DJs the choice to play the track their audience preferred. The flipside was 'Underneath the Arches', a quaint slice of English music-hall whimsy, written way back in 1932, and subsequently recorded by Londoner Max Bygraves, among many others. Bygraves was the type of light entertainer that Sambell envisaged Johnny becoming.

'We hope the oldies will like "Underneath the Arches",' Johnny explained, 'and the kids will like the pop number. We'll cop it both ways.'

Together, 'Friday' and 'Arches' reached the Top 10 in Sydney, Melbourne, Brisbane and Adelaide in early April 1968, while 'Sadie' was still in the charts. Johnny again had stellar company, from Manfred Mann with 'Mighty Quinn (Quinn the Eskimo)' to Tom Jones ('Delilah') and the Small Faces ('Tin Soldier'). Fellow Aussies The Masters Apprentices, whose bassist was an ambitious fair-haired up-and-comer named Glenn Wheatley, were also charting, with their psychedelic rocker 'Elevator Driver'.

One of Johnny's more peculiar appearances promoting his new hit was a TV spot in which he shared the set with an antique car, driver and all. For reasons best left unexplored, and little understood, Johnny and chauffeur spent much of the performance awkwardly sharing the front seat, before they finally drove off into the darkness of the studio. Anything to sell the song appeared to be the attitude of Darryl Sambell and EMI. But if credibility was something Johnny craved, this was no way to achieve it.

Hans Poulsen, who'd tipped off the guys in Strings Unlimited to Johnny, had by now left the 18th Century Quartet to focus on songwriting. After a couple of indifferent releases under his own name, he turned his hand to writing songs for others. Poulsen, with his Van Dyke beard and granny specs, was a curiosity, described in the *Australian Encyclopedia of Rock and Pop* as the era's 'resident hippie eccentric'. Hippies weren't yet a common sight in Oz, especially in the company of middle-of-the-road pop stars like Johnny Farnham. Quality homegrown pop songwriters were even thinner on the ground. But Poulsen had some good songs that seemed a perfect fit for Johnny, among them 'Rose Coloured Glasses' and 'Jamie'. They'd be Johnny's next two singles, the first time he'd recorded local compositions.

On the release of 'Rose Coloured Glasses' in late July 1968, Johnny put in yet another *Uptight* TV appearance. He wore shades as a reminder of the song's title, but it was a mistake: why hide Johnny's smiling eyes, the very thing that made teenage girls swoon? At least Johnny's mega-watt smile never left his face – even when he was confronted with the challenge of what to do during the song's instrumental break. He opted for a nervous jig, which just went to show that Johnny Farnham was a singer, not a mover.

Awkward spots such as this didn't impede his success. As Johnny's star continued to rise, so did the commotion outside his parents' Noble Park home, night and day. It didn't seem to matter that Farnham was rarely there; young girls gathered on the front step of Chateau Farnham, or in the nearby street, and refused to leave, chanting Johnny's name. Rose and John Sr, who remained rock-steady, community-minded folk, had no idea what to do when confronted with Johnny's ardent admirers. Should they make them a cup of tea? Invite them inside for a chat? Chase them off with the hose? And Rose definitely didn't know what to say when one particularly enthusiastic fan asked her what colour socks Johnny was wearing that day. Why would anyone want to know that?

Their phone rang off the hook, 24/7.

'[But] they never did any damage,' said Rose. 'They never did anything wrong.'

She was enormously proud of her son, the pop star. But Johnny, every inch a mother's boy, was worried that Rose might find the pressure too much.

'I'm fine,' she reassured him. 'I think it's great.'

Johnny's younger sister Jackie had been buying into her sibling's success, introducing him excitedly to all her friends as 'Johnny Farnham the singer – my brother!' But it left Johnny a bit uncomfortable, as he told a reporter at the time. 'I just have to stand there feeling like a real idiot.'

As successful as he was, Johnny was still unsure about all the adulation. Did he really deserve it?

In early 1969 Johnny decided it was time to find a place of his own. It would ease the pressure on his parents – maybe his fans would stop besieging their family home – and also give him a base closer to the city. He'd befriended Glenn Wheatley, the bassist of The Masters Apprentices, and they agreed to share a flat. Johnny and Glenn had plenty of common ground: both had, for a time, juggled a regular job with the life of a musician – Wheatley, a photo-lithographer in training, had been the Queensland Apprentice of the Year in 1965, but eventually threw it in for music – and both came from steady working-class families. And Wheatley, with his former band Bay City Union, had almost signed with EMI, Johnny's label.

But unlike Johnny, Wheatley was business-minded. He'd started booking gigs and hustling for work in and around Brisbane as early as 1963, when he was 15. In December 1966, aged 18, Wheatley and the band headed south, first to Sydney and then Melbourne, the epicentre of the music biz, but found things tough going. While Farnham's 'Sadie' was assaulting the charts and airwaves of Australia, Wheatley and the guys from Bay City Union were barely scraping together the $6 required for their weekly rent at St Kilda's unglamorous Seaside Lodge. On bad weeks they'd swipe milk money to get by. But Wheatley's fortunes improved again when he was poached for The Masters Apprentices in 1968, so much so that he was fast getting used to the same kind of fan frenzy that Johnny often experienced – once, after a Masters gig at Festival Hall, Wheatley barely made it out alive, his shirt ripped to shreds.

'We were engulfed,' Wheatley wrote of the experience, 'and I found myself in a very scary situation.' But Wheatley was a survivor.

The Masters were also managed by Sambell, although Wheatley suspected, with good reason, that Sambell might be too preoccupied with Johnny to help The Masters Apprentices fulfil their potential.

Sambell's other clients included pop/rock band Zoot, who sometimes shared bills with Farnham and were locked in a lively rivalry with The Masters Apprentices. Zoot's curly-haired bassist Beeb Birtles, like Wheatley, would get to know Johnny Farnham very well.

Wheatley's 21st birthday fell on 23 January 1969, and the celebrations that ensued helped develop a powerful and lasting bond between him and Farnham. Wheatley's mother had sent him a bottle of Great Western champagne, which, unwisely, her son had forgotten all about, leaving it to ferment in the back seat of his car while he and Farnham worked their way through some beers at the party held at Sambell's penthouse apartment. The summer sun had done its work by the time Wheatley remembered his mother's gift and popped the cork. Soon enough, he was clinging tight to the toilet bowl, vomiting profusely and frequently. From time to time, Johnny would check on him, ensuring that 'Wheat' hadn't passed out, or worse.

'I saved his life you know!' Johnny boasted about that night. 'I rescued him from drowning in the toilet bowl. We became good mates.'

Could there be a better way for two young blokes to connect?

What neither knew was that what seemed like harmless drunken bonding was the beginning of a relationship that would, over time, rescue both their careers – perhaps even save their lives.

3

THE LONELIEST NUMBER

Johnny's first TV special aired on 10 April 1969. The hour-long show, hosted by Jimmy Hannan, also featured fellow pop artists Ross D. Wyllie, The Strangers and Yvonne Barrett. But it was not a success. 'Channel 0 presented us with a Johnny Farnham special last night,' noted a reporter in *The Age*, 'an hour show which took every minute of an hour to pass by. Farnham did well, but it was a pity he had to mime most of his songs.' The reviewer went on to criticise the lack of a studio audience, some odd decisions regarding non-musical parts of the show – a skit in which Johnny dressed as Robin Hood was tartly described as 'almost a comedy spot' – and the young man's lack of presence. 'He looked a little lost,' the reviewer surmised. It seemed that Johnny wasn't quite ready for the transition from the pop charts to a TV special, which was all part of Sambell's master plan.

Johnny learnt another lesson about the harsh realities of a performer's life when he toured Queensland, soon after, with Johnny O'Keefe. Since his Sydney Stadium heyday in the 1950s, O'Keefe had been on a career roller-coaster. His rocky journey had included a near-fatal car crash, several spells in psychiatric hospitals, a divorce, a disastrous US tour, a fall from public favour – and occasional chart success. O'Keefe's star was in decline yet again when he and Farnham went on tour, but that didn't stop O'Keefe from reminding audiences that he wasn't called the Wild One for nothing. Johnny got to learn why at very close range.

Early on in O'Keefe's set, the audience grew restless and started booing. 'We want Johnny,' they yelled, referring to the other, younger Johnny on the bill. Farnham looked on from side-stage, his concern growing, heckle by heckle, for O'Keefe.

'Get off, you old fart,' some members of the audience yelled, spilling their beers. 'Bring on Johnny Farnham.'

This commotion only inspired O'Keefe to work harder. As Farnham watched, his respect growing by the minute, the old stager pushed his band to play harder, louder, while he urged the audience to get involved. The ripples spread through the room. A handful of songs later, the Wild One had the entire crowd hanging on his every roar, loving him unreservedly. They gave him a standing ovation when he finally left the stage after an hour, dripping sweat, the strains of 'Shout', O'Keefe's big closer, ringing in everyone's ears.

'The audience [at first] didn't care who he was,' Farnham would recall. 'It was a tough crowd. But by the third song, he had them. He was unbelievable – a remarkable man, a fantastic bloke.' And a handy mentor for Johnny, too; he would be inspired by performances like this when his own career started to flatline. Often, when confronted with a surly crowd, Johnny would flash back to this rowdy night in

Queensland and channel the Wild One. Never give up, he'd tell himself. Don't let the bastards drag you down.

Perhaps a little bruised by the tepid response to Johnny's TV special, Sambell and EMI chose his next single releases carefully. These were songs that would become as much Farnham staples as 'Sadie' – although this time they would have quality going for them, something you couldn't say about the dear old thing with red detergent hands.

Harry Nilsson was an American singer whose wild streak was almost as legendary as his knack for killer melodies. When not running amok with John Lennon, Keith Moon and other large-living rockers, Nilsson was a red-hot performer: his 1969 cover of Fred Neil's 'Everybody's Talking', a centrepiece of the film *Midnight Cowboy*, earned Nilsson his first Grammy and a US Top 10 hit.

Nilsson was also a crack songwriter. His song 'One', which found its way to Johnny in the winter of 1969, had a curious creative genesis. The song – already a number five hit that year for America's Three Dog Night – opened with a simple piano note, repeated over and over, not unlike the Bee Gees' timeless 'Spicks and Specks'. With it, Nilsson was trying to capture the sound of an engaged telephone line – for the broken-hearted, there's nothing lonelier than the sound of an unanswered phone.

In Johnny's recorded version, that sound was even starker, bleaker – somehow more desperate. Johnny then launched into the lyric with real gusto; for perhaps the first time in his career he was testing his ability to deliver genuine, deeply felt emotion. And he did it brilliantly. The production was slick, too, loaded with energy and just a hint of psychedelia.

'One' – backed by the truly awful 'Mr Whippy', a shameless plug for the ice-cream peddler – peaked at number four on *Go-Set*'s national chart in early October 1969, below the Rolling Stones' 'Honky Tonk Women', Johnny Cash's 'A Boy Named Sue' and Russell Morris's great 'Part Three into Paper Walls,' another potent slice of homegrown pop.

When Johnny appeared on *Uptight* to sing 'One', the response – even before he opened his mouth – was euphoric. His female fans screamed the house down. Host Ross D. Wyllie did his best to keep things in check, but he might as well have been trying to hold back the tide.

'As you can hear by all the noise,' Wyllie half shouted, 'we've got Johnny Farnham coming along for you.'

It was another slightly uneasy appearance by Farnham. This time around he was backed by a long-haired four-piece rock band – there wasn't a dancing cleaning lady in sight – but Johnny stuck with his supper-club-friendly suit and high-wattage smile. He wasn't quite ready to let his hair grow out, or lose the formal threads. And any edge the song had was undermined by the feverish response of his fans, who threw streamers and stuffed toys at Johnny, as if he was on the deck of the *Oriana*, about to hit the high seas. Still, it was a great song and an inspired vocal, and it would stay in Johnny's live set for several decades. 'One' was a keeper.

The success of 'One' returned Johnny to the top of the pop pile – only weeks earlier he'd been anointed King of Pop, his first of five consecutive crowns. (Normie Rowe had claimed the crown in 1967 and '68.) The award, established by *Go-Set* and *Uptight*, was fan-driven; readers could vote for their favourite pin-up by clipping a coupon from the pages of *TV Week*. In 1969, Johnny romped it in.

At the awards ceremony, staged at Melbourne's Chevron Hotel, Johnny had some trouble with his oversized crown, which kept slipping while he tried to sing. It didn't help that he had tears welling in his eyes.

The first song he chose to perform as King of Pop was his next hit single, 'Raindrops Keep Falling on My Head'. It was yet another cover, this time of a recent BJ Thomas hit, composed by the highly rated team of Hal David and Burt Bacharach. The song featured prominently in the huge box office hit *Butch Cassidy and the Sundance Kid*, a vehicle for dynamic duo Paul Newman and Robert Redford. With that kind of pedigree, how could Johnny miss? His version was unavoidable throughout the early months of 1970, topping the *Go-Set* charts from 24 January to 13 March: another massive hit single for Australia's favourite son. When he took the stage at Melbourne's Festival Hall, Farnham-mania reached new heights, as his fans screamed, shrieked, threw streamers, waved and cried. Some passed out, overcome by the moment. Once revived by medical staff, they'd leap back into the fray.

Johnny also appeared on Channel 9's *Bandstand* to plug 'Raindrops'. Three years after 'Sadie', he was now 'the man who needs no introduction', in the estimation of *Bandstand*'s bookish host, Brian Henderson. This time around, instead of a long-haired rockband backing him up, the thoroughly wholesome, G-rated Johnny Farnham was surrounded by a team of dancers. As Johnny sang and glowed and broke hearts from coast to coast, their steps looked more like a test for drunkenness – 'Okay, place your hands on your head while touching your nose, now walk a straight line' – than actual choreography. At one point, a female dancer exchanged a goofy smile and a laugh with Johnny, as if to say, 'I know, it's dumb, isn't it?'

Bandstand loved Farnham; between 1967 and 1968 he made six appearances, singing all his singles, plus obscurities like the Clinton Ford / Charlie Chester nugget 'In the Old Bazaar in Cairo', and Engelbert Humperdinck's 'Miss Elaine E.S. Jones'. Henderson was right; after so much exposure, Johnny didn't need an introduction.

Yet, despite being a big hit, 'Raindrops' typified the tendency of Johnny (and Sambell) – during the first decade of his career, at least – to flip-flop between credible songs and safe mainstream choices. This was done, certainly in part, to keep the hits coming, but also to ensure Johnny didn't alienate any part of his audience. Yet it was short-term thinking at best: eventually his teen fans would move on to someone newer and even prettier – teenager Jamie Redfern was already starting to make waves. If Johnny wanted to genuinely establish himself as a 'real' singer he needed to start taking control, yet he seemed to leave the key decisions in the hands of his manager and record company. 'One' was a terrific choice, as was 'Friday Kind of Monday', but in between there was a mix of clunkers and crowd-pleasers. It was unclear if Johnny was set on becoming a great vocalist or an old-fashioned entertainer.

Johnny's life was a whirlwind, a situation he'd grown to grudgingly accept. 'Just point me at the stage,' he'd wearily tell Sambell most nights. There was hardly a day when he didn't have a radio commitment, a TV spot or a charity event, another single to record, a concert to play, more hands to shake, cheeks to kiss, autographs to sign. The turnover rate at the time was remarkable; even serial chart-toppers The Beatles and the Bee Gees crafted new singles every couple of months for fear of being swamped by a tsunami of new pop acts. Johnny understood this, but he also had a dangerous inability to say no – to pretty much anything. He aimed to please.

A typical day for Farnham at this time might begin with an early morning flight from somewhere to Melbourne, where he'd be driven straight to the studio. He'd arrive without knowing what he was to sing; he'd learn the songs on the fly. Then by six, with the session done – he recorded his first couple of albums in a matter of days – he'd be off to that evening's gigs. Sometimes there were two, even three appearances per night. The next day the cycle would start all over again. He'd keep his head down when out in public, trying his best not to be mobbed. It was fantastic to have supportive fans, but he would have loved some sort of normal life.

And in spite of a succession of hit singles, constant touring and the incessant pushing of a very entrepreneurial manager, the King of Pop was hardly raking in the cash. On a good night, he might return home with $30, sometimes $40. As he was resigned to writing nothing more than the occasional B-side, he wasn't earning much from songwriting royalties either. Johnny Farnham was generating money, but it was for his label and other writers – not so much for himself.

An exhausted Johnny turned 21 on 1 July 1970. Many years down the line, at the age of 50, he was asked about himself as a 21-year-old: What was going on in his life? Who was in charge?

'I never had much control of what was happening – I tended to be led around a lot,' he admitted.

When pushed for what advice he'd have given his 21-year-old self, Johnny figured it would have been something about seizing the reins, making some of his own decisions, choosing his own direction. *Learning to say no.* But that didn't happen, not in 1970.

'I was never given the opportunity to sit down and consider my position, my music, what I wanted to do,' Johnny confessed. 'I took my advice [only] when I finally grew up enough to take control of my life.'

By contrast, his flatmate Glenn Wheatley had recently fired Sambell and taken over management of The Masters Apprentices. *He* was calling the shots.

On dark days, Johnny missed his old job with plumber Stan Foster and the guys on the building site: life was more predictable back then.

4

THE PRINCE OF PANTO

Johnny's next career move pushed him a step closer to being the type of all-round entertainer Darryl Sambell had dreamed of creating. In late December 1969 Johnny performed at the Sydney Stadium, Johnny O'Keefe's old stomping ground. But Farnham wasn't humping the microphone stand and rolling his eyes à la the Wild One; no, he was treading the boards in the very mainstream panto *Dick Whittington and His Cat*. This was fizzy family entertainment. Even advertising for the event had a warm, cosy feeling: in a newspaper ad, beneath the ticket prices ($1.20 for adults, 60c for kids) was the slogan 'A commonsense price for all'. With 'Raindrops' still high in the charts, Johnny then took *Dick Whittington* to Melbourne, playing Festival Hall for several days, and then to Adelaide in late January.

Johnny was all over the production: he played the lead role, the kid with a dream who runs off to London with his feline buddy, and sang 'One', 'Raindrops' and 'Sadie'. He told jokes, he grinned, he hammed it up. The production was pure vaudeville, a combination of song, dance and slapstick, with an inevitable happy ending. His adoring public lapped it up. But edgy it wasn't.

Only a few months earlier, Sydney impresario Harry M. Miller had staged the first local production of *Hair: The American Tribal Love-Rock Musical*, which would run for two years, raise many eyebrows – it included nudity, fruity language, drug references and 'free love' – and kickstart a theatrical revolution in Australia. *Dick Whittington* was from a completely different age; it had first been performed on stage in 1877.

Soon after treading the boards as Dick W., Johnny found himself the subject of controversy, proving just how closely his every move was scrutinised. When he arrived late for two events – the presentation of a gold record to boxer Lionel Rose in Melbourne (for Rose's surprise hit single 'I Thank You') and the Festival of Perth – the reaction was over the top. Melbourne station 3UZ, until then a big supporter of Farnham's, banned his records for a week (the kiss of death in those days); they even threatened legal action. The Festival of Perth organisers also stamped their feet, resulting in a whisper that Johnny – 'the golden boy of entertainment', in the words of *TV Week* – had become unreliable.

'I travel thousands of miles a year to engagements all over Australia,' Johnny stated, 'and pride myself on getting to them on time.'

The misunderstanding, he explained, was that he hadn't properly digested the Rose invitation, thinking it was a reception, not a full-scale concert. He had been told he was due to appear at 10.15 p.m.; when he arrived a few minutes late, the concert had already wound up. His delay was brought about by a visit to an Adelaide children's hospital en route to the airport, and a delayed flight to Melbourne.

None of this mattered to the organisers, who gave Johnny the cold shoulder when he arrived. One fellow performer gave him a gobful. Who did he think he was?

A similar mishap occurred during his Perth trip. He arrived on 2 February, as per his contract, only to discover that he'd been expected the day before, to attend a charity barbecue.

'Where have you been, Johnny?' a reporter snapped on his arrival.

Johnny was lost; it was only when he read the newspaper the next day that he learnt about his supposed 'snub'.

'I had no idea what anybody was talking about,' an understandably defensive Farnham said. 'They were all accusing me of arriving late, but as far as I was concerned I was there right on time.'

Johnny offered up yet another unnecessary apology. Anything to keep the peace. Being King of Pop had its disadvantages: Johnny was under the microscope.

With the help of the ever-present Sambell, Johnny spent much of 1970 consolidating his place at the top of the pile; it was all about the work. He started hosting a recurring TV spot called *Johnny Farnham's Revolution*, appeared regularly on *In Melbourne Tonight*, and released another album – his third, *Looking through a Tear* – in late July; it sold 50,000 copies – a gold record. *Happening '70*, which Ross D. Wyllie hosted in the wake of *Uptight*, dedicated a four-hour special to Johnny, in September the King of Pop crown was placed atop his blond head for the second year running, and 'Comic Conversation', one of his better singles, was released in November, just days before another Channel 0 TV special, *The World of Johnny Farnham*.

Looking Through a Tear contained two Farnham originals, 'What Can I Do' and 'Two', something of a revelation. But the bulk of the LP was existing hits ('One', 'Raindrops') and cautiously chosen covers. Sambell was no great advocate of Johnny's original songs; he found them boring. Once, in a drunken rage, he smashed Johnny's guitar, as if to say, 'Don't bother with this' – not quite the vote of support Johnny had hoped for. How could he escape being seen as some sort of human jukebox, a singer of other people's songs, when his own manager rejected his songs? (It's not widely known that Johnny wrote the B-side to 'Sadie', a song titled 'In My Room'. He performed it at least once on a Channel 9 soundstage, surrounded by a team of dancers who appeared to be listening to a completely different song, throwing themselves about the set like whirling dervishes. Johnny, meanwhile, sang his heart out.)

A spot in *Charlie Girl*, a hit musical from London's West End that was opening in Australia in 1971, was Johnny's next engagement. But first Johnny, along with Sambell and Ian Meldrum, travelled to the UK. Johnny needed to audition for the show's West End producers, while Sambell was trying to drum up some enthusiasm about Australia's biggest pop star in EMI's London HQ. What ensued was more the Darryl and Molly show, with Johnny a bemused, sometimes annoyed, onlooker.

First point of business for Johnny was to read for the part of Joe, *Charlie Girl*'s young romantic lead, with the show's director, 62-year-old expat Aussie Freddie Carpenter. Carpenter had worked with such greats as Noël Coward and Danny La Rue and had been treading the boards – as dancer, choreographer and director – since his stage debut way back in Melbourne in 1924. He was a veteran, a 'lovely old chap', in Johnny's words, although Carpenter's ill-fitting wig was a bit of a distraction. It kept slipping about his head as he spoke. Maybe it was too much of a distraction, because Johnny fluffed his lines the first time around.

'Can I try again?' he pleaded.

A second read was unheard of, especially for stage novices like Johnny, but Carpenter understood the lad's marquee value back in Oz, and acquiesced. Johnny nailed the reread and the part was his.

Yet any joy Johnny felt at the opportunity was gradually eroded by the bickering between Sambell and Meldrum, which had begun pretty much as soon as their Singapore Airlines 707 left Tullamarine, and intensified as the trip wore on.

'They were like two old ladies,' said a dismayed Johnny.

At one stage Johnny pulled their rental car over on the side of the road and grabbed the squabbling pair by their collars. 'If you two don't shut up,' Johnny roared, 'I'll throttle the both of you.'

After one long day, Johnny decided he needed a bath. He luxuriated in the tub, having finally escaped the turbulent twosome. Or so he thought. After closing his eyes and shutting out the rest of the world for several minutes, Johnny was given a rude shock. Meldrum jumped into the bath to join him.

'I was gobsmacked. I got out pretty quick, got my towel, let him have the dirty water. It was a pretty unpleasant experience,' recalled Farnham.

Johnny and Meldrum would go on to share many things – stages, awards, breakdowns, breakthroughs, a strong friendship that spanned six decades – but this was the first and last time they shared a bathtub.

Safely back in Oz, Johnny went into rehearsals for the show, which was due to open in late September 1971 at Her Majesty's Theatre in Melbourne and run for nine shows a week. 'It's flippin' well marvellous!' proclaimed a print ad for the show. *Charlie Girl*'s producer was Kenn Brodziak, a wily operator best known as promoter for The Beatles' 1964 Australian tour. He'd seen them in the UK in 1963 and spotted their magic straight away, quickly booking them for their first (and only) Australian visit. The 16-date tour cost Brodziak all of £2500, an absolute pittance. By the time they made it to Oz, The Beatles were being offered 50 times that amount to tour America. 'So you're the one got us at the old price, are you?' George Harrison chuckled when he met Brodziak.

In a wild coincidence, Johnny had met Brodziak before – when he was apprenticed to Ken Foster, he'd worked at Brodziak's apartment.

Johnny, meanwhile, had a new distraction in his life.

It was her legs that got him first. Johnny was deep into rehearsals for *Charlie Girl*, which were being staged in an old church hall on Batman Avenue in the city, when he spotted Jillian Billman, a 16-year-old dancer from Glenroy. Though six years younger than Johnny, she had already performed in the chorus lines for *Casino* and *Promises Promises*. With her long dark hair and doe-like eyes, it was hard not to spot Jillian. She was gorgeous. Johnny was lovestruck. And those legs …

'I was a bit of a leg man,' he admitted, 'and she had great pins, so I just gravitated to her.'

Johnny had not yet had a serious romance in his life, although he had more than his fair share of public and prominent admirers, including Olivia Newton-John and one of Sir Reg Ansett's daughters. A long-legged dancer from *Bandstand* arrived unexpectedly at a Farnham family Easter get-together and stayed for the weekend. He'd also been linked with April Byron, a sexy, raven-haired Adelaide-based singer. And of course there were the occasional hotel stowaways – more prevalent when he played shows out of town. Those country girls really knew how to let their hair down. But Jillian was a different matter altogether. Johnny was in love.

Jillian was also immediately drawn to Johnny.

'I love bottoms,' she laughed. And she certainly took note of Johnny's pert derrière as he went through his paces at rehearsals.

But his name and celebrity were lost on Jillian, who'd been almost completely focused on her dancing career for the past couple of years. 'Sadie' meant nothing to her: she didn't know the song. A fellow member of the cast produced a photo of Johnny, whispering something about him being a big pop star. Jillian knew him only as the one with the 'cute bum'. 'Shame he's gay,' she told her friends.

Despite their mutual admiration they kept a polite distance until one day, during rehearsals, Jillian was struggling with the rusty door to the toilet, which was at the back of the church hall. A chivalrous Johnny came to her rescue, kicking the door open. He smiled and went back to work. Finally, a connection.

As the cast got even further into rehearsals, they moved base, relocating to Her Majesty's. There, Jillian would arrive each day to find a single red rose on her dressing-room table. Sometimes there'd be some biscuits, or a hot chocolate. Small but heartfelt gestures from Johnny. Jillian's mind was changed: maybe Johnny wasn't gay after all.

Producer Brodziak could be strict. He drafted a memo that banned dancers from fraternising with the cast (which also included expat British comic Derek Nimmo and West End star Anna Neagle). As opening night grew closer, Jillian was summoned to the producer's office, and directed to stop talking to Johnny. Immediately.

'If you don't,' the producer warned, 'I'll fire you.'

'Oh yeah, really?' Johnny responded when Jillian told him.

Johnny stormed into Brodziak's office, all red-hot fury, in a rare display of assertiveness. 'If she goes,' he insisted, 'I go.'

Brodziak may have been tough, but he was no fool. He chose to let is pass. After all, Johnny was a surefire guarantee of bums on seats. And *Charlie Girl* was a tough gig: there were six evening shows and two weekend matinees, so there was no point in losing one of his principals this close to opening night. After the Melbourne run, there was a season booked in Auckland, beginning in May 1972; it was a long haul. And he admired the young guy, a kid really, who was willing to stand up for himself.

Brodziak's pragmatism paid off: the show was a hit.

In a curious footnote, during the run of *Charlie Girl* Farnham came to the attention of ASIO – for the first and probably last time. On 26 March 1972, Aboriginal activists announced that Johnny was going to play a charity gig to raise funds for the 'tent embassy', which had set up base in front of Canberra's Parliament House in January as a protest against Prime Minister Billy McMahon's refusal to recognise Aboriginal land rights. This was way out of character for Farnham and it's unclear if he actually agreed to the appearance.

Sambell rejected all requests for Johnny to align himself with anything vaguely political or controversial, seeing it as bad for his boy's public image. And there's no record of Johnny gigging in Canberra at this time, so it seems that if the activists did reach out to Johnny, he didn't perform in the end. It's unclear how deeply ASIO explored his activities, but Farnham's name appeared in a report unearthed in 2012, which documented a 1972 student meeting where plans for the charity gig were mentioned. 'The singer of hits including "Sadie (The Cleaning Lady)" came to the attention of the Australian Security Intelligence Organisation in the 1970s as a potential supporter of the Aboriginal tent embassy, which the spy agency feared could have been a front for a Maoist-led, armed overthrow of the Australian government,' stated the 2012 report, disclosed by Fairfax's Andrew Taylor.

Farnham has never spoken about the event. But he did put in an appearance, also while in *Charlie Girl*, at the far more ASIO-friendly Night of the Stars, a fundraiser for Freedom for Hunger, put on at Dallas Brooks Hall, Melbourne, in September 1971. Also appearing that night were irreverent Brits Peter Cook and Dudley Moore.

Around this time, Johnny made his second promo appearance for TAA, but this time he was not just given a credit, he was the star. It was a relentlessly upbeat, almost frenetic TV promo, spruiking the airlines' 'friendly people doing their thing the friendly way'. Trailed by an ever-present camera, Farnham was chirpier than a chipmunk as he burst into a sprint inside the airport terminal, waving and smiling every which way. This led to an all-in dance routine on the tarmac – Johnny mixing it with mechanics, hosties and passengers – before he finally found his window seat and kicked back, reminding everyone how 'you get a little more the friendly way' as his plane disappeared over the horizon. All of this in a touch under 30 seconds of screentime.

Johnny fast became a go-to guy for advertisers, spruiking everything from Sunblest bread – 'Use your loaf,' Johnny suggested, 'say Tip Top Sunblest' – to Bushells tea. He was now in every kitchen of Australia.

The appeal of a pop idol, especially in the 1960s and '70s, diminished greatly when – heaven forbid – they met the love of their lives and the relationship became public knowledge. Beatle John Lennon had suffered this fickle backlash twice: first when he married Cynthia Powell, his college girlfriend, in 1962, then again – and even more feverishly – when he married Japanese artist Yoko Ono seven years later. Elvis Presley fans were mortified when the King wed Priscilla Beaulieu in 1967. Closer to home, Johnny O'Keefe's marriage to his first wife, Marianne Renate, at the height of his success in 1958, radically altered the way his fans saw him. The crowds of girls that once gathered on the nature strip of O'Keefe's house faded faster than you could say, 'Do you take this woman…' If you were a hormonally charged teenager, why bother? There were other, unattached pop stars in the ocean.

In 1971 Johnny Farnham wasn't married – not yet, anyway – but Darryl Sambell understood only too well the potential dangers of Johnny's relationship becoming public. The screams would fade; the allure would be gone. Johnny would become untouchable. Taken. The Army had stolen Normie Rowe – Sambell had met with influential people in Canberra to ensure the same didn't happen to Johnny – and he wasn't going to let some dancer 'steal' Australia's latest pin-up boy. It was a potential career killer – his fans were besotted with him. ('I was in love with Johnny Farnham,' read a typical fan letter, 'he was my first "boyfriend".').

If Johnny was going to date Jillian, what he needed was a 'beard', someone to distract the hungry media, keep them off the scent of the real story. Lesley Shaw, a producer at *Uptight*, had gotten to know Johnny and she became a go-between to keep the press off the trail of this hot new romance. Reporters were confused: if Johnny was going out with the dancer they'd heard whispers about, why had he been seen in public with Shaw? It was a little bit complicated, however, because Lesley was actually attracted to Johnny but he made it clear he had feelings only for Jillian. Still, Lesley provided 'cover' when Johnny wanted to step out with Jillian; she even helped him when he needed saving from Sambell's wild parties, which happened more than once. Johnny wasn't comfortable with the more over-the-top behaviour he witnessed at Darryl's place.

Sambell could be overbearing.

'Where are you going tonight?' he'd demand of Johnny.

'I'm going out with Lesley,' Johnny would tell him. But Sambell knew something big was brewing between Johnny and Jillian, and he didn't like it.

Ian Meldrum said that Sambell was 'possessive and obsessive' about Johnny, and this was becoming more obvious by the day. On the surface, it seemed like a crush – who wouldn't develop feelings for a young guy as pretty as Johnny? – but it was a tricky thing to add to the mix of a business partnership. It seemed as though

Sambell was hung up on keeping Jillian away from Johnny. And clearly he disliked all the attention Johnny was giving his new love. He was jealous.

There were flashpoints, clear signs that all was not well between Sambell and Farnham. Johnny, hardly the most physical of men, threw a rare punch at his manager when Sambell referred to Jillian as a 'slut', an insult that would have dire ramifications. (Johnny later said he could forgive just about anything from Sambell, 'but not his treatment of Jillian'.) Jillian herself stood up to a verbally abusive Sambell during a barbecue on the Yarra. When Johnny and Jillian planned a quiet getaway on Brampton Island, Sambell got the news and arranged for a reporter from *TV Week* to 'visit', which forced Jillian to hastily leave the island.

During *Charlie Girl*, producer Brodziak was forced to intervene when he felt that Sambell was overworking Johnny, not necessarily to maintain his public profile, but to keep him at a distance from his new girlfriend. Sambell denied this, naturally, when challenged by Brodziak, but it wasn't hard to read between the lines. Sambell had already lost The Masters Apprentices; now it seemed he was on shaky ground with Farnham. He was letting his emotions intrude upon business. Not smart.

But Sambell was relentless: some nights Johnny and Jillian would be at Farnham's South Yarra flat when the phone would ring or there'd be a knock on the door. It was Darryl. It was always Darryl. The courting couple were forced to hide out at the apartment of a friend of Johnny's, Geoff Reynolds. Or sometimes they'd go down to the St Kilda marina and take off in the small boat Johnny had moored there. 'We'd go out and cuddle for hours,' said Johnny.

The Farnham–Sambell alliance was showing cracks. Even the racehorse Johnny and Sambell co-owned, a grey mare named Seascape, ran last at its first two outings. Surely this was a bad omen.

There were other more public problems: Johnny's three latest singles, 'Acapulco Sun', 'Baby, Without You' (a duet with Allison Durbin) and 'Walking the Floor on My Hands', released between May and November 1971, barely grazed the Top 40. The King of Pop was being overtaken by the likes of new kids Daddy Cool, pin-up Russell Morris and pop sirens Colleen Hewett and Olivia Newton-John (whose 'Banks of the Ohio' was a worldwide smash). The lustre on the King's crown was starting to fade.

'Sambell's not doing right by you,' EMI's Cliff Baxter told Johnny. The label boss thought Johnny could do better if he and producer David Mackay co-managed him.

Johnny wasn't having it; he defended Sambell. Despite everything, Johnny was loyal to his manager; after all, this was the man who got him started, who believed in him. And loyalty was paramount to Johnny.

He was shocked that Baxter could be so upfront.

'You can't say that,' Johnny said. 'You can't talk to me like that.'

But it was clear that time was just about up on the relationship that had transformed a plumber's apprentice into the nation's biggest star.

5

WEDDING BELL BLUES

Several months into their relationship, the bond between Johnny and Jillian was profound; he'd never felt like this before. In mid-1972 Johnny approached his *Charlie Girl* co-star, Englishman Derek Nimmo, to discuss his feelings for Jillian.

'Why don't you marry the girl?' Nimmo asked. It was clear that Johnny was deeply in love; Blind Freddy could see that.

With that, John ran down the corridor to Jillian's dressing room, and closed the door.

'I'm madly in love with you,' he said, dropping to his knees. 'Will you marry me?'

Jillian didn't think twice.

'Of course,' she said, tears welling in her eyes.

'Right then,' said John, 'I'll see you after the show' – and with that he tore back to his dressing room to prepare for the next performance.

They planned to marry in April 1973.

Every performance of *Charlie Girl* required Johnny to belt out a song called 'Give it a Go'. It was fast becoming his mantra. 'I guess that sums me up okay,' he'd say about the song. 'I'll have a go at just about anything.' 'Anything' now included married life.

But before that, Johnny had two problems to deal with: a head-to-head with his future mother-in-law, Phyllis, who he sometimes quietly referred to as 'the dragon', and the fury of an increasingly angry, erratic and overbearing manager.

Phyllis Billman believed that her daughter was too young to marry; Jillian was only 17, six years younger than Johnny. Johnny talked Phyllis around, but they did clash.

'You're not marrying my daughter, you Pommie bastard,' she'd roar at Johnny, when some new wedding planning problem arose. She even threatened to tear up the marriage licence. Johnny, typically, would smooth things over, so much so that he and Phyllis grew very close.

But Sambell still presented problems for the soon-to-be-newlyweds. He would pull Johnny aside and whisper, 'Don't do this. It'll ruin your career.' He even insisted that Johnny lie to the press: 'Wedding? What wedding?' he instructed his charge to say when asked about it.

Jillian's parents had planned a double wedding; Jillian's sister Judy was to marry her partner, Vincent Grech. But Sambell stepped in and insisted this mustn't happen; if this wedding was going to take place – against his wishes – he could at least ensure his star wasn't deprived of the spotlight. Sambell had big plans, he wanted to turn the wedding into an event starring Johnny, and he nitpicked virtually every aspect of the wedding day, all in the name of his protégé, angering the Billmans more and more with each change, and driving Johnny and Jillian nuts.

One round table at the Billman household left Jillian in tears. Who was getting married, she wondered? It was starting to feel like Sambell's wedding, not hers – he'd even insisted on being Johnny's best man. And as if Sambell wasn't enough trouble, some of Johnny's more besotted fans had been hassling her, sending threatening notes through the post. She was accosted in the street by a woman wielding a knife. It was all way too much.

Ian Meldrum became a go-between, and tried his best to mediate. He liked Sambell, but, having grown close to Johnny and Jillian, could appreciate the chaos Darryl was creating. However, it muddied the waters that Meldrum was a journalist and now had his mitts on the biggest scoop in the Australian entertainment world – Johnny Farnham was about to get married. He even had proof: the wedding invitation.

In the end, Meldrum couldn't resist. He broke the news in *Go-Set* in February 1973, running a 1000-word story and a copy of the invite. Sambell leapt into action, denying the story, undermining Meldrum's supposed 'exclusive'. This put Molly's nose way out of joint; he spoke with 3AK, saying that he'd stake his entire career on the veracity of the story. He and Sambell argued – a 'rather fierce argument', as Meldrum told the Melbourne press.

The whole thing was a mess. Johnny and Jillian just wanted to get the wedding over and done with, which wasn't really the ideal way to approach one of the most significant days of their lives.

On 17 April, just days after Johnny was declared Victoria's Youth of the Year, he was riding in a taxi when talk turned to his upcoming nuptials. Tomorrow was his wedding day.

'I have one piece of advice,' the cabbie told Johnny, glancing at him in the rear-view mirror. 'Always fall asleep in each other's arms. It'll keep your marriage strong.'

It was wise counsel – and something Johnny never forgot.

The worst-kept secret in Australian music had now been made public by Meldrum, and several thousand eager fans gathered outside St Matthew's Anglican Church in Glenroy on 18 April. Onlookers clamoured for any and every available vantage point, craning their necks to catch a glimpse of Johnny and Jillian as they arrived. The wedding party included both sets of parents, as well as Johnny's assistant, Jean Nair, matron-of-honour Judy Grech, Johnny's sister Jean, bridesmaid Lynette Bateman – a close friend of Jillian's – and flowergirl Tracey Bateman. Among Johnny's groomsmen was his brother, Alan. Sambell stuck close to Johnny's side.

'Don't do it, Johnny!' yelled a few heartbroken fans, their voices ringing loud and strong. Some got close enough to tear at Jillian's dress; they just couldn't believe the King of Pop was getting hitched. The cries and wails of Johnny's grief-stricken fans could still be heard by the wedding party as the ceremony began.

Several hundred more fans staked out the reception at the Dorset Gardens Hotel. Two hundred guests had been invited and as everyone eagerly awaited the newlywed Mr and Mrs Farnham, the sun set against a picture-postcard backdrop of rolling green hills and sturdy eucalypts, like something from a McCubbin painting. It was undeniably romantic.

Then it happened: there was a whirling roar in the distance

and a tiny speck appeared in the sky, growing larger by the second. Neither fans nor guests could believe what Sambell had conjured up: an orange chopper was transporting the Farnhams from church to reception, a ride of two minutes, tops. A limo be damned, Sambell figured – what could be more impressive than a helicopter? (*The Australian Women's Weekly* went so far as to describe their arrival as 'all very glamorous – even slightly James Bond-ish!')

A chant erupted, shattering the bucolic serenity – 'We want Johnny! We want Johnny!' – as the chopper hovered overhead. The local police who had gathered to keep the peace shifted a little uncomfortably; they'd seen Festival Hall crowds run amok and prayed it wouldn't happen here. Not today. Please.

Johnny was visible in the jump seat, waving at his fans and friends. As soon as the chopper reached terra firma, Johnny leapt out and ran to the other side, where he took Jillian's arm and helped her through the scrum of photographers and fans that had formed. Blue was Jillian's colour of choice: she wore a long-sleeved gown and matching blue lace colts and shoes. A blue lace headband held back her mane of wavy hair. She looked great, if more than a little nervous. As for Johnny, he turned on the charm, waving and mouthing 'hello' and 'g'day' as he joined his guests, trying his best to downplay how stressful the whole event had been.

Sambell might have had major issues with the wedding itself, but he couldn't pass up the chance to throw out a few tasty whispers to the press. Speaking with journos outside the reception, he revealed that Johnny and Jillian had plans to build their first house, a love-nest, possibly in rural Kilmore.

'And I'm off to London shortly,' Sambell threw in, 'to discuss a new musical for Johnny.' Sambell also talked up a proposed TV show for his charge, not a one-off special this time, but possibly as many as 26 half-hour shows. The sky was still the limit for his number-one client.

'Why the helicopter?' someone asked.

'Why not?' Sambell replied. Anything for Johnny.

In the lead-up to the event, Johnny hadn't thought much about Sambell's warning, that marriage was the worst possible career move; he loved Jillian too much to even consider this. But it did start to eat away at him when he and Jillian returned from their Brampton Island honeymoon and he plunged back into a new, hectic schedule. The crowds started to thin out; his records didn't sell.

'I was naive enough to think people who were enjoying my music would have been happy for me,' Johnny later admitted. 'I soon learnt that getting married was sudden death for a pop star. My career went very quiet; nobody wanted to know me.' Johnny Farnham was about to discover that Sambell had been right.

Not that he was short of work – anything but. In early June, Channel 9 screened the clumsily titled special *Ted Hamilton and Johnny Farnham Together Again for the Very First Time*. Logie-winner Hamilton was currently starring on Channel 9 as police constable Kevin Dwyer in *Division 4*.

Johnny also lined up for a variety show with Colleen Hewett at the Sydney Opera House, which had only been open for a matter of weeks. Farnham's relationship with Hewett extended beyond music; they became partners in a Melbourne restaurant named

Backstage, located in Spring Street, along with Hewett's partner, Danny Findlay. Johnny admitted that food was an industry 'I didn't know about' and that he 'wasn't a businessman's arse' – and over time, Backstage would prove as onerous as Johnny and Sambell's nag Seascape.

Johnny's grasp of the charts continued to slip. He released a flurry of singles between April 1973 and early 1974 – 'Everything Is Out of Season', 'I Can't Dance to Your Music' and 'Shake a Hand' – of which only one, 'Season', reached the Top 10. 'Shake a Hand' peaked – if you could call it that – at the very unflattering position of 91, and promptly disappeared from the charts. It was a very tangible warning sign for Johnny: he'd lost his magic touch. It would be another six long, empty years before he'd record his next Top 10 hit.

Johnny looked on as the more successful Australian acts of the moment, such as Helen Reddy, Rick Springfield and Olivia Newton-John, shifted overseas in the early 1970s, having outgrown the small Australian market. Newton-John won her first Grammy, and scored her debut US Top 10, with 1973's 'Let Me Be There'; Reddy was fast-tracking her way to becoming the world's biggest female act, on the strength of hits like 'I Am Woman' and 'Delta Dawn' and headline-grabbing moves like referring to God as 'she' in a Grammy acceptance speech. Springfield broke into the US Top 10 with the whimsical 'Speak to the Sky'; soon enough he'd be starring in his own cartoon series. Another expat, Peter Allen, was working on 'I Honestly Love You', a future worldwide number one for Newton-John.

Domestically, the rise of such rock reprobates as Skyhooks and AC/DC was but a few power chords away. Former Easybeat Stevie

Wright was poised to record the epic 'Evie (Parts 1, 2 & 3)', arguably the greatest single in Oz pop history, while William Shakespeare, John Paul Young and Ted Mulry (with and without his Gang) were busily cornering the pop market. Even ageing rocker Col Joye, who'd been another early mentor of Johnny's, had returned to the charts with 'Heaven is My Woman's Love', while Johnny O'Keefe had done the same with 'Mockingbird'. Farnham's label EMI were having far more success with breakout acts such as singer-songwriters Ross Ryan, whose 'I Am Pegasus' was huge in 1973. Russell Morris, who recorded for EMI subsidiary label Harvest, did equally big business in 1972 with the soaring 'Wings of an Eagle', which clung to the charts for the best part of five months. But Johnny was adrift in a commercial wilderness, short of hits and ideas.

And how did Sambell and Johnny counter this? They retreated to the safety of the theatre. Johnny took refuge in a production of *Pippin*, again produced by Kenn Brodziak, slated to open at Melbourne's Her Majesty's in February 1974. Johnny was cast in the titular role, one of Charlemagne's sons, and was paired with the equally golden Colleen Hewett. Farnham also struck up a friendship with the English actress Jenny Howard, a venerable theatre veteran.

'The show's young star, Johnny Farnham, and I get on so happily together,' Howard gaily told a reporter backstage. Johnny and Howard would reminisce about England; they discovered they shared Essex roots.

Billed modestly as 'the most breathtaking, stunning, star-studded musical comedy in a decade', *Pippin* Oz-style did reasonable business in Melbourne, ran briefly in Sydney and bled money in Adelaide. But it didn't match the success of *Charlie Girl*. And it came nowhere near the success of the Broadway original, directed by stage legend Bob Fosse, which ran (and ran and ran) for almost 2000 performances and won five Tonys. It seemed that Australia's theatregoers were tiring of Johnny Farnham. Apart from the obligatory Carols by Candlelight spot, Johnny wouldn't return to the theatre until 1992, when he'd be cast as no less a character than Jesus Christ himself.

In late July 1974 Channel 10 began screening *It's Magic*, a variety show aimed at a younger audience. Johnny co-presented the program with Hewett. It was billed in the press as a 'fully integrated music show', based upon an idea by Johnny Young and his partner Kevin Lewis. *It's Magic* was filmed in and around *Pippin* rehearsals and performances, hardly the perfect scenario for a new project. When shooting was over for the day, as Hewett related, 'we'd then rush to the theatre to put the wigs on'. It was a relentless schedule. Johnny, always politic with the press, admitted, 'it was a bit of a strain – but worth it'. A Fairfax photographer snapped the pair popping the cork on a bottle of champagne, toasting their new show. The headline declared: 'Bubble and Fizz Before Work', but their smiles seemed a bit forced. This was work, hard work.

There was a fun segment on the show, mostly ad-libbed, called 'The Kids', in which Johnny and Hewett would sit in a sandpit and grumble about 'grown ups'; sometimes Johnny would hoon around the studio on a kid's pushbike. Yet despite some solid press – 'I've run out of superlatives to describe this show,' gushed a reporter for *The Age*, 'it is a great day when Australians can watch their own talent on screen' – *It's Magic* screened for only 13 weeks and then quietly faded into Oz television obscurity.

Proving far more popular, Channel 10's *Young Talent Time*, hosted by Johnny Young and featuring stars-on-the-rise like Jamie Redfern and Debbie Byrne, was a couple of years into its record-breaking 18-season, 800-plus-episode run. When the *Young Talent Time* troupe visited Sydney's Luna Park, the crowd response was so fervent that the cast was forced to escape through a tunnel in the park's scenic railway. In 1973 the newly crowned King of Pop, *Young Talent Time*'s Jamie Redfern, packed Melbourne's Festival Hall, until recently Farnham's happy hunting crowd. Johnny's old fans had found a newer, fresher face to love. Farnham agreed to cameo on *Young Talent Time*, but it was a big comedown.

How could he break his career slump? Was Cliff Baxter right – was it time to move on from Sambell?

In late 1974, Glenn Wheatley, Johnny's former flatmate, was en route to Melbourne, where his future lay with a group under development that would become the Little River Band. Wheatley's plane reached Darwin on 23 December 1974; he was travelling with his wife, Alison. The next day, having been warned of a huge storm heading Darwin's way, they caught what turned out to be one of the last flights to leave the city, headed for the Gold Coast, where Wheatley's parents lived.

Flicking through the local newspaper the next morning, Wheatley was shocked to read of the apocalyptic Cyclone Tracy, which killed 71 Darwinians and pretty much flattened the northern capital soon after his flight departed. He turned on the TV and 'watched with horror the devastation of Darwin': he and his wife had come close to being among the victims.

Still reeling from the news, Wheatley found a distraction: his old housemate and buddy, Johnny Farnham, had a gig in town, a New Year's Eve bill with Colleen Hewett, on the beach at Southport. Wheatley decided to see what Farnham was doing. What does a King of Pop get up to, he wondered, when he isn't the king anymore? Wheatley was about to experience his second shock of recent days.

Five years earlier, while still with The Masters, Wheatley had shared a big bill with Johnny, and others, called Operation Starlift, which played to full, frantic houses in Adelaide, Hobart, Melbourne, Sydney and Brisbane. Johnny's fans sometimes had to be dragged away from the stage; the backstage area was like a battlefield, littered with the bodies of young girls who'd passed out. Seventy female fans in Hobart needed treatment during Johnny's set. (Wheatley had to step over the bodies to reach the stage.) Operation Starlift drew 6000 punters to Brisbane's Festival Hall, a bigger crowd than The Beatles had pulled in 1964. And now *this*? Wheatley asked himself, as he looked on. Johnny's gig was a disaster.

Wheatley was a man on the move. Having sacked Sambell in early 1969 after it became apparent Johnny was absorbing too much of his manager's energy, he established Drum, an agency that managed acts on the rise (The Sect and The Expression, among others) and promoted local shows. Wheatley also took over the management of The Masters Apprentices; he and the band travelled to the UK in May 1970, courtesy of a contact at the Sitmar cruise line, who offered them working passage on the *Fairstar*. The Masters remained in England long enough to record two influential albums, *Choice Cuts* and *A Toast to Panama Red*, before splitting in 1972.

After a moment of pure clarity in the wake of a sold-out Masters' gig – 'Where did all the money go,' he wondered, 'if not to us?' – Wheatley then turned his attention full-time to the business of music. He worked for the Gem-Toby Organization in the UK and also spent time in America, where, among other things, he helped arrange concerts for Richard Nixon's 1973 presidential inauguration. He worked with Michael Jackson; they shared a dressing room at the Academy Awards. And Wheatley had a green card, a priceless document for someone in his position, organised for him by US Vice President Spiro Agnew. Impressive. Wheatley returned home and set up The Wheatley Organisation.

Wheatley had two key sources of inspiration. The first was a book entitled *The Business of Music*, which he carried with him like a talisman. The second was an article called 'The Day Radio Died', written by an American music industry exec named Stan Cornyn, and published in *Billboard*. Cornyn's story became Wheatley's MO: 'How do you think outside the box?' Cornyn wrote.

'His article had a profound effect on me,' admitted Wheatley. He needed to be imaginative to succeed in the music biz.

Wheatley had developed a very simple philosophy as a manager: he treated the artist as he would have liked to have been treated when he was a musician. He also had a clear goal, to manage the first Oz band to conquer the United States, while still operating out of Australia. Wheatley would achieve this with Little River Band.

But he also didn't forget about Farnham. 'There has to be something more for him,' Wheatley figured, as he headed back to Melbourne. 'There just has to be.'

6

A FADING STAR

Friday 8 November 1974 is a significant date in Oz pop history – the start of an institution that over time would launch dozens of careers, local and international. It was the debut of *Countdown*, an ABC music program that, despite the influence of UK's *Top of the Pops* and numerous US 'clip' shows, was presented with a distinctly homegrown Australian spin. *Countdown* was MTV before the notion of music television even existed. It was the brainchild of the ubiquitous Ian 'Molly' Meldrum – soon to become the face of the show – and collaborators Michael Shrimpton and Robbie Weekes. The first episode screened on a Friday evening, but *Countdown* quickly settled into a Sunday night routine and became essential dinnertime viewing for pretty much every Australian under the age of 25. *Countdown* was different to precursors *Six O'Clock Rock* and *Bandstand*; it was more tribal and homespun, a bit looser and less starchier than those early pop shows. And much of the music was original, a huge step forward for Oz pop and rock. No more dodgy covers of overseas hits.

'I was so nervous,' Farnham said of his appearance on the first episode of the program. 'It was national – it was the ABC.'

Farnham was to sing 'One Minute Every Hour', and to prepare himself – and walk off his nerves – he paced around the ABC dressing room in Ripponlea with a tape deck, playing the song over and over again.

'I didn't want to make a complete idiot of myself.'

But anyone could see that Farnham was out of step during those early *Countdown*s. 'One Minute Every Hour' had a strong pedigree – it was the handiwork of Harry Vanda and George Young, the former Easybeats who were fast turning Sydney's Alberts studio into a house of hits – but the song wasn't their finest few minutes. Johnny dug deep and sang as if his very life depended on it, but it was no 'One', nor could it compare with Vanda and Young's remarkable mini-symphony 'Evie'. And by comparison with the offerings of Johnny's fellow guests on that inaugural episode of *Countdown*, it was positively humdrum.

Sherbet's Daryl Braithwaite crooned his hit power ballad 'You're My World', while his band, Sherbet, also appeared, sweetly harmonising 'Silvery Moon', decked out in satin and platforms, their voices in great shape, their hair even better. But more crucially, Skyhooks left the deepest impression with 'Living in the 70's'. This was the title track to their monster album, a smart, risqué record that documented life in Melbourne's fast lane, with an unmistakable undercurrent of dissent. Skyhooks' key songwriter, Greg Macainsh – later a Farnham bandmate – tapped into the sense of disquiet felt by young men who'd been aware that the random drop of a ball could result in them becoming a human target in the jungles of Vietnam.

Over time, the LP would sell 250,000 copies and top the charts for 16 weeks, setting new Australian records.

So here were Skyhooks on *Countdown*, telling it like it is, how it felt to be 'living in the '70s'. Guitarist and agitator Red Symons, his face splashed with Max Factor, stood as still as an Easter Island statue, casting disdainful stares at the shrieking teenyboppers, while singer 'Shirley' Strachan, perhaps even prettier than Farnham at his peak, was breaking hearts left, right and centre with his every pout. They were a pop band, but they were cutting-edge, mixing their astute insights into modern life with shock tactics and a splash of funny, macabre cabaret. And on the other side of the cultural divide was Johnny Farnham, a fading King of Pop, warbling 'One Minute Every Hour'. It was no contest. Johnny remained a great singer, without doubt, still packing loads of charm, but musically he was lost, directionless.

By the time Johnny returned for the 13 December 1974 episode, *Countdown* had hosted Stevie Wright, Renée Geyer, AC/DC, Daddy Cool, Madder Lake – and Skyhooks again, during the show's first outdoors shoot, at Melbourne's Luna Park, performing their new hit, 'Horror Movie'. *Countdown* was capturing the zeitgeist; these acts were all making huge waves. But not Johnny: it had now been 20 months since his last Top 10 hit.

During that 13 December episode he appeared immediately after Skyhooks – a tough spot, the 'Hooks being one hard act to follow – and sang the heavy-hearted 'Things to Do'. It was a sudsy ballad, more a show tune than a contemporary pop song like Sherbet's 'Silvery Moon' or William Shakespeare's 'My Little Angel'. Yet another misstep. At least he'd lost the suit: Johnny sported blue denim and a yellow tank top, his hair swept gently back from his face. But the live audience's response was polite, muted. Soon after, leather-clad vixen Suzi Quatro stepped up and tore a hole in 'Wild One', her bass slung low, her voice a sexy growl. Johnny's earnest performance faded away quicker than Molly Meldrum could say 'do yourself a favour'.

The unfortunate trend continued when Johnny fronted for the first colour episode of the show, screened on 1 March 1975. He now had to intro the band that had stolen his thunder.

'Hello, I'm Johnny Farnham,' he announced, 'and this is *Countdown*, the first edition for 1975 in glorious colour. Throughout the year we're going to bring you the most exciting people in Australia. Let's kick it off now with one of Australia's fastest-rising groups, Skyhooks.'

Bloody Skyhooks! It must have felt as though he was being stalked by the red-hot Melburnians. Other locals, such as Debbie Byrne, Hush, Linda George, Stevie Wright and The Captain Matchbox Whoopee Band, also featured on this special edition of the show.

Johnny returned later to count down the Top 10, a feature of each and every *Countdown*, reciting a list that featured Skyhooks (yet again) and such big international names as Elton John and the Sweet. Number one was William Shakespeare's 'My Little Angel'. Noticeably absent was the name Johnny Farnham.

Johnny spent much of 1975 in a commercial holding pattern. He did the usual rounds, including an appearance with Johnny Young and his Young Talent Team (and old stagers Bobby Limb and Dawn

Lake) at a Night of the Stars, staged in Adelaide on 1 July. He also contributed to charity events, including a Cyclone Tracy benefit in May.

Johnny even put in an unlikely TV cameo, playing the part of a bank robber by the name of Tom, in an uncharacteristically light-hearted episode of cop show *Division 4* entitled 'Once Upon a Time' and screened on 1 September. But Johnny Farnham was no bad guy; this was very much a one-off. And the dodgy wig he sported on screen, which left him looking like a frightened clown, did Farnham no favours.

Regardless, Crawford Productions, the trailblazing creators of *Division 4* and other local TV shows, continued searching for a vehicle for Johnny. In late 1975 Johnny filmed a pilot for a Crawfords TV comedy with the working title of *Me & Mr. Thorne*, playing the lead, a character named Bobby Fletcher. The plot was a twist on the Sherlock Holmes story; Bobby was the Watson character, the sidekick of Thorne, antique bookseller and amateur sleuth.

'I don't know what it will do for my image,' Johnny told a reporter on the set. 'The minimal music in it gives me a chance to do some serious acting.'

Yet despite the presence of well-known actors Gordon Chater (fresh from *My Name's McGooley, What's Yours?*) and Chuck Faulkner, some good reviews – 'Farnham could very soon become one of Australia's top acting talents,' *TV Week* proclaimed, 'the sooner it becomes a series the better' – and the muscle of Crawfords, *Me & Mr. Thorne* didn't get picked up as a series. The 90-minute pilot was put on the shelf. It didn't air for another year and duly died a quick and relatively painless death.

Johnny set to work on a new album. But if this was intended to be the musical statement that would reposition him at the top of the pop ladder, someone, somewhere didn't get Sambell's memo.

There were some wonderful Australian releases in 1975 – Skyhooks did it again with *Ego Is Not a Dirty Word*, another daring collection of songs, which became the country's fourth bestselling album of the year (their *Living in the 70's* was the number one bestseller). Ariel's *Rock and Roll Scars* featured the timeless hit 'I'll Be Gone'; AC/DC delivered the double whammy of *High Voltage* and *T.N.T.*; Stevie Wright pumped out 'Black Eyed Bruiser'; Sherbet, with their, 'Life ... Is for Living' (and their first greatest hits set) was unstoppable; Hush were *Rough, Tough 'n' Ready*. All these albums were great in their own way – okay, maybe not the Hush record overall, but their take on the rockin' chestnut 'Boney Maronie' was a massive hit. *J.P. Farnham Sings*, however, was not a record to get excited about.

Credit where it's due: it was an attempt on Johnny and Sambell's part to present a more mature sound and image, targeting an older audience. The days of 'Sadie' and other novelties were long gone. Each track on the album was an Australian composition, Johnny singing cuts from Brian Cadd ('Show Me the Way'), Vanda and Young ('Things to Do'), Russell Morris ('Don't Rock the Boat'), a cover of Billy Thorpe's 'Most People I Know (Think That I'm Crazy)' and a Farnham original, 'To Be or Not to Be'. The back-cover shot, of Johnny's denim-clad legs and an acoustic guitar, looked like something straight from the singer-songwriter handbook – even the album title implied a more sophisticated Johnny. But nothing worked. EMI pulled two singles from the album – the Russell Morris and Vanda/Young songs – but neither charted, nor did the album. It was apparent that Johnny's days as the label's poster boy, a dependable hit-maker, were well and truly over. His time with EMI was about to expire, along with another key relationship.

Clearly, if Johnny was to continue making music, it was time for a change. In early 1976, the relationship between Johnny and Darryl Sambell, begun in Cohuna in 1967, was finally, acrimoniously annulled by Farnham. It's hard to pinpoint one particular event that brought things undone, although it's likely that the deathblow was dealt on New Year's Eve, when Darryl insisted that Johnny perform a midnight Melbourne show, even though Johnny had already made plans to see in the new year with his family. After the gig, an angry Johnny went home, late, while Darryl drowned his sorrows – in booze and tears. (On a bad day, Sambell could work his way through an entire bottle of Scotch. He was also prone to the occasional nervous breakdown; he'd had nine while working with Johnny.)

Jillian, on the other hand, laid the blame on a drunken drive with Sambell after a party at the home of his business partner, Kevin Lewis.

'He could have killed us all,' she said. She'd had enough of 'Dazzling Dazza'.

The formal showdown took place in the office of Johnny Young.

'I'm quitting the business,' Sambell added, a tad shrilly, after Johnny told him of his decision.

'No, you're not quitting the business,' Johnny replied. 'I'm sacking you. You can work with someone else.'

But Sambell's mind was made up. He was done.

The demise of the partnership was announced in *The Age* in mid-January 1976. 'Farnham Sambell Split' roared the headline.

This wasn't the first time a Sambell/Farnham row had been covered by the dailies; in June 1969 they'd even gone to court, briefly, when Farnham filed a writ claiming Sambell owed him a substantial sum of money ('Singer Asks for $30,000'). The writ, filed by John's father, sought a court order demanding that Sambell produce all books and records of their accounts. It was resolved, but that didn't matter now. They were through.

There's no denying that while together, Sambell and Farnham had made history. By his unique blend of nous, hype and sheer bloody-mindedness, Sambell had helped transform a shy apprentice into the country's biggest star since Johnny O'Keefe, a star of stage, small screen and the pop charts, the idol of a good chunk of under-20 Australia. Sambell had played a key role in Johnny's unprecedented run of hits, starting with 1967's 'Sadie' and ending with 1973's 'I Can't Dance to Your Music'; Farnham cut 13 Top 20 songs during that red-hot run. 'Sadie', the song Sambell claimed as his discovery, was still the biggest-selling single in Australian music history. Johnny was crowned King of Pop for five years running. And Darryl was always in the wings at Johnny's many shows, concerts that generated the type of weak-kneed teen hysteria rarely seen since The Beatles' tour of Oz. Sambell was actively involved in every aspect of Johnny's career, from his wardrobe to his song selection, to his work in the theatre and on TV. He lived and breathed Johnny Farnham.

'He was the youngest manager in the pop business,' Melbourne's

Herald once noted of Sambell, 'and his property was of sun-surface temperature – Johnny Farnham.'

But now there was too much personal baggage, there'd been too many conflicts, and Johnny's career was flat-lining. Almost immediately after the split, Sambell moved to Auckland, while Johnny also took a break.

Johnny and Jillian flew to America in April, where he had the chance to sit in on a recording session with a personal hero, Motown great Stevie Wonder, perhaps his biggest musical influence. It was bliss, the perfect escape from all his hassles back in Oz. Once back home, Farnham would sing Wonder's 'All Is Fair in Love and War' during an appearance on the *Dave Allen Show* and, in another killer performance, Wonder's challenging ghetto drama 'Living for the City'. He'd already covered 'Ma Cherie Amour', back on 1971's *Johnny* LP. He was a rusted-on Wonder fan. They'd also get to tour together, a dream fulfilled for Johnny.

Kenn Brodziak, the man who'd produced *Charlie Girl*, agreed to manage Johnny, but in a very different manner to Sambell. Brodziak chose to be hands-off, business-like; he wouldn't involve himself with Johnny on a day-to-day basis. Theirs was a strictly professional relationship. There'd be no haggling and no late-night, post-gig dramas. He'd ensure that promoters always paid upfront. Farnham wasn't going to do any more TV ads, at least not on Brodziak's watch. 'They're just not right for a star of Johnny's stature,' Brodziak believed. And as far as Brodziak was concerned, Johnny's personal life was just that – his own. There'd be no unplanned drop-ins or after-hours phone calls. It was all about business.

Johnny's first move with his new manager, however, was yet

another miscalculation. It seemed as though he just couldn't take a trick.

Johnny may have admitted that it 'wasn't the best comedy in the world', but *Bobby Dazzler* wasn't a completely terrible TV show. The local television industry, especially sitcoms such as this Crawfords production, was still relatively young. Until now, dramas had been dominant – *The Sullivans* had just begun its eight-season run – and cop shows were as common on the small screen as certain actors' faces: *Homicide*, *Matlock Police*, *Bluey* and *Solo One* were all either in production or still screening during 1976. *Number 96* and the long-running rural soap *Bellbird* rated highly. But well-scripted sitcoms were rare; the order of the day comedy-wise was variety shows such as Paul Hogan's regular specials and *The Norman Gunston Show*. Comedy benchmarks like ABC's *Mother and Son* remained way off in the future.

The plotline for *Bobby Dazzler*, which began production in April 1976, was uncomplicated. This wasn't Chekhov; hell, it wasn't even *Kingswood Country*. Essentially, a young man reconnects with his errant father; easy laughs ensue. End of story. At least Crawfords got the casting right. Johnny played Bobby Farrell, the male lead, but there wasn't a lot of acting required: Bobby was a pretty young pop singer on the rise, searching for a manager to build his career. This was almost reality TV.

'The series is not based on my life and career as a singer,' insisted Johnny, 'but obviously there'll be material based on the sort of experiences I've had.'

Fred, Bobby Farrell's wayward old man, played by veteran actor Maurie Field – who'd just been seen in *Bellbird* – was a former vaudevillian, which provided plenty of opportunities for he and Johnny to sing, or at least ham it up, song-and-dance-man-style. In the pilot they mugged their way through 'Won't You Come Home, Bill Bailey'. Also in the pilot was a very young, extremely green Sigrid Thornton, playing a gushing, weak-at-the-knees fan of Bobby's who seemed on the edge of a breakdown.

Interestingly, the pilot originally closed on a slightly different note. At its close, Bobby (Johnny) announced that his father might be staying 'for a night – or two', his smile fading noticeably as the credits rolled. But that bittersweet ending was modified for the finished episode, as was Farmham's Christian name, which was briefly billed in the credits as 'John' but then reverted to 'Johnny'.

The pilot was successful enough for Channel 7 to commission a 13-episode series, with production starting in November 1976. Screenwriter Terry Stapleton, who'd later hit pay dirt with *The Flying Doctors*, wrote all 14 episodes. There was easy-going chemistry between old-stager Field and Farnham; Hector Crawford himself talked it up to the press. 'It's a great vehicle for Johnny Farnham and the rest of the very talented crew,' the producer stated. 'We are looking forward to this with great optimism. We think it's sufficiently amusing and different to be a top-rater.'

Yet the show seemed doomed from the start. It didn't screen in Melbourne until 20 November 1977 and then ran through summer, the non-ratings period – the cricket season – which was not a huge vote of confidence from Channel 7. When its ratings were briefly monitored, *Bobby Dazzler* cornered only 14% of the viewing audience – hardly must-see TV. Also, its timeslot was tweaked, which confused viewers. The show was canned after one season.

Farnham's attempts to reboot his career as a TV actor, though not entirely without merit – he had a knack with wholesome comedy – had fallen flat. He was treading water, yet again, and the tide was rising. *Countdown* hadn't invited him back since 1975, his place now taken by other Jo(h)ns – as in, English, St. Peeters and Paul Young. Skyhooks, meanwhile, made at least a dozen appearances in the show's first 12 months.

And Johnny's most recent singles, 'You Love Me Back to Life Again' and 'Rock and Roll Hall of Fame', had come and gone without a murmur, this time on Infinity records, Sherbet's label, EMI having not renewed his contract. The 'Hall of Fame' single was an interesting diversion, with just a hint of disco groove lurking beneath the pop-rock surface. Johnny's vocal was tougher than usual, grittier – but it hardly mattered. No-one was listening.

In the late 1970s there was unfashionable, and then there was Johnny Farnham. He resorted to occasional work as a radio DJ, pulling a few day shifts at Sydney's 2GB, sitting in for regular host Jimmy Hannan. He also did a week at Gold Coast station 4GG. He even judged talent quests.

'It was tough,' Farnham said of this incredibly difficult time. 'I couldn't get a job.'

He spent a lot of time at home on the couch, packing on a few pounds, watching his bills pile up. Johnny's restaurant was still in the red, his records weren't selling and a hefty, unpaid tax bill pinned to the fridge kept catching his eye. Sometimes he'd go fishing, one of the few things that truly relaxed him, or he'd disappear into the garden. When he was on the road, no matter where he was or what the situation, he'd call Jillian before he went to sleep.

'It's all fine,' he'd reassure her, even if the opposite was true. 'Everything's going great.'

Jillian remained the only true supporter he had, the love of his life.

She sometimes found herself protecting her husband. At a show in Adelaide, during a break between sets, Jillian snuck away to the bathroom, where she overheard a conversation.

'I can't stand that Johnny Farnham, he makes my skin crawl,' slurred one woman.

'Oh, I hate him,' replied her friend.

This was too much for Jillian, who approached them.

'Oh, I love him,' Jillian announced. 'I think he's great.'

'How could you?' the two asked in unison. They seemed shocked.

'I'm his wife,' Jillian snapped back.

The bathroom emptied quicker than you could say 'foot in mouth'.

'I love being married,' Johnny said in an interview from these bleak days. 'I wouldn't be single again for anything. Jill is a terrific person ... she keeps me in line.'

Despite the ongoing disappointments, Johnny didn't consider quitting the business. He was a singer, an entertainer. What else could he do?

7

HELP IS ON ITS WAY

Johnny changed managers yet again early in 1978, hooking up with his friend Danny Findlay, Colleen Hewett's partner and a former member of the band M.P.D. Limited. Findlay was the third member of the Backstage restaurant troika, which remained a problem – the venue was bleeding money. Findlay was surprised to learn how insecure Johnny was feeling about his career – though, considering its sad state, it shouldn't have been a shock. Farnham was no longer recording, his TV career had flopped; all that remained were endless, soulless nights on the club-and-pub circuit, trying to sway punters' attention away from the pokies.

Glenn Wheatley, now making a huge splash as manager of the Little River Band, caught Johnny playing at Twin Towns RSL at Tweed Heads, and felt the same quiet despair he'd experienced after witnessing that concert on the beach a few years back. As Wheatley watched, the RSL gig started badly and didn't get much better. A few songs in, Johnny stopped the incompetent house band and was forced to count them back into the song. They played with no feeling, no soul and the couple of hundred people looking on turned away, disinterested.

Wheatley was stunned. He knew that Farnham was much, much better than this, yet here he was, adrift in pop purgatory, picking up a few hundred dollars a night.

'This is the great Johnny Farnham,' he thought to himself, nursing a drink, watching the train wreck continue, 'singing with a band who can't play. What's going on?'

Johnny was recognised by some in the business as the 'Man Who Can't Say No', and here was tangible evidence – he was performing with a dud group to a bored, distracted audience. It was a big comedown.

Wheatley hung in long enough to check in with Johnny after the show. Johnny had changed into his street clothes; his stage suit was hanging nearby. Without saying a word, Wheatley grabbed Johnny's tux and threw it into a garbage bin. Farnham didn't protest. Nothing said middle-of-the-road like a penguin suit. Johnny's wardrobe needed an update.

Wheatley left him with some advice: 'From here on in, we're going to have to forget all this. You have to start again.'

Though he didn't make any specific promises on the night, it was clear that Glenn Wheatley could well be the key to Johnny's future.

Though he lacked confidence, Farnham remained an optimist at heart. He believed that someone would throw him a lifeline, and he was proved right. It came in the form of a popular TV show. Johnny couldn't sell records, he had no record deal, and he was finding it hard to grab the attention of club-goers, but he did have the support of Don Lane. And for once Johnny's timing was spot on.

Lane, the so-called 'Lanky Yank', began hosting his hugely popular *The Don Lane Show* on Channel 9 in 1975. Over its eight years and hundreds of episodes it would become the highest-rating variety program in Oz TV history; Lane became the highest-paid celeb on the small screen. He won a Logie for Most Popular Personality on Australian TV in 1977 – 'The Lanky Yank Takes the Gold,' proclaimed *TV Week*.

John's thing – it would always be John from now on – for big ballads and show tunes made him a natural for the program. Right now he was a much better fit with the blue-rinsers who watched and loved Don Lane than he was among the screaming teens of *Countdown*.

One of his earliest appearances on Lane's show took place on 22 November 1979. John, accompanied by a lone pianist, wrapped himself around Paul Simon's epic, aching, gospel-ly 'Bridge over Troubled Water'. His suit was a sombre brown, his tie only as wide as his collared shirt would permit, his hair not quite the super-mullet that would soon be his trademark, but getting there, inch by sneaky inch. He looked great. John's eyes were closed much of the time, and he enunciated every last word carefully, soulfully, singing as though his life – not just his career – depended upon it. Just as he'd done with Harry Nilsson's 'One', all those years ago, John had found a song that allowed his voice to soar, and a lyric he connected with deeply. Love, loss, despair – 'Bridge' had the mother lode.

John absolutely nailed it – and just for a moment, as the song came crashing to a close, the Don Lane Orchestra having chimed in during the final verse, it seemed as though Lane's audience was about to jump out of their seats – a stretch, given their vintage. The applause was deafening. John smiled and nodded, as if to say, 'There. Told you I could sing.' Farnham had found his audience.

John heaped praise on Lane: 'He helped me over my nerves on being on live TV, he always had something positive to say and always gave me much-needed advice, which I still rely heavily on today.' They became good friends, very tight.

Lane always introduced Farnham in the most fulsome manner – John was the best vocalist in the country, he was a terrific guy, a great friend, a good family man and so on. And behind the scenes John had the backing of Kate Halliday, a producer on the show, someone who also had total faith in John's ability. (She'd go on to work with Glenn Wheatley.) Yet sometimes John's pre-show nerves were so bad he'd ask for cue cards, even when he was singing a tune he knew inside out. Other times he had a song's lyrics scrawled on his hand. Memory was not his strong point.

The problem with the Lane show, if there was one, was simple: after a run-through with the band at around 6 p.m., and a final rehearsal, John was left with several hours to kill before making his live, late-night appearance. He'd pace up and down, up and down, wearing a hole in the green room carpet. Still, the audience was huge, Lane's support was undeniable, and the pay – $250 per spot – was very handy.

John forged other friendships on the show. After one appearance, he came home with quite the surprise for Jillian: half a dozen visiting test cricketers, his co-stars on that night's program. Fortunately, Jillian, like John, was a cricket fan – and thankfully they had a decent-sized couch.

In August 1979 John and Jillian scraped together enough money to take a holiday in Las Vegas, travelling with none other than Lane himself. Coincidentally, on 17 August the Little River Band was playing the Aladdin in Vegas, midway through their latest American tour. They filled the 7000-seat concert hall for three nights running. The band was on fire in America. Their latest single, 'Lonesome Loser', was yet another Top 10 hit in the States. It would be nominated for a Grammy.

John tried and failed to get a ticket for the sold-out show, so he called his old friend Wheatley and managed to swing some freebies. That night John sat in the hall, a face in the crowd, absolutely blown away by what he witnessed. This 'little' Aussie band was killing it: the crowd went nuts, they knew every number that LRB performed. John was blown away. Why didn't he know about this?

John and Jillian caught up with Wheatley afterwards. It was midnight and they sat and talked as the crew bumped out the group's gear. It was a warm night in the desert – but temperatures ran even hotter backstage, as John briefly witnessed the hard-to-please band pick apart each other's faults. Still, John was astounded by what he'd seen on stage.

'Is it always like this?' he asked Wheatley.

'What do you mean?' Wheatley replied.

'The crowd, the madness. The way the people responded. They blew me away. It was great.'

Wheatley assured him that yes, it was the same wherever they went in the States. The band was at their absolute peak; America couldn't get enough of them. They'd just filled the Universal Amphitheater in LA five nights running. Their records were selling in huge numbers.

'I just never knew the Little River Band were this big in America,' gushed John. 'It's incredible. They're superstars. You must be incredibly proud of what you've achieved.'

Wheatley *was* proud. He also had an idea.

'What if I were to manage you?' he asked.

Wheatley had seen how low John's career had sunk in Australia. He firmly believed in John's talent as a vocalist. As Wheatley wrote in his memoir *Paper Paradise*, John was 'probably the greatest interpreter of songs Australia has produced'. He knew John had the chops, charisma and stage presence to do much more. On the flipside, Wheatley also knew what he was getting into: the Farnham name was poison with record companies and record buyers back in Oz. It would be a tough battle to get him a deal, let alone get his music played on radio. Still, he couldn't just sit on his hands and watch his friend's career implode.

John was very tempted by Wheatley's proposal, but was still working with Danny Findlay. And, as always, his sense of loyalty came into play: how could he sack Danny, who'd hung in with him during the toughest time of his career? Findlay was also a friend – and a partner in Backstage. John didn't know which way to move, but he did agree to meet with Wheatley again, back in Australia.

That meeting took place in early 1980. By this time, Wheatley had formed a company with his brother Paul, simply known as WBE: Wheatley Brothers Entertainment. Their client roster was impressive; they repped LRB, Australian Crawl, Ross Wilson and Stylus. John, meanwhile, had finally accepted that it was time to part ways with Danny Findlay, although, typically, it had taken him some six months to decide it was the right move. Loyalty was one thing, but Wheatley, clearly, had the contacts and drive – and the score on the board with LRB – to take John's career in a new, better direction.

'I knew how America worked and that was a big factor,' Wheatley wrote, reflecting on John's decision. 'He also desperately wanted to get back on top in Australia. He did not want to end up doing clubs for the rest of his life.'

John's old mentor, Johnny O'Keefe, had been stuck on that seemingly endless treadmill when he died in October 1978, aged just 43. His last gig, in fact, had been at an RSL in Bathurst, to an enthusiastic yet small crowd. Farnham loved O'Keefe but didn't want to head down that path.

'That meeting with Glenn was the turning point in my life,' he said of their sit-down, 'both personally and professionally. It was not only the start of my public resurgence, it was also the beginning of a lifelong friendship. In fact, he is like a brother to me.'

But even the most cursory once-over of John's accounts made it clear to Wheatley that his new charge had big problems. Backstage was still haemorrhaging money, for one thing. John owed more money than he owned. Wheatley brought in lawyer Ken Starke, along with accountants from the reputable firm Ernst & Young, to help put John's finances in order.

Business-wise, the first point of order was to sell some assets, which meant John and Jillian were forced to flog the two houses they owned, in Melbourne's Surrey Hills and Bonnie Doon. Only a year before, John and Jillian had been talking up their Bonnie Doon 'haven' to a reporter from *The Australian Women's Weekly*. 'This is the only place where we can share everything and we can be ourselves.' Now, out of necessity, it was gone.

For someone raised by solid, sensible working-class parents, selling his properties was a huge sacrifice for John, especially at a time when he 'felt like a washed-up singer'.

'To lose that dream and have to rent was soul-destroying for him,' Wheatley wrote.

John was devastated but had no choice. It was time to cash things in – and to man up. There was also the matter of finding a new home for their dogs, a borzoi named Laczar and a Great Dane called Bonnie, as well as their four cats. The Farnhams had lost what was a fair menagerie.

'Wheat, Jillian and I are broke, clean broke. I'm in real trouble,' John admitted during one of their earliest meetings.

'How much do you need?' Wheatley asked him.

John gave him a figure and Wheatley proceeded to write a cheque for $50,000, no further questions required. John couldn't have asked for a greater show of faith.

Wheatley's commitment gave John the sense he might yet get out of this mess.

Wheatley tried to negotiate a new record deal for John, but without success. No-one, from John's former label EMI down, was willing to gamble on a Farnham comeback. They simply didn't believe it could happen. After a few months of knockbacks, John signed directly to WBE Records, Wheatley's own label. In an interesting twist of fate,

WBE was distributed by EMI, the label that had just rejected their former biggest star. The irony wasn't lost on John or Glenn. They'd show them.

Farnham reinforced Wheat's faith when he appeared on the Royal Charity Gala Concert TV 'spectacular' in May 1980, which aired on Channel 9. Wheatley approached director Peter Faiman and suggested that John perform 'Help!'. Faiman wasn't so sure.

'Why a Beatles song?' he asked. 'Can't he do something contemporary?' But eventually he accepted that it might work. It did much more than that. John was no master of the ivories – 'this is the only song I know how to play on the piano,' he'd tell audiences before playing 'Help!', 'and then not very well' – but there was something unique and intriguing about the way he played, and sang, 'Help!'. Jillian had heard it hundreds of times at home, John plunking away on the piano in their lounge room.

As a vocalist, John was at his best when he tackled a lyric with which he could genuinely connect, emotions like the despair of 'One' and 'Bridge over Troubled Water'. 'Help!', given his circumstances, couldn't be more poignant: if anybody needed a leg up, it was John Farnham, flat broke and stuck in music biz limbo. Sure, there was more than a whiff of melodrama to the arrangement – he didn't so much give it the kitchen sink treatment, but the entire kitchen, dishwasher and fridge included – yet the effect was powerful, overwhelming. John Farnham stole the Gala Concert.

His co-stars, Peter Allen, Julie Anthony, Olivia Newton-John, Helen Reddy and ocker comic Paul 'Hoges' Hogan, watched on in amazement, as did the resident royal, Queen Elizabeth. Farnham shone even more brightly than Liz's jewels.

The Royal Charity concert pulled a huge audience of more than six million viewers, making it one of the most viewed TV shows of all time (just a little south of the Moon landing). And many of those six million watching wisened up to the fact that the country's best singer was back in action.

Wheatley was in Germany with the Little River Band when the show took place. The next morning, his telex machine clicked into life, the message making it very clear how great Farnham's performance had been. It was then that he knew they were on the road out of hell.

8

UNCOVERED AND REBORN

What John now needed to do was make a musical statement, to really drive home the fact that he was back. Farnham agreed to Wheatley's idea of teaming him with Little River Band's Graeham Goble, a huge Farnham fan. The feeling was mutual; Farnham was a big admirer of Goble's LRB hits. Maybe together they could come up with some musical magic. Goble needed an outlet for his songs; the battle to get his own material on LRB albums was one of the more challenging aspects of a band not short on internal friction. And perhaps Goble could help 'update' John's sound and image, something he desperately needed.

Uncovered was an album of firsts: the beginning of John's professional relationship with Wheatley, his first release for WBE and the first (but not the last) time Farnham worked with Goble. It was also the public 'coming out' of John Farnham: now, finally, he was Johnny no more. *Uncovered* marked the start of his 'adult contemporary' career. There'd be no more novelty songs or show tunes in his repertoire from now on. The release of *Uncovered* in July 1980 was the first time John had been anywhere near the business end of a chart since 1973.

Goble, clearly in the midst of a creative purple patch, wrote or co-wrote nine of the 10 tracks that made the final cut – the only other song included was Lennon and McCartney's 'Help!', a no-brainer after John's standout rendition for the royals. Goble also produced the album, which was recorded over three weeks at Balance studios in Melbourne. For John's studio band, Goble assembled an impressive line-up: guitarist Tommy Emmanuel, keyboardist Mal Logan, who'd played with LRB and the Renée Geyer Band, and bassist Barry Sullivan, who'd been part of Chain. Guitarists Ric Formosa and David Briggs – both past members of LRB – contributed to the album, as did current LRB members Derek Pellicci and Wayne Nelson. With their involvement, and Goble's, the album was an accidental dry run for Farnham's near future. Inspired, John nailed his vocals in the rapid time of three days.

Clearly inspired, Farnham even co-wrote one track with Goble, 'Jillie's Song', an ode to his wife of seven years, a woman who'd been by his side as his career bottomed out – a 'pretty lady', in Farnham's simple words. When he played it to her, Jillian wasn't sure how to react: she felt he'd been a tad generous with his praise. John had idealised her. 'I'm not *that* great,' she told him.

Still, the emotions were heartfelt and John sang the hell out of it, proving that, when inspired, he had a fair grasp of the songwriter's trade. John's claw-fisted playing on 'Help!', which he thrashed out on a pianola at home, helped give that track, a feature of *Uncovered*, a distinctively Farnham flavour. These two contributions alone proved he wasn't taking the same approach as in the past, when he'd rock up to the studio, sing what he was told to, and then race off to the next engagement.

John appeared on *The Don Lane Show* once again, around the time of *Uncovered*'s release, crooning Goble's piano-powered ballad 'Please Don't Ask Me', a song that would be a staple of his live set for years to come. This was the more sophisticated, grown-up John Farnham on full display: his fair hair was shining, not a strand out of place, his jacket was a conservative ash-grey, and he wore a blue collared shirt underneath. Eyes closed most of the time, he sang as if it was the last song on earth – by the final note he seemed close to tears. Once again, John proved just how great an interpreter he was.

Come July 1980, 'Help!', *Uncovered*'s first single, was scaling the charts. It would peak at number eight and chart for almost four months. Finally, a Top 10 hit. John hadn't had that experience since 1973's 'Everything Is Out of Season'. The Top 40 in July was a curious mixture of rock stalwarts (Paul McCartney's 'Coming Up', Billy Joel's 'It's Still Rock and Roll to Me') and new wave acts, including locals Flowers and The Dugites. But with such sonic melodramas as 'You've Lost That Loving Feeling' from Long John Baldry (featuring Kathi McDonald) and Bette Midler's 'The Rose' both riding high in the Top 40, and with belters like Michael Bolton and Whitney Houston soon to pounce, John, for the first time in his career, was slightly ahead of the game. At its essence 'Help!' was a precursor to the power ballads that would dominate the 1980s.

'This is, quite simply, the best thing Johnny [sic] Farnham has done,' wrote Fairfax music critic Madeleine d'Haeye. 'It sets a high standard in phrasing, timing and expression. This is no longer a pop hit – Farnham has turned it into a cry from the heart.' High praise.

Three other singles, 'Please Don't Ask Me', 'She Says to Me' and 'She's Everywhere', were lifted from *Uncovered* over the next 12 months; none were big sellers, but they proved the record had depth. *Uncovered* sold 55,000 copies, not a bad return for Farnham and Wheatley, a steady first step together. The album hung about the charts for three months.

John, however, wished he'd been a bit more bullish in the studio, admitting that he let Goble 'lead me by the nose. [*Uncovered*] was the first album I put any serious input into, but looking back, I didn't do as much as I could have.'

He was being a bit tough on himself; it would have been incredibly difficult for anyone, let alone a guy staging a return, to challenge the opinion of the man who wrote 'Reminiscing' and whose work with LRB had dominated the US charts the past few years.

In the press, the words 'comeback' and 'resurrection' were mentioned in every article relating to Farnham and *Uncovered*. 'John Farnham Veteran at 31' announced *The Sydney Morning Herald*. This sometimes upset John.

'If the public see this as a comeback,' he said to Peter Dean of *The Australian Women's Weekly*, 'then that's the way it is.' He hastened to add that he felt it was nothing but 'journalistic bull'. Rare strong words. John, to his mind, hadn't been away; he'd just fallen out of favour.

'Farnham and his advisers,' noted Dean, 'have set their sights [with *Uncovered*] on a wider market, particularly the 18-to-35-year-old album-buying public.' Farnham hinted at an assault on America, although 'the right overseas offer hasn't come along yet'.

The album artwork, an image of John's face obscured by a woman's hands, one of his eyes partly visible between her brightly polished talons, seemed to be a comment on his recent invisibility. He looked like a man slowly, hesitantly, emerging into the light. It was an apt metaphor for where he was at in his career in 1980.

Albums reviews were mainly favourable. 'John Farnham's *Uncovered*,' noted *The Sydney Morning Herald*, 'firmly underscores the professionalism of this articulate singer.' The heavy involvement of LRB alumni did not go unnoticed. 'The albums bears the Little River Band stamp of quality.'

In the wake of the positive response to the album, and the fact 'Help!' was a hit, John returned to the road, but this time with a rock-solid band, including guitar wizard Emmanuel, himself a big Farnham fan, who described his new boss as 'the best pop singer in the world'. The once empty houses now started to fill, but with a new audience.

'What I'm doing now is totally different,' John told a reporter backstage at a gig at Sydney Uni. He admitted that at some gigs older fans had rolled up expecting to hear 'Sadie'. That wasn't going to happen. 'I'm not doing a cabaret act now; I'm doing a more contemporary thing. It's virtually starting again.'

'The atmosphere [at the gig],' noted one reviewer, 'was closer to AC/DC than Burt Bacharach. Gone is the middle of the road cabaret singer. Superseding him is a keener, stronger and more ambitious rock and roll performer.' John covered songs from Toto, Christopher Cross and Bob Seger.

When the John Farnham Band packed Melbourne's Billboard nightclub in late September 1980, one of the many people sardined into the room was the striking actress Gaynor Martin, who'd become hugely popular through her role on the hit Crawfords soapie *Skyways*. Glenn Wheatley met Martin for the first time that night. It seemed that John wasn't alone; Wheatley's future was also looking pretty damned bright.

Oddly, after the successful 'rebranding' that was *Uncovered*, John's next step was a sideways move. *Uncovered* may have been an original work (even the reworked 'Help!' felt new) and a clear creative step forward for John, but *Farnham and Byrne*, the show that debuted on ABC TV on 16 August 1980, was a flashback to John's middle-of-the-road past, a safe commercial bet. That's not to say it was a bad show; it was a smartly produced 50 minutes of family-friendly good times, directed by Grant Rule (one of the brains behind the trailblazing *Countdown*) and Ric Birch, later to find fame as executive producer of the 2000 Sydney Olympic Games ceremonies. Four choreographers assisted with the many musical set pieces, which featured 30 dancers and a sizeable crew. But *Farnham and Byrne* blazed no creative trails.

As *The Australian Women's Weekly* noted when the show premiered: '*Farnham and Byrne* centres on two artists doing what they do best – singing. There are no corny comedy sketches or fool-around scenes to create boredom. Just lots of music and dancing, which makes for good solid entertainment.'

Guests included Kiwi cabaret king Ricky May, Doug Parkinson, Angela Ayers and Normie Rowe, as well as Farnham's friend and former Queen of Pop Colleen Hewett – all dependable crowd-pleasers.

Debbie Byrne was a recent Queen of Pop, winning the *TV Week* crown in 1974 and 1975.

It wasn't an easy gig. For three months straight John's working day would begin at 6.30 a.m. with several hours of make-up and then he was straight onto the set. Taping continued until 5.30 p.m. Then the two stars would sit down to chew over likely music for future episodes. Each show comprised 12 songs, mostly covers of contemporary hits; they needed loads of music.

'It was hard work, bloody hard work,' said John.

The stars fulsomely talked up each other's talents.

'[Debbie's] singing and dancing up a storm,' John said from the ABC set. 'I'm knocked out by her talent. [And] everyone's having a ball.'

'This is the first time I've worked with John,' added a beaming Byrne, who brought her young daughter, Arja, into the studio every day, perhaps stirring up some paternal feelings in John. 'I've just discovered I can dance better than I thought I could.'

The show's set pieces were slick, '80s-style TV. For their take on Billy Joel's 'The Stranger', the producers recreated a retro-looking diner, Farnham and Byrne surrounded by gyrating teddy boys and rockers, decked out in winklepicker shoes (deja vu for John, who sported a pair as a teenager) and stovepipe pants, their hair slick with product. So far, so *Happy Days*. John, his own hair sculpted into an eye-gouging pompadour, even briefly nursed a ciggie, à la Olivia Newton-John in *Grease*. As always, he dug deep for the song, which was a good fit for his voice.

For a 'Superstition' production piece – reaffirming John's love for Stevie Wonder – things got a little more risqué. John's sensible pullover and slacks were in stark contrast to the dancers' skin-tight lycra, drag-queen make-up and blatantly homoerotic overtones – four shirtless Village People types in leather pants was quite a bold statement for Auntie ABC in 1980, let alone for a show starring John Farnham. John spent much of the clip warily keeping his distance, quite literally, from the hairy-chested dancers, who came on like back-alley hustlers.

John got in a plug for *Uncovered*, singing Goble's 'She Says to Me' during one episode, with the utmost earnestness. There were no topless male dancers in sight this time. Afterwards, John explained that 'She Says' was inspired by Goble's young daughter, Alicia.

'Can I have one please, Graeham?' Byrne asked.

'What, a baby?' Farnham joked.

'No – a good song.'

Despite the show's obvious polish and broad appeal, *Farnham and Byrne* lasted only one season. Farnham's partner was on the brink of a major heroin addiction, which would soon become big news: Byrne was busted in 1982 and fell off the radar for some time. And John? He was just a few steps away from some major changes of his own.

9

PLAYING TO WIN

John had a dream start to 1981. He and his band opened for his idol, Stevie Wonder, when the African-American soul and pop superstar toured Oz, for the first time, in April. Wonder was riding high on the success of his latest hit album, *Hotter Than July*. John was thrilled to simply be in the same room as the man; yet here he was, sharing the bill. Better still, Wonder invited Farnham up on stage each night to help with the encore. It was a career high for John, a huge moment. He couldn't believe his good fortune.

Off stage, John and Jillian had been trying, and failing, to have children pretty much since the time they were wed. They'd grown close to Findlay and Hewett's kids, and hoped for a brood of their own. Jillian had miscarried in 1979 and they'd tried artificial insemination, working with a doctor who'd had success with primates at the Melbourne Zoo, but so far they remained childless.

'There was nothing wrong with either of us,' John pointed out, '[but] it was something that just didn't happen.' They decided to adopt.

Then in early 1981, very soon after the death of Jill's father, Robert, the couple discovered with surprise that Jillian was pregnant. Their finances were a disaster – they'd finally offloaded their restaurant, Backstage, losing something like $500,000 on the investment – but becoming parents, well, that was priceless, way more important than anything else. They were thrilled.

John had a theory about when and where their son was conceived. He was sure that it happened one night in the country, when he and Jill excused themselves from a party, went for a walk and 'one thing led to another'. Before you could say 'chain reaction', John's bum was protruding from the back of his car as he and Jill got down to business.

Robbie Farnham was born on 27 September 1981.

In early February 1982 John, just back from a vacation with Jill and baby Robbie, fielded a call from Glenn Wheatley.

'John,' his manager asked after a quick catch-up, 'how would you feel about joining the Little River Band?'

The line went quiet for a few seconds.

'When can I start?' John asked.

LRB? He was in. The opportunity was too good to resist, for a number of reasons. First and foremost, he loved the band, having seen them in action in Vegas. John also saw it as a chance to perform to new, international audiences, Wheatley having tried and failed to garner an overseas deal for *Uncovered*. John was growing weary of the same Aussie clubs, the same faces. He knew some of the LRB guys – Goble, Birtles and Pellicci – from *Uncovered*, which would help his transition into an established band. And maybe he could offset some of his recent financial disasters by joining such a successful group. There were loads of positives.

'Farnham Joins Million Dollar Band' read the headline when John's news went public. But the bottom line for his new venture proved a little less tantalising than John, or the press, could have realised at the time.

The Little River Band had already come a long way by the time John officially joined the group. Wheatley had first spotted them in a dingy London pub in 1974 operating under the name Mississippi. Their members at the time included singer-songwriters Birtles and Goble, as well as drummer Pellicci. Some of the guys, like Farnham, were from immigrant families – more ten-pound Poms – so there was some common ground.

Glenn Shorrock, yet another offspring of ten-pound Poms, was also in London in 1974. Shorrock was a vastly different character to those in the band, especially Goble – he was a piss-taker, mouthy, always on the lookout for a party, whereas Goble was pedantic and detail-orientated, with a keen interest in numerology – but Shorrock sensed a kindred musical spirit and a fellow traveller and agreed to join the group as singer.

As for handsome Dutch-born Birtles, whose real name was Gerard Bertelkamp, he'd been a member of Oz pop-rockers Zoot, who were once managed by Darryl Sambell and sometimes shared bills with Farnham. The Zoot were The Masters Apprentices' key rivals, so he and Wheatley had some lively history.

In 1974 Farnham's old housemate Wheatley was only passing through London; he was about to slowly make his way back to

Australia. (During his return journey he witnessed the train wreck that was Farnham and his band on the beach at Surfers.) But by the time Wheatley and the four musicians reconnected back in Melbourne, their master plan was in place: America or bust. Wheatley's experiences with the Bay City Union and The Masters Apprentices would prove incredibly helpful in fulfilling his dream of managing the first Oz band to crack America while still based in Australia.

Birtles, Goble, Pellicci and Shorrock bonded over poverty and ambition, especially ambition. Everyone, Wheatley included, had served their apprenticeship. And when their voices joined in harmony, well, it *was* pretty special. They also had a good stock of new songs ready to unveil. They had a sound that seemed tailor-made for the US market.

'We were unified through the music we were writing and performing,' said Birtles. 'We were also friends in those early days because we started with nothing between us.'

While still on the dole – seemingly another rite of passage for a struggling Aussie band with big dreams – they played their first gig as the Little River Band at Melbourne's Martinis Hotel on 20 March 1975. By the end of April the Little River Band had already played 20 shows. They'd barely stop to take a breath for the next 10 years, playing more than 1300 concerts and recording 10 albums, a hefty load that would break the toughest of bands. Yet LRB, as they came to be known, seemed to revel in the work.

Their debut single, 'Curiosity Killed the Cat', was a Top 20 Oz hit in September 1975, around the same time John Farnham's career was starting to flounder. But America was their shared destiny, their common goal, as Birtles recalled.

'We all felt that our style of music was more suited to the States.'

Showing the type of relentless commitment that he would display when working with Farnham, Wheatley maxed out his American Express card in the States in 1975, as he wore a new path up and down the Sunset Strip, trying to sign LRB directly to a US label. This would be a first for an Australian band. By early 1976 he had a deal in place with the LA-based Capitol Records, the label of the legendary Beach Boys and the US home of the Beatles. Helen Reddy, too.

LRB soon also had the ear of influential Florida radio vet Bill Bartlett, a programmer for stations WPDQ-FM and WAIV. Bartlett was a big fan of Australian music – he'd also ardently promoted the work of AC/DC and Skyhooks – and repeatedly played the eight-minute version of 'It's a Long Way There', a standout from the band's debut album.

LRB didn't waste any time in getting to the States. They played their first American show on 15 October 1976 at the Madison University in Harrisonburg, Virginia, opening up for the Average White Band. Wheatley had exactly three dates locked in when they arrived that winter, but the band stayed for months, operating at a loss but gaining vital exposure.

As 'Long Way' started to climb the US charts, breaking into the Top 30, the band was ecstatic. Wheatley travelled with a suitcase; inside was a copy of *Billboard*, a sales sheet and a map of America. Like a general marshalling his troops, he was forever plotting the band's next move.

That first US tour alone, which kept LRB on the road until the week before Christmas 1976, encompassed 50 shows. They returned in June 1977 for another 50 gigs, opening up for everyone from the Eagles to Fleetwood Mac, the Steve Miller Band to America and Supertramp. The biggest names of the 1970s.

LRB could turn it on live, but group hugs were rare backstage. Goble was a perfectionist; Pellicci a hypochondriac; Birtles had found religion; Shorrock was a party animal.

'There was always a multiplicity of agendas,' said guitarist David Briggs, who came on board prior to their first US tour. 'The politics and social dynamics of a band on a personal level can be quite different to how a band performs. The Little River Band was a business.'

The band crisscrossed America in two band buses – the rowdier named 'Pete's Disco', the other 'God's Bus'. When they returned to Australia in November 1977 for – surprise, surprise – another run of dates and more recording, 'Help Is on Its Way' was fast-tracking its way into the upper reaches of the US charts. Their first big hit.

It was a great payoff for Wheatley, especially, who was in yet another hotel room when he got the news. He poured himself a stiff Scotch, drank it slowly and savoured the moment. They'd arrived.

John Farnham, meanwhile, was spinning his wheels, wondering when – or if – *Bobby Dazzler* would ever be screened. As LRB's star was rising, his was crashing.

By late 1977, LRB's rise was complete: 'Help Is on Its Way' actually overtook Fleetwood Mac's 'You Make Lovin' Fun' as it climbed the Top 200. It was the beginning of LRB's purple patch, the first in a stretch of 10 consecutive charting singles in the US and American sales of 25 million records.

The band took just one day off every fortnight, every second Sunday. That continued for the best part of a decade.

'Whatever it takes. That was our mindset at the time,' said Birtles.

It helped that Birtles, by his own admission, was an 'easy-going guy', a bridge between the more volatile members of the band. This came in particularly handy when tension started to build between Shorrock and Goble, which would eventually bring John Farnham into the mix.

Sometimes, minutes before they were due on stage to perform in front of thousands, Shorrock would be curled up in a corner, catching up on his sleep. A belt of whiskey later and he was good to go. Goble was not so relaxed. He'd take notes to sharpen their performances, sometimes while a gig was in progress, which he'd later share with the band. This didn't sit so well, especially with Shorrock.

'My analytical nature drove him completely mental,' Goble would later confess.

LRB wasn't just a touring band; they were also prolific composers and recording artists. With a variety of in-house songwriters – Goble, Birtles and Shorrock wrote together and alone, while Briggs also contributed songs, including 1979's Grammy-nominated hit 'Lonesome Loser' – they had no shortage of quality material. All this creativity came to the fore on *Diamantina Cocktail*, their third album, which dropped in 1977. It was the band's strongest LP, containing their best songs: Shorrock's 'Help Is on Its Way'; a Briggs–Birtles co-write, 'Happy Anniversary'; Birtles' 'Witchery', a bespoke song for a fashion store of the same name, commissioned by Wheatley; and a great Birtles–Shorrock co-write, 'Home on Monday'.

The success of each release from the band was reflected in incremental increases in audiences. 'Help Is on Its Way' peaked at number 14 on the *Billboard* chart in late 1977, 'Happy Anniversary' reached a similar mark a few months later, and the band's crowds – and the venues they filled – grew in size. The *Diamantina Cocktail* LP was the first album from an Australian band to 'go gold' in America, selling over 500,000 copies.

In 1978 they recorded 'Reminiscing', which hit a band high of number three in the US charts. It was a monster hit. LRB was now in the A league, headlining arena shows. 'Reminiscing' was the recipient of an elite Five Million AIR award for that landmark, recognising five million plays on American radio, the only Australian-made song to achieve that mark. (Paul McCartney's 'Yesterday' was a fellow recipient.)

When 1979's *First Under the Wire* LP shipped a staggering one million copies on the day of its release, Wheatley swiftly renegotiated the band's recording contract. Capitol re-signed LRB for an impressive $8 million, with a $1 million advance. Serious rock-and-roll money.

In 1979, with a run of full-house shows all over America, it seemed the band's star couldn't rise any higher. Promoters laid on the limos and other favours: in Dallas, one promoter supplied a high-class escort with each vehicle. Another provided the band with a backstage hot tub, complete with naked women. Cocaine was rampant, even though much of the band weren't interested in the high life. But those who were went at it, feverishly.

'From late 1978 through '79 and '80,' wrote Wheatley, who admitted to a dalliance with Bolivian marching powder, 'we saw some dizzy heights and situations that most bands could only dream about.'

Over time, sackings and voluntary resignations were pretty commonplace within the band's ranks, the result of their heavy workload, internal friction and insular lifestyle. When drummer and co-founder Pellicci suffered extensive burns in 1978, they found a replacement and played on. Bass player George McArdle saw the light and left the band to become minister of a Pentecostal church.

Capitol upped the recording budget significantly for LRB's next long-player, *Time Exposure*, allowing the band to record during April 1981 in the Caribbean with the legendary George Martin, but it didn't prove to be the career peak they'd anticipated.

During the recording sessions, Shorrock returned from a media commitment to find out that McArdle's replacement, American bassist Wayne Nelson, had cut the vocal for a new song (and future single) called 'The Night Owls'. This came as quite a surprise.

'He can do the singing on the rest of the album, as far as I'm concerned,' an incensed Shorrock informed his bandmates. He was already unhappy that most of his songs had been rejected by producer Martin; now he felt he was being ousted as lead singer. Shorrock retired to his room and wrote a letter to his bandmates, stating that the rivalry among LRB's songwriters had become a 'cancer', driven purely by money. 'The beast is sick,' Shorrock wrote, referring to the group, 'and needs to be made well again.' However, Shorrock didn't want to leave the band.

Goble and Shorrock had never been close – Goble considered him a 'square peg' within LRB, set apart from the rest of the band – and after the *Time Exposure* drama, Shorrock began lobbying to make a solo album. Meanwhile, in the wake of their collaboration on *Uncovered*, Graeham Goble had been doing some lobbying of his own, pushing for John Farnham to replace Shorrock.

In late 1981 Goble invited Wheatley to his property in Glenburn in rural Victoria.

'Shorrock has to go,' Goble said firmly. 'I want John Farnham to replace him.'

Wheatley wasn't comfortable with the idea. While he knew that his client and friend Farnham was up to the job, he also believed Shorrock was an integral part of LRB's success. He was the band's frontman, a singer who could project all the way from the front row to the punters way up in the nosebleeds. Shorrock had presence. Wheatley also worried that any change would give their label, Capitol, the impression that he didn't have control of his group.

But Goble dug in, pointing out that Wayne Nelson had sung their most recent Top 10 hit, 'The Night Owls', and their fans hadn't raised a fuss. Why couldn't a new singer do an equally good job? As far as Goble was concerned, Farnham was Australia's best singer. His mind was made up.

A few months later, in early February 1982, a band meeting was called in Wheatley's Melbourne office. Goble spoke for everyone in the group.

'We've discussed it and we want John Farnham to replace Shorrock. With him we could be the best band in the world.'

Wheatley was told in the strongest possible way that if he didn't accept this new move, then he, like Shorrock, might also be given his notice.

Farnham got the call from Wheatley the next day.

Wheatley was surprised by how quickly John accepted the offer, but, truth be told, it was a priceless opportunity. He'd be fronting one of the biggest bands on the planet, and playing to new crowds – American crowds. A big step up from playing RSLs.

While Farnham and his new band started work on 'Down on the Border', the first taste of the new LRB, Shorrock recorded a reply to his dumping. Its name? *Villain of the Peace*.

10

REINED IN

Many years after John's tenure with the Little River Band, TV comics Roy Slaven and HG Nelson playfully encouraged him to spill about the first track he cut with the band, 'Down on the Border'.

'Is it the worst song ever recorded?' Nelson asked, adopting his default poker face. He had a point, at least lyrically: what, exactly, was the song about: drug smuggling? A clash of cultures? Long hair? It wasn't clear.

'Actually,' John replied, suppressing a chuckle, 'that was a very big hit, but it's not one of my favourites. I wouldn't choose to record it, but I was in there, I joined the band.' Then he added, after a pause: 'It was my fault.'

Roy persevered.

'When you were with LRB, did you have Graeham Goble and his other half-baked mate …'

'Beeb?' offered John.

'Beeb! I can't work those guys out at all, they're cod ordinary, never got on with them. Are you of a similar mind, John?'

'Do you hate their guts?' enquired HG, getting straight to the point.

'No, no, not their guts,' John insisted. 'We don't talk much ... I don't have anything against them but I don't talk much with them either. I found it difficult because I'd been a solo performer all my life, but I also love to be a team player – as long as I'm the captain!

'I felt very restricted within the band, often because the material we were recording I wasn't comfortable with. But because the other guys liked it I had to ... it's like being the managing director of a company whose product you don't believe in.'

Hindsight, of course, is a wonderful thing, but it's fair to say that John began his LRB odyssey in 1982 with nothing but positivity. This was it, a successful band, an internationally renowned act. His big shot.

On 8 August 1982, John appeared with the group – Birtles, Goble, Nelson, guitarist Stephen Housden and drummer Pellicci – on *The Don Lane Show*. It wasn't merely an appearance; they effectively had the run of the entire program. What better way for John to make his LRB debut? Lane's audience loved him. It was as good as a homecoming for John.

They began with an unplugged, virtually a capella rendition of 'Man on Your Mind', Farnham standing and singing, absolutely belting it out, while the rest of the band remained seated. It elicited a standing ovation from the audience, many of whom knew Farnham well from his many solo spots on the show. Wheatley strode out to join 'the boys' on the set, his hair brightly blond, in jeans and suit jacket, looking every bit as good as his star client.

Wheatley and Farnham, who was rocking a blousy, aqua-coloured shirt and black pants, chatted amiably with Lane.

What changes were brought to the band with John's recruitment, especially someone with John's stature? asked Lane.

'Well, I guess the nervous part of the whole thing, Don,' Wheatley replied, brushing some invisible fluff from his tie, 'is that we don't know yet. Since John's joined the band we've basically been in the studio. Time will tell. We're all very confident, of course, we feel that it's going to work.

'No matter what the band does now, they're going to be coming under the biggest microscope in the world. There's a lot of attention being put on the thing. There's a lot of pressure on the guys to go out and deliver.'

Talk turned to testing the new line-up on the road; Wheatley revealed the band was about to head out on tour for five weeks. Briefly, the camera flashed to a beaming Gaynor Martin, Wheatley's wife, in the studio audience. She and Wheatley had wed on 14 July, with both Farnham and Shorrock stepping up as groomsmen, showing there was no acrimony between LRB's past and present singers. Shorrock's issues were with the rest of the band.

The first part of the roadtrip, Wheatley added, was a quick tour of Oz and then an equally short run in the States.

'The shortest tour of America we've ever done,' added Wheatley. 'The problem is we're running into the winter and we really don't like touring America in the wintertime. It's quite dangerous.'

Their immediate plans were made clear: the new single 'Down on the Border' was about to drop, but the album wouldn't appear until the new year. They needed to be in the US to back it up, Wheatley explained; they'd already sold out three shows at LA's 7000-capacity Universal Amphitheater. Not bad numbers for a band working in a new lead singer.

The conversation moved to Farnham, who looked a little starstruck, like a guy who had finally drawn all the aces.

'Mate, I can't believe it, I really can't,' John said, when asked about joining the band. 'It's inconceivable to me.'

Lane added how he'd talked up John to some American friends, who said they were 'hugely impressed' with the singer. Farnham, typically, downplayed this.

'I think a couple of them thought I was a bad comedian,' he said.

Glenn Shorrock, who Wheatley continued to manage as a solo act, was then mentioned by Wheatley. He explained that American audiences expected to hear the hits, the songs Shorrock was famous for singing, and this was perhaps Farnham's biggest challenge. The band had been forced to change the keys of some of the songs, in order to work with John's voice.

'But it's not John Farnham and the Little River Band, is it?' asked Lane. 'It's the Little River Band, right?

'And that's the way it should be,' Farnham replied. 'The only reason [my recruitment] had any impact was because I'm an entity here in my own country. The rest of the world doesn't know who I am; it's not so important over there. The thing I do have to do is fill Glenn Shorrock's boots, and they're pretty big boots; he's a hard act to follow.'

Wheatley added that John was the only person they considered worthy of replacing Shorrock. John, typically, had the last laugh, just as the rest of the band joined them on the set.

'Maybe I was the only person they knew,' he said, his eyes sparkling with laughter.

Jokes aside, it was clear that he was up for the challenge. America. The unknown. A brave new musical frontier.

'Fitting in with the guys hasn't been hard,' John said in another early interview, with George Moore, for *The Australian Women's Weekly*, 'they have made it so easy for me. But recording and on stage things are quite different from what I've been used to,' he added, subtly alluding to Goble's notorious fastidiousness. 'On stage you have to sing the same thing the same way each time, as there are four other voices expecting to join in. And in the studio there are six opinions about the way something should be done.'

In his solo career, John explained, he was the one who often made those calls, usually alone, sometimes in consultation with Wheatley.

'But it does mean that there's great input,' he added quickly. 'We're all mates – although we have to make allowances for Wayne.'

It seemed that the sole American in the band, not the new kid, was the target of piss-taking.

John concluded, 'I've always been a fan of LRB, and it's great being able to get up there and say, "This is a favourite LRB song of mine" – and getting to sing it!'

Moore then raised a tricky subject: John's new gig meant a lot of road time. How would this affect his life with Jill and their new baby?

'I will never let strain come into my marriage,' said John, turning serious. 'I'm in love with my wife and I love my son and I'll have them on the road with me as often as possible.'

LRB were workaholics. After an opening run of 40 Australian appearances, from August to October 1982 – which also included two *Countdown* spots and five other Oz TV appearances – they launched their latest American sortie, John's first, at the Denver University Arena on 28 October. The band raced through the Midwest, then headed to the west coast, where their mini-tour (a mere 15 dates) ended with the three-night stand at the Universal City Amphitheater they'd talked up with Don Lane.

What to do next? Keep touring, of course. They began another Australian tour, in Coolangatta, on 17 November – barely three days after the end of their run in LA – and rolled on until they reached the Myer Music Bowl, for a televised Carols by Candlelight special, on Christmas Eve. That wound up some 30 dates in five weeks. After a year-end break they were back on the road in late January, crossing the ditch for shows in New Zealand in February, then back to Oz for more shows through April. The momentum never let up.

In February 1983, during that latest Australian run, the band convened at Beeb Birtles' home in Malvern, Victoria, to prepare themselves for three shows at the Melbourne Concert Hall, which were to be filmed for an HBO US TV special. But this was not your regular pre-gig rehearsal; the band had recruited a string section for the event, from the Melbourne Symphony Orchestra. The

MSO – along with much of the group, Beeb's wife, Donna, the HBO crew and assorted Little River babies – convened in the Birtles' music room, as the camera rolled. It was a very full house. Framed gold and platinum LRB records dotted the walls.

Goble stood throughout, walking from band member to band member, talking through the song they were preparing, 'Sleepless Nights', and occasionally stopping to whisper something in the ear of MSO conductor Graeme Lyall. There was no question that Goble was in charge.

John seemed to be working straight from Glenn Shorrock's how-to-be-a-mellow-frontman textbook: at first he sang as he casually walked the floor, as if he'd been taking a morning stroll, heard the music and decided to join in. Then he took a seat, one arm draped over a nearby chair, all the while belting out the song, even though he seemed to be one short breath away from a nap. Every now and then he'd take the time to drag on a cigarette or sip from a mug of coffee. Fully aware of the presence of the HBO crew, John occasionally shot a wink or a sly nod in their direction, playing to an invisible audience.

It was an intriguing contrast between showman Farnham, always ready for a laugh, and the controlling Goble, a contrast that would grow more apparent during John's time with the band.

John was in great form at the third of those Concert Hall gigs, on 9 February. Drenched in sweat, his hair falling in his eyes, he led the band through a roaring take on the late-era Easybeats' belter, 'St. Louis', their final song of the night. By now the crowd was out of their seats, throwing themselves about the place. This was a very different LRB in action: high voltage, high energy, claiming an Oz rock great as their very own. Even Goble, in cut-off shirt like the rest of the guys, flashed a grin as they tore it up.

'Come on,' yelled John, gesturing towards the crowd, and, duly inspired, they went crazy. It was a big night; the band was at its best.

John and band soon returned to *The Don Lane Show*, for Lane's opening program for the year. The Lanky Yank, just like LRB, had recently returned from America.

'I was at Universal Studios,' Lane told his audience on 14 February, 'and I gotta tell you, all everyone talked about was Little River Band's performance at the amphitheatre there. They packed it out.'

This time the band was plugging 'The Other Guy', their next single. Farnham, as usual, looked great, sporting a casual dark jacket, jeans and white shoes; Goble to his left, beamed, while Birtles moved in from Farnham's right to join in the chorus. There was a genuine sense of musical communion in action; they were the holy trinity of harmonisers.

The over-the-top audience response made it clear than Farnham and the band were on safe home turf; this was their crowd. John in particular was treated like their adopted son, just back from the rock-and-roll frontline.

Lane asked the band whether they'd had any apprehension about their recent US tour, John's American debut.

Goble said no, but Farnham felt otherwise. 'Speak for yourself, mate,' he laughed, glancing at Goble. 'I get fairly toey, anyway, but that was an amazing experience, just great. Credit to the guys.'

Lane mentioned how he'd spotted John and his son, Robbie, in the Channel 9 canteen earlier in the day.

'He looks exactly like him,' Lane said of Robbie. 'Even sings like him.'

At this point baby Robbie was brought in from the wings, a dummy lodged in his mouth, as the crowd oohed and aahed. Robbie clapped his hands and then shrieked into his father's microphone. Farnham was genuinely chuffed, the proudest parent in Australia.

But he didn't have much downtime to savour with his family; between joining LRB in 1982 and his eventual departure in early 1986, John would front the band for a staggering 385 live shows. He barely had time to draw breath.

There were complications early on for John and LRB. On stage, Farnham had always been a man of the people – physical, dynamic, very willing to get the audience in on the action. An entertainer. For Goble and Birtles, however, that was a little too flashy for LRB 1980s-style; they may have been rocking much harder, but they feared not being taken seriously. However, this didn't stop John – until one night he pulled up abruptly on stage, like a lame horse. His microphone lead had been shortened, without John knowing. There'd be no Farnham antics tonight. And no joking with the crowd, either.

As Glenn Wheatley later revealed, John had been given orders. 'The word was handed down from Beeb and Graeham [to John] not to be funny.'

In that slyly revealing Roy and HG interview, John admitted he'd heard the 'same rumour' about Goble and Birtles' rules and regulations, eventually confessing that it was true.

'Some nights, though, I'd have 60 feet of mic cable and I'd take off, but the next night I'd have six feet and I'd take off like I'd been roped.' His microphone stand was sometimes secured to the stage with gaffer tape, which he angrily ripped off.

'The gaffer tape wasn't going to stop John Farnham,' wrote Glenn Wheatley.

Every night, John would leave the stage soaked; he worked incredibly hard, regardless of the length of his microphone cable.

American audiences didn't seem to mind the switch of frontmen – Farnham laughed about it, wondering if they even noticed – but the same couldn't be said for Capitol, the group's North American label. The Capitol suits preferred Shorrock. According to Wheatley, Capitol 'liked the blend of harmonies created by Glenn, Beeb and Graeham. It had been a successful formula.' John needed to work extra hard to keep the label onside; he knew that without their support, LRB would struggle to be heard.

If this wasn't enough for John to contend with, there was also the matter of songwriting and publishing royalties, the most lucrative aspect of life in the band. The power struggle between Goble, Shorrock and Birtles had been tough enough, with each competing to get their own songs recorded and earn more royalties. John wasn't in their same league as a songwriter; it took two albums before he had a song cut by the band, the dynamic title track of 1985's *Playing to Win*. (Admittedly, the songs for 1983's *The Net* had already been written by the time he joined the band.)

Even though 'Playing to Win', a rocking anthem and a real statement of intent, was John's, by the time it had been through the LRB production blender, every member of the band had a share. Goble broke down the lyrics, word by painful word, to determine who owned what and what percentage of royalties they deserved. John eventually received just 55.5% of the best song he'd ever written. It was ludicrous.

There was also the issue of the band's deep debt to Capitol. Even though their records had been selling strongly, they'd racked up some serious studio costs – hiring George Martin, for instance, didn't come cheap; ditto, recording in the Caribbean. Keeping them on the road was also hugely costly – pretty much everything they earned through the turnstiles went towards paying their bills. There was also the matter of 'earning out' the substantial advances paid when Wheatley renegotiated their recording contract, completed before John was in the band.

Joining LRB wasn't proving to be lucrative for John – not unless they had a monster hit record. He continued to struggle financially – at one lowpoint, he and Jill couldn't afford to take their son, Robbie, to McDonald's to celebrate his birthday. It was that tough.

The Net, the first LRB album recorded with Farnham out front, was released in June 1983. It definitely offered up a different band to the one best known for 'Help Is on Its Way' and 'It's a Long Way There', a group that had built its reputation as a vocal guitar-pop outfit. Surprises came from the get-go, via the juicy horns and slightly disco-tinged guitars of the opener, 'You're Driving Me out of My Mind'. 'Mr Socialite' and 'Easy Money', meanwhile, with their ever-so-jaded, end-of-night feel, hinted at late-career Eagles. 'The Danger Sign' and 'Falling' were also left turns for the band, favouring heavy guitars, dark undercurrents and hints of prog-rock.

To his credit, whatever John was handed by key songwriter Goble, who had a hand in seven of the album's 11 tracks, he tackled with his usual commitment and depth of emotion, even when the song did not necessarily seem to fit him as a singer. His voice is barely recognisable on the plodding title track, with its weirdly prescient lyric about the Big Brother-ish dangers of 'The Net'.

That's not to say the band neglected the things it did well: such standouts as 'We Two' and 'Down on the Border', despite John's shortcomings, capitalised on their trademark blend of voices and harmonies and platinum-plated guitar hooks. 'The Border' was swiftly added to a concurrent *Greatest Hits* release, while 'We Two' was the first North American single lifted from the album, reaching a so-so peak of 22 in the US charts. (It also became the name of a company formed to represent LRB a few years down the line; clearly it resonated with the band.) 'You're Driving Me out of My Mind', *The Net*'s second single, struggled to 35 in America.

In Australia, 'Down on the Border' reached the Top 10, while the album made it to number 11. But 'We Two' barely scraped the Top 50. The figures didn't lie: LRB was on a slow decline, even with a shiny new singer in place.

The music press were never LRB's biggest fans – most American scribes wrote them off – and they didn't hold back when *The Net* dropped.

Their new sound 'seems forced and somewhat strained', noted *AllMusic*'s Mike DeGagne.

'The blame can't be put completely on Farnham,' he added, instead pointing the finger at the changing musical moods of the time, as new wave and slick pop started to rule the charts. Michael Jackson, The Police and Culture Club all dominated year-end lists for 1983. The heyday of The Eagles and that distinctive West Coast sound, mined so brilliantly by LRB, were over.

Rolling Stone magazine, meanwhile, slammed *The Net* with a one-and-a-half star rating. 'Little River Band,' they wrote, 'produce a sound that has tremendous commercial appeal but only minimal artistic value', thereby condemning them to the uncool pile for eternity.

As was their nature, the Little River Band kept touring around *The Net*'s release. They wrapped another Oz lap of honour in April 1983 with a televised Royal Gala Performance. John, who was fast getting used to singing for royalty, looked very sharp in a pink sports jacket and black leather duds, as he and the band rocked the song 'D' with gusto. They then toured Europe during May, before returning to the US in late June. The high-rating TV show *Solid Gold*, until recently hosted by expat Aussie Andy Gibb, was their first port of call. Then there were almost 50 more North American dates, which took them through to the end of August 1983, rounding out a very lively 12 months for John.

He barely had time to reflect, though, because the band flew to Japan and then back to America, where they toured heavily until late October. This time they topped their previous efforts, ending with four nights at the Universal Amphitheater – shows attended by such stars as Rick Springfield, Dionne Warwick and Olivia Newton-John.

Yet backstage at the Universal there was no love in the green room. None at all. By the night of the final show, John was fed up. He'd had enough of the bickering, the restrictions placed on him by Birtles and Goble, and the pressure to keep touring while still not earning any real money. He also missed his family, terribly. Another interminable band meeting began, but rather than quietly absorb the latest airing of grievances, as he'd normally do, John exploded. Farnham directed his anger at Birtles, but he was really addressing the entire group.

'Get out of my way,' he roared. 'You are stopping me getting on with my job and doing what I want to be able to do.'

According to Glenn Wheatley, John then turned around, headed for the stage and put in 'the performance of his life'.

John was still seething after the Universal show. Fortunately it was the last night of the tour.

'I'm sick of this bullshit,' he growled backstage. 'I'm not going to get dragged into this thing. I'm going to get on and do something.'

'It was a major turning point in John Farnham's career,' noted Wheatley, and he was absolutely correct. For perhaps the first time, John was taking control, tolerating no bullshit. It was this clarity that would soon help him reignite his solo career.

Within days of that backstage dust-up, John Farnham returned solo to *The Don Lane Show*. But this was no ordinary episode; this was the final show of the Lanky Yank's record-breaking series. It wouldn't be a swan song without one more Farnham appearance, something the tuxedo-ed Lane made very clear in his intro, even if he couldn't quite let go of the 'Johnny' tag.

'I have to say, honestly, I have been a fan of Johnny Farnham since the days when I had my show in Sydney. He had a hit record called 'Sadie (The Cleaning Lady)' and boy I tell you, he has come a long, long way since then. He's been involved with us for a long, long time, too.

'I've always loved him as a solo performer; I thought he was one of the greatest talents ever produced in this country. So did the Little River Band, who decided he was going to be their new lead singer. The truth of the matter is that Johnny returned home early, just three days ago, to be with us. He's been on a very successful tour of the USA with LRB. Like I said, only the best voice produced in this country. Ladies and gentlemen – Johnny Farnham.'

Backed by David Hirschfelder on piano, Farnham belted out 'Help!'. A single spotlight was focused on him throughout, as he kept his eyes closed, lost in the song, squeezing every last emotional drop out of Lennon and McCartney's cry of pain. Sure, the mustard-coloured jacket was an eyeful, but his performance was, as ever, heartfelt, and note perfect. Little did the enthusiastic studio audience know that John related to the lyric even more strongly now – he needed help to get through his current crisis with LRB.

'What about that? Johnny Farnham!' yelled Lane, as the song ended. The two embraced.

'I gotta tell you, as long as I've done this show, it always frightens the life out of me,' Farnham confessed, in a post-song interview.

'Why is that?' Lane asked.

'Live television. I'm shaking like a leaf. I haven't worked on my own for three years. If something goes wrong, I can't turn around [to a bandmate] and go, "Ha! You blew it." I can't do that.'

'How was the tour?' Lane asked, after a beat.

'Fantastic,' insisted Farnham. But his forced smile suggested something else entirely.

It was during this fallow time with the Little River Band that John recorded what is now known within Farnham circles as the 'lost album'.

In order to earn some extra cash while LRB was recording *Playing to Win*, John recorded 10 vocal tracks at a Hollywood studio without the band. American label Curb had intended to release some of this material on an album tentatively named *Break the Ice*, after the strongest track among the selection, but it never came to pass. Instead, most of the tracks gradually made their way onto film soundtracks, under John's name, over the next few years – 'With You' became the love theme from the 1986 movie *Rad*, while 'Justice for One', which John co-wrote with American Sue Shifrin, turned up on the soundtrack to the movie *Savage Streets*, as did 'Innocent Hearts'. 'The Quiet Ones You Gotta Watch', a track John and Wayne Nelson wrote for LRB but was rejected by the band, also made it to the *Savage Streets* soundtrack. A duet with the pop singer Rainey, 'My World Is Empty Without You', featured on the soundtrack to 1985's *Voyage of the Rock Aliens*; 'Running for Love', meanwhile, made it to the Chevy Chase flick *Fletch*. The film *The Slugger's Wife* featured 'Love (It's Just the Way It Goes)', which John sang with Sarah M. Taylor.

Most of these tracks were archetypal '80s pop-rock in the style of such bands as Mr. Mister and Toto, more glossy than gritty, but with powerhouse vocals from John nonetheless. It's interesting to think that if the *Whispering Jack* phenomenon hadn't happened soon after these releases, John probably could have built a career in Hollywood, providing the type of lucrative voice-for-hire work from which such vocalists as Christopher Cross, Kenny Loggins and The Doobie Brothers' Michael McDonald prospered greatly.

It was a very different LRB that resurfaced, three months after John's *Don Lane Show* performance of 'Help!', for their next Australian odyssey, a solid five weeks of touring the east coast. Co-founder Birtles had quit, having lost his desire to keep touring, and underwhelmed by the harder sound the band was chasing. Drummer Pellicci was on his final lap, soon to be replaced by Cold Chisel drummer Steve Prestwich, who would supply John with 'When the War Is Over', a great, soulful showcase for his voice. Keyboard whiz David Hirschfelder was now a permanent fixture, having joined the band for their previous, tumultuous tour. He, too, would have a big impact on John's musical future.

When the thoroughly made-over LRB stepped out again on *Solid Gold* on 26 March 1985 to plug 'Playing to Win', the changes were impossible to miss. Gone were the practical denim and collared shirts of yore, in their place a day-glo assortment of colours and styles (and sounds, too; this was the most tech-heavy, high-energy song they'd ever record). Goble's change was the most abrupt – with his oversized specs, skinny tie, boofed-out hair and square-shouldered outfit, he could have passed for one of the Buggles. Hirschfelder, in a silver suit (or was it tinfoil?), was sporting a thinking-man's mullet and sculpted facial hair, and when he leapt to centre stage to rock a solo with his keyboard axe – a keyboard worn with a strap, just like a guitar – the effect was pure 1980s, for better or worse. Bassist Nelson looked at least part pimp in his sinister wraparound shades.

John's hair was now a frizzy perm, the top he wore on the *Solid Gold* set somewhere between a bomber jacket and a parachute. While he didn't appear entirely comfortable with the new LRB image, he still sang the song with both heart and soul. He did likewise with the more sombre 'Blind Eyes', which they also performed, along with 'Don't Blame Me', all from the *Playing to Win* LP.

The *Solid Gold* spot was part of LRB's latest American tour, their 13th, which, over two months, had taken them from coast to coast – and bled cash. It cost them more money than they earned, an unfortunate first for the group. It was a diabolical situation: in order to pay off debts they needed to keep touring. If they didn't tour, the debts remained. Only the songwriters in the band made any real money – and in John's case, when he did write something worthy of the band, such as 'Playing to Win', he'd lost out when Goble divvied up the publishing spoils.

LRB, 1985-style, were stuck: in a desperate attempt to shake things up and cast off the past, they'd now become interchangeable with a dozen other bands, both in look and sound. From Starship to The Hooters, there were more than enough bands plying the designer-pop route. 'Playing to Win' may have been an exceptional song, a frantic few minutes of dynamic pop, but it wasn't a hit, struggling to number 60 on the Billboard Hot 100. Its companion album limped to number 75 in North America and number 38 in

Australia, not coming close to gold status in either country, their key markets. *Rolling Stone* slammed it with a one-star review, calling it 'drearily forgettable'.

Yet the band's live performances received good press. The influential trade magazine *Billboard* covered a two-night run in mid-June at a San Diego venue named Humphrey's, and singled John out for praise. 'Not only is Farnham a much better singer than former frontman Glenn Shorrock,' stated writer Thomas K. Arnold, 'he is also far more charismatic on stage, jumping about like a madman and enticing the rest of the group to do the same. Farnham's delivery brought a new sense of passion to the old hits.' Arnold had obviously caught the band on a night when John's microphone cord hadn't been tampered with.

Regardless, John could see quite clearly that the Good Ship LRB was listing badly. He would return from the road to the rented, nondescript house in suburban Bulleen he shared with Jill and Robbie. The high life was somewhere else.

By mid-July 1985 John and the band were rocking 'Playing to Win' at the Oz for Africa appeal, staged in Sydney. One of their fellow acts on the bill was INXS, who were poised to seize the momentum that the Little River Band had established for hard-touring Australian bands. LRB drummer Derek Pellicci had been right when he said that he and the band had 'created a four-lane highway right across America for other acts to follow'. But for LRB, things were different. After three final Melbourne dates in August 1985, John and the band went to ground. They seemed as good as done.

'John Farnham was incredibly unhappy,' Glenn Wheatley wrote of this major crossroads in Farnham's career. By early 1986 John was quietly talking with his manager about another album under his own name; he felt the time was right. John wanted to get back to the solo life, and the sooner the better. Wheatley, of course, was in the awkward position of answering to both John as a solo act and to LRB as their manager.

Events helped hasten John's move. After another LRB album, 1986's nondescript *No Reins*, came and went, the inevitable happened: Capitol dropped the band from their roster. Wheatley didn't receive so much as a phone call, despite the amazing run he and the band had experienced with the label. But Capitol had other priorities in the mid-1980s: a rejuvenated Tina Turner, up-and-comers Crowded House, Canadians Heart and Brits Duran Duran. They were all conjuring up hits, unlike LRB.

Inadvertently, this disaster actually proved beneficial for Farnham and Wheatley. While Goble and the remaining remnants of LRB attempted to make one more charge at America – remarkably, they managed to convince Glenn Shorrock to re-join – both John and Glenn opted out, quitting the band, agreeing the time was right to move on.

Farnham had come a long way over the past few years – 385 live shows, three albums, countless TV spots, interviews, close encounters with royalty and entertainment greats – yet his LRB tenure ended with little more than a shrug. As his last hurrah, John played a week's-worth of low-key shows with the band, ending with a 13 April 1986 gig at the Olympic Hotel in Melbourne's suburban Preston. And that was it.

Glenn Wheatley, admittedly, had accomplished his dream of turning an Australian band into superstars in America, while still maintaining a base in Oz. But for John, his dream of success with LRB had turned very sour; there was too much bickering, too many restrictions. He'd become little more than a hired hand.

Glenn Wheatley knew what had to be done.

'Now it was time for me,' he wrote, 'to pursue other challenges – the main one being to put John Farnham up where he belonged.'

11

WHISPERING JACK PHANTOM

John's difficult stretch with LRB had taught him that he needed to be his own man; he had to go his own way. He wasn't a natural team player; decision by committee wasn't his style. As he explained in an interview soon after leaving the band, 'We used to sit down as a seven-man unit, including Glenn Wheatley. Everything was done democratically and diplomatically, majority ruled. I think that was good ... but that can be hard, too.'

John admitted to not always relating to their songs' lyrics; he also questioned the band's song selection. As a solo performer, he'd be able to control the latter. As for the former, he could also be a bit pickier as a soloist with the lyrics of the songs he chose to record. John needed to feel a song in order to sing it well. And he didn't always feel the LRB songs.

From Graeham Goble's perspective, John's time fronting the band gave him 'the motivation that focused him on his own career'. David Hirschfelder agreed, saying that LRB 'strengthened' John and gave him the drive to find his own voice – quite literally. Wheatley said something very similar, stating that LRB 'hardened' Farnham – it had to, especially when it became clear that at least one Capitol exec was lobbying to get Glenn Shorrock back into the group. That kind of pressure could only toughen a guy up. Yet there remained a part of John, as always, that figured he was somehow at fault for the band's poor returns.

For a long time after his departure, John would hold himself responsible for LRB's lack of success during his time, but as usual, he was shouldering way more than his fair share of guilt. The band was past their commercial peak, and no number of makeovers, line-up changes and / or backstage brawls could alter that inalienable truth.

'John blamed himself for the relative failure of Little River Band after he joined,' Glenn Wheatley told a Fairfax reporter not long after the split. 'I kept telling him there's always a downturn after an original combination breaks up or changes around.

'It was no reflection on John that Capitol Records in America became negative about LRB, but he felt he had something to prove [as a solo artist]. This time he put himself very much on the line.'

Still, Wheatley went as far as to admit that if Farnham's first post-LRB effort didn't connect, his career could prove 'extremely difficult to resurrect.' That potential downside was unavoidable: what if LRB, despite their chronic problems, was as high as John would ever climb? He still had no Australian record deal. It had been that way since the late 1970s. *Uncovered* had been rejected by virtually every local label only to be rescued by Wheatley, who released it himself. And now that John was back to working solo, what kind of music should he be recording and performing? He couldn't retreat to playing the old 'Sadie'-era hits; nor could he tap into LRB's hefty back catalogue of songs. His 1985 setlist, such as it was, would comprise *Uncovered* tracks and covers of hits by ZZ Top and Toto. Hardly what would become the definitive John Farnham songbook.

'I don't set out to portray any kind of image; it's just me,' John said as he got his solo house back in order. He figured his problem was credibility. 'People never saw me as a credible singer. Being tagged with soft music like "Sadie" … but that after all was years ago. That's not in my set anymore.'

The musical mood had shifted considerably since he cut *Uncovered* in 1980. The mid '80s were ruled by the polished sounds of such local acts as Real Life – also managed by Wheatley – and Mondo Rock and INXS, while internationals like a-ha, the Eurythmics, Madonna and Foreigner were everywhere. 'I Want to Know What Love Is', 'Take on Me' and 'Would I Lie to You?' were all huge records in 1985, both in sound and sales. The commonality between all these acts was their studio slickness; in order to get played on the radio, and thereby compete on the charts, a record needed to sound huge – even blue-collar rocker Bruce Springsteen had embraced the latest technology. His smash 'Born in the USA' typified the type of rolling sonic thunder that John needed to capture in order to compete. He had come close with his solo recordings in LA, when he was moonlighting from LRB; he knew what was required.

The introduction of MTV, which launched in 1981, now meant that a record simply sounding good was no longer enough: if a song was to become a hit, it needed an accompanying flashy, airbrushed, attention-grabbing video. It was an entirely new world. Making music, clearly, had come a long way since John's one-take-and-you're-done, hit-and-run beginnings. What he now required were collaborators, people to help him find the right songs and then give them a radio-friendly sheen. He also needed to update his look.

Regardless of the challenges, John was up for it.

'Bugger it,' he told Wheatley in a quiet moment, 'I'm getting older. What else can I do?'

'I think he was very hungry,' said Jill, in a rare interview, 'financially and for his own self – to prove to himself [that he could succeed on his own terms].'

Wheatley's immediate task – while John hit the road during winter 1985, with a new John Farnham Band, a tour so successful it was extended by a week – was to recruit the right producer for John. He needed someone with real empathy, who would give his voice the chance to shine. American great Quincy Jones, who'd made magic with Michael Jackson, was on Wheatley's long-list, as was David Foster, a solid-gold American hitmaker who'd worked with Boz Scaggs, Chicago and Kenny Loggins. Despite being a big Farnham fan, Foster passed; he couldn't commit to working with someone without a label deal. Jones, too, was a no.

A few years earlier, during a New Year's Eve bash at Melbourne's Billboard nightclub, John had met Ross Fraser, who worked for Wheatley. Fraser was blown away by John's performance and his friendly demeanour.

'Jeez, I'd like to work with that guy one day,' he told Wheatley as they headed off into the night.

Fraser tour-managed Real Life, but had aspirations to produce. He struck up a deal with Wheatley: if he could find the right songs for John, perhaps they could then entice a 'name' producer to travel to Australia to record with John; until then Fraser could continue working with Farnham. That agreed, Fraser and Farnham sat down and started listening to demo tapes, searching for songs; over time they combed through something like 4000 recordings. 'Boxes and boxes' of tapes, as Fraser would recall. They agreed that a song had to 'smack them in the face' before it made their shortlist. One song the team rejected, curiously, was 'We Built This City', a number one in January 1986 for Starship. Clearly it smacked the Americans harder than it did Farnham and Fraser.

Wheatley also helped with this search for songs, using the clout he had established in the world of music publishing – he repped Arista Music in Australia, as well as the Bob Seger, LRB and John Lennon catalogues.

'I got on the phone and used whatever leverage I could to get some songs,' Wheatley wrote of their ongoing search.

In October 1985 work began in earnest on the album, in the humble suburban garage of Farnham's rented house. Wheatley was covering all their costs; John remained a man without a label deal. (Over the 12-month genesis of *Whispering Jack*, Wheatley shelled out $150,000 of his own money, extending his home mortgage to cover the costs.) With ace guitarist Brett Garsed – a fellow former plumber, in his early twenties, now a member of John's band – and LRB alumnus Hirschfelder, a guy with a feel for cutting-edge technology and sounds, John started to record some basic tracks on a four-track recorder, with Fraser producing. They assembled some rudimentary equipment: a drum machine, a Yamaha keyboard, Hirschfelder's sequencer and his Fairlight, very much instruments of the moment, capable of generating big sounds. Any disagreements – and there were very few – would be negotiated over a game of table tennis. Producer Fraser usually won, although he'd admit to 'throwing' a few games for Farnham.

Farnham and Fraser grew close. 'We understand each other,' the singer said.

As for the bearded Hirschfelder, 'He and I have a great working relationship,' Farnham said. 'With him I can sit down and he can interpret my ideas, which is fantastic.'

To mark their bond, John and Hirschfelder let their hair grow out into serious-looking mullets; it wasn't just the sound of the album that was big.

Fraser craved making a modern-sounding record, something truly cutting edge.

'I was dying to do a high-tech album,' he admitted, 'lots of computers, drum machines. I wanted to take all these tacky machines and put it together in some sort of whiz-bang sound – so did John.'

At the heart of all this technology was one very human ingredient: John's voice. *The voice.*

Among the early songs demo-ed were 'Pressure Down', 'Reasons' (written by Sam See, who'd toured with John) and 'A Touch of Paradise', a Ross Wilson co-write previously cut by Mondo Rock. John had written a rare song, entitled 'Let Me Out', but, as usual, found it hard to come up with quality compositions of his own. Still, it wasn't a bad start to what was essentially a garage recording. After a month in the Farnham sleepout, the team moved into Melbourne's AAV Studios.

There was no great anticipation within Oz music circles about the album in progress. When Fraser told anyone he was working with John Farnham, there'd be an unmistakable pause, a nervous silence.

'Oh. Really? So what else are you doing?'

'The radio stations weren't exactly waiting for the next John Farnham album … to add to their playlists,' admitted Glenn Wheatley. He knew it was going to be a tough sell.

Yet recording continued in the knowledge that those on the inside – Fraser, Farnham and the players – were fully aware they had something special in the works.

Wheatley, meanwhile, continued to try and get a record label on board. First port of call was Capitol in America, who, under a clause in LRB's existing deal, could pick up John's solo work if so inclined. But they passed, as did the various local labels Wheatley approached. All the while, as the months passed – suddenly it was early 1986 – Wheatley kept covering the recording costs, keeping John, Fraser and the others on a retainer. Wheatley was worried, not just about his mounting bills, but the fact no label was willing to commit: didn't they hear the record's potential in these early recordings? Did they have tin ears?

In order to stay strong and maintain his resolve, Wheatley would flash back to his early days with LRB, who'd been knocked back by virtually every US label – most famously by United Artists' head Artie Mogull, who compared LRB's music to the sound 'your nails make when you scrape them down a blackboard'. And look what happened next: Capitol got on board, swiftly followed by a bounty of Top 10 singles and album sales of 25 million. Lightning might just strike twice.

'I did it then,' Wheatley said of the time, 'so I knew I could do it again.'

Still, the bills were starting to hurt. And when Farnham agreed that Fraser was the right guy to produce the entire album, Wheatley's worries intensified: what label would touch a record by a novice producer? He hadn't given up on the idea of having the record produced by a 'name', someone that would make it easier to sell. That wasn't Ross Fraser.

'Now,' Glenn noted, with more than a little concern, 'not only did I have a singer that no company wanted, I had a first-time producer as well.'

Work on the record continued well into the new year. While the album was taking great shape, it still lacked that one key song that could become the focal point for the entire LP. That was soon to be resolved in a very random fashion, the happiest accident of John Farnham's career.

Doris Tyler worked as Wheatley's label manager, and she'd been helping John and Fraser sort through the seemingly never-ending tapes of potential songs. Buried deep on a cassette gathering dust in a bottom drawer was a song called 'You're the Voice', which caught Tyler's ear. When she got it to Ross Fraser, he was hit by a thunderbolt: this was it! He'd found the killer song they needed to round out the album.

Fraser jumped in his car and drove straight to Farnham's house in suburban Bulleen, the demo tape blasting on his car stereo for the entire 30-minute ride.

He and John sat down in the garage and played the anthem-in-waiting on a boombox.

'What do you think?' Fraser asked.

'I love it,' John replied. He connected deeply with 'You're the Voice'; it was one of those songs that he felt had been written specifically for him.

'And you know what it needs?' John said, clearly enthused. 'A bagpipe solo!'

'That's not very rock-and-roll,' Fraser said, shaking his head.

'Oh yes it is,' insisted John. As a long-time fan of AC/DC, he had their epic 'It's A Long Way to the Top' in mind. At the heart of that ode to the tough times of 'playin' in a rock roll band' was a blazing pipe solo, courtesy of the late, great Bon Scott. As bizarre as the idea sounded, John proved to be totally on the money.

'You're the Voice', unlike many of the songs John recorded with LRB, had an empowering lyric that he totally related to and wanted to be identified with. It was a vaguely political song of the people – nothing too overt, but punchy enough when necessary, especially just before the chorus kicked in.

'When you hear a singer interpret a piece,' John explained, 'whether he wrote the song or not, you automatically attribute that meaning to that voice, that face' – and from 1986 on, John and 'You're the Voice' would be inseparable.

'You're the Voice' almost didn't make it to John. The song was a four-way co-write: its creators were New Zealander Chris Thompson, who'd sung the hit 'Blinded by the Light' for Manfred Mann's Earth Band and worked on Jeff Wayne's musical version of *The War of the Worlds*; keyboardist Andy Qunta, who'd done time in Oz band Icehouse; Keith Reid, a lyricist par excellence, who'd written for Brit band Procol Harum, including their epic 'A Whiter Shade of Pale'; and Maggie Ryder, an English session muso who'd worked with the Eurythmics and Queen. As creative CVs went, theirs were hard to top.

Chris Thompson told his label he wanted to record 'You're the Voice' for a solo album, but they rejected the idea. Only then did it go onto a tape for music publishers to shop around. His record company's loss proved to be Farnham's very big gain. (In a told-you-so footnote, American David Foster, who rejected the idea of recording with Farnham, included the song on a 1990 album he produced entitled *River of Love*. As for Thompson, he cut his own version in 2014. Farnham had proved its worth.)

Finding the song addressed the first part of the puzzle. But Farnham and his team needed to get 'You're the Voice' down on tape and prove that their instincts were correct. The demo recording of 'You're the Voice' was great – passionate and powerful. Farnham and Fraser then cut the song in AAV. They spent three days mixing the results, a significant amount of studio time for one song. They knew it was the key track and they worked incredibly hard to get it right.

Finally, it came time for John and Fraser to play 'You're the Voice' to Wheatley. Wheatley's wife, Gaynor Martin, was also there that night in the South Melbourne studio, a bottle of champagne at the ready to toast their imminent success.

Everyone went deadly quiet as 'You're the Voice' blared from the speakers. The song was a hit, that was evident to all in the room, but this version was missing ... *something*. Wheatley felt it in his gut; his well-developed musical instincts told him that the song wasn't quite there. Close, but not quite.

Farnham sat pensively on the other side of the room, his eyes burning a hole in his manager and friend. He knew Wheatley well enough to know something was up.

'You don't like it, do you?' John asked – no, demanded – to know.

Wheatley explained that there was something about the demo that was better than this more polished version. The song was a hit, for sure, but it lacked the same magic.

'It's the vocal, isn't it?' Farnham said.

He didn't wait for Wheatley's response; he already knew the answer.

John walked away, back into the studio, instructing Fraser to turn out the lights and turn up the volume in his headphones. Then, as Wheatley later wrote, 'He put in a vocal performance as only John knows how' – the vocal performance that many million listeners around the world now know intimately. In some ways, it was a replay of the scene backstage with LRB at the Universal Amphitheater, when John unleashed on the band and then went on stage and sang his heart out. The new John Farnham thrived in heated situations such as this. 'You're the Voice' was now ready to roll.

John, by his own admission, wasn't an easy man to live with during the making of the album. He understood its significance to him, his career and his family. And to Wheatley, who'd literally staked his house on the album. If it failed, Wheatley could potentially end up as broke as John currently was.

John's father suffered a stroke during the time of recording, which didn't help Farnham's fragile state of mind.

John lived *Whispering Jack* 24/7 throughout its lengthy creation; his commitment was unlike that for any record he'd made before. By the time he and Fraser handed the finished version to Wheatley in mid-1986, John felt he'd become a 'basket case'. He attached a simple handwritten note to a cassette of the final album mix: 'Dear Boss, This is the best that I can do. Thanks for the chance. Love, John.'

Album done, John went home and crawled into bed, rarely eating, let alone surfacing, for the six weeks that passed between the completion of the record and its release. He was so neurotic about how the public would respond to the album that he didn't want to leave the house. For such a naturally gregarious man, this was entirely out of character.

Jillian understood what John was going through, but her tolerance could be stretched only so far. While John was off making his masterpiece, Jillian had been learning tae kwon-do. When they clashed one day at home, during this difficult post-recording/pre-release period, she shaped up to John, threatening to kick his neurotic backside. John backed down immediately; he knew she'd flatten him if he pushed things any further. When their anger subsided, Jillian got John to see a naturopath – anything to help him get through the turmoil. It helped. 'I cried for an hour and a half,' recalled John, 'and he gave me some herbs and spices.'

'I'm in every beat and every bar of this record,' John said of the album. 'I think it's the best record I've ever made. I don't wince when I hear the tracks on this album, and I'm proud of it.'

Wheatley, meanwhile, had finally broken through and secured John a label deal. He'd sat down with Brian Smith, MD of RCA Records, and played his ace – the final version of 'You're the Voice'. Smith was no fool; he could recognise a hit record when a single like this was served to him. And RCA needed 'You're the Voice', as they had little in the way of local acts, preferring to rake in the royalties generated by having ABBA, Elvis Presley and, more recently, the Eurythmics, on their books. Wheatley sweetened the deal by adding his own label, WBE, to the mix, which meant that RCA could soon claim John Farnham, Moving Pictures and Real Life as their own. Financially it was a good deal, but still not quite enough to recoup Wheatley's $150,000 stake in *Whispering Jack*.

A release date was set for 20 October 1986. This was still a record without a title. But John recalled an incident during one of his trips to America, when he checked out a nightclub with some friends. One of those friends, a woman named Loretta Crawford, became, in John's words, a 'megamouth' after a few glasses of wine. She tracked down the club's MC and told him that 'famous Australian singer John Farnham' was in the house. John's name meant nothing to the host, and his friend's red wine–induced slurring didn't help, but he agreed to share the news with the patrons.

'Ladies and gentlemen,' the MC announced during a break in proceedings, 'we have an Australian great in the club tonight. Maybe he'll step up and give us a song. Here he is, folks: Jack Phantom!'

As soon as John related the story to the guys in his touring band, 'Jack Phantom' was given an additional twist. John did a brilliant impression of 'Whispering' Ted Lowe, the voice of TV snooker show *Pot Black*. Jack Phantom was now Whispering Jack and the nickname had stuck like glue. Voila, an album title.

John still wasn't in the best of psychological shape when the time came to give *Whispering Jack* its first public airing. Jillian had to drag him out to the car, and then John spent much of the drive to AAV in Melbourne in the passenger seat, sobbing. He was an emotional wreck, hopeless.

'What if no-one likes it?' he asked between sobs. 'What then? We're done for.'

Jillian shot him a hard look. 'Come on, pull yourself together. You've come too far with this record. You've got to go through with this.'

John's main concern wasn't whether it'd be a hit, but that it would at least be judged on its merits. He hoped 'that it would get a fair look at, a fair listen to, by the people who had preconceptions about me.' He wanted to shake off the stigma of 'Sadie' forever and start anew.

John brightened up at the party, thanks to a hefty slug of his favourite tipple, brandy – he had several slugs as the night went on – and the gift of a CD player. Times were so tough for the Farnhams that they didn't even own one. RCA and Wheatley had decided that *Whispering Jack* would be the first Australian-made album to be released on CD; at least now he could play it at home.

John's mood had improved noticeably by the time of filming the 'You're the Voice' video. With the rise of MTV, video budgets were already running into the six figures – in 1987, Sony forked out a staggering $2.2 million for Michael Jackson's 'Bad', directed by Martin Scorsese. 'You're the Voice' didn't compare; its budget was a measly $10,000. But it was money well spent.

Based on an idea from Ross Fraser, who'd envisioned the clip in black and white with splashes of colour, Farnham opened 'You're the Voice' with a spot-on impression of newsreader Brian Henderson, horn-rimmed specs and all. He announced austerely, 'Good evening, here is the news' as images of war and tragedy and bloodshed exploded behind him. As the video continued, outspoken journo Derryn Hinch and his then wife, actress Jacki Weaver, convincingly played a warring couple from the 'burbs, while Farnham's agent Frank Stivala turned up, as did Vince Leigh, the drummer from Melbourne pop band Pseudo Echo. Even John's make-up artist got a gig.

Skyhooks' bassist Greg Macainsh, who'd just signed on for Farnham's touring band, also appeared in the clip. A few years back, the idea of John working with Macainsh, the most politically motivated songwriter to ever infiltrate the Oz mainstream, was highly unlikely, but 'You're the Voice' changed everything. It wasn't quite Skyhooks' 'Whatever Happened to the Revolution', but when 'You're the Voice' did hit, it hit hard and wide. People connected with the lyric and the raw, real emotion of the song.

John, dressed in a full-length grey Driza-Bone – again on the suggestion of Fraser – looked like a man primed for action, his windswept hair seemingly taking on a life of its own. In five minutes flat he'd established his signature look for the next couple of decades: rock-and-roll stormtrooper.

As for the bagpipe solo, Farnham was right, it was just what the song needed. 'You're the Voice' was a no-holds-barred call to arms, every bit as emphatic and rocking as AC/DC's 'It's A Long Way to the Top', if a bit more polished.

A great clip and single now in the can, getting it heard was the next hurdle for Wheatley and his team. Some early media was set in place, first with Derryn Hinch, who was working at 3AW (perhaps the scoop was payback for his video cameo) and then with Richard Zachariah on his daytime TV chat show, Wheatley once again recognising the power and influence of the small screen. Soon enough, the *Daily Telegraph* had syndicated a story revealing John's 'tough times' with LRB and his new challenges as a solo artist and a father. John was concerned; he hoped the record would be judged on the quality of its music, not coloured by his recent roller-coaster ride.

'The last thing I wanted,' he said, 'was a sympathy vote.'

But working in John's favour was a recent change in the state of play in Australian radio. The old dominance of AM stations like Sydney's 2SM and 2UW and Melbourne's 3XY was fading. A new wave of FM stations, including Melbourne's 3FOX and 3EON (part-owned by Wheatley and just sold to Triple M Sydney for $37.5 million) and Sydney's big two, Triple M and 2DayFM, were fast taking control. 'Character' DJs such as Triple M's Jonathon 'Jonno' Coleman and Ian 'Danno' Rogerson, and 'Uncle' Doug Mulray, who ruled the airwaves in Sydney, and *Countdown*'s Molly Meldrum and Gavin Wood, who teamed up on EON's breakfast show, were more responsive to the slick sounds of *Whispering Jack* than their AM predecessors, who had trouble shaking off their perception of John – Johnny – as the lovely bloke who sang 'Sadie'.

'You're the Voice' was a totally different Farnham, in look and sound and approach.

Still, anything new from John Farnham was not going to be embraced by the FM networks with the same fervour as the latest release from Jimmy Barnes or INXS, no matter how good it was. Wheatley had to fight to get his client heard. He resorted to presenting the new record in a paper bag, sans the artist's name.

George Moore was among the more high-profile DJs on 2DayFM. One morning in October 1986 he came into the Sydney studio for a programming discussion about new releases. He was told a new Farnham record was on the pile; he couldn't miss it, it was the record in the brown paper bag.

'What's it like?' he asked with vague disinterest.

'It's not bad. It's called "The Voice", or something like that.'

Moore gave the record a spin and was converted straight away.

'As soon as we heard it,' he said in 1988, 'we knew it was going to be big. But now "big" seems such an inadequate word to describe it.'

Over at Triple M, program manager Charlie Fox had a blunt message for Wheatley.

'Glenn,' he said, 'this station does not play "Johnny" Farnham.'

But once 2Day put the song into rotation, and requests came pouring in, Triple M had to fall in line, in order to compete and stay relevant. The groundswell was beginning. And 'Johnny' prejudices aside, 'You're the Voice' was a natural fit for FM radio, resting comfortably on playlists alongside 'Listen like Thieves', the latest from INXS, Boom Crash Opera's 'Hands up in the Air' and Jimmy Barnes's 'Good Times' (which he cut with INXS), all big local songs of late 1986. Perhaps for the first time in his recording career, John was on the cutting edge. Triple M wised up to the extent that within a year they'd be 'simulcasting' a 90-minute *Whispering Jack* in-concert special, backed by a hefty $350,000 budget, as 'Jack's Back' mania hit its peak.

Chart-wise, early August 1986 had been the time of Madonna's 'Papa Don't Preach', as it began its six-week-long stint at the top of the Australian singles list. Bananarama's cover of 'Venus' did one better, ruling for seven weeks from mid-September. But as of late September, the ladies of Bananarama had a windswept rival, as the 'You're the Voice' juggernaut began its chart ascent.

John celebrated with a few late-October dates in Melbourne, playing the Palace, the Flight Deck, Cramer's and the Village Green Hotel. He was billed by *The Age* as a 'pop star of old who has managed to keep his popularity afloat without having to resort to nostalgia'. It would be the last time for a long time that he could play such intimate venues.

By 3 November 'You're the Voice' was the national number one and it wouldn't budge from the top for seven weeks. Despite its late-year release, it outstripped Wa Wa Nee's 'Stimulation' and Martin Plaza's cover of 'Concrete and Clay' to become the biggest Australian single of the year. It also became the top-selling single of the year in Australia overall, besting Billy Ocean's ubiquitous 'When the Going Gets Tough, the Tough Get Going', among others. It was a monster.

'You're the Voice' was John's first Top 10 hit since 'Help!' back in 1980, and his first number one since 1969's 'Raindrops'. It had been a long and often challenging 17 years, but now, finally, he was back on top. At the same time, John was surprised to learn that an LRB single, 'Face in the Crowd', had just been lifted from *No Reins*, his final album with the band. Suddenly he was competing with himself – and 'You're the Voice' won by a landslide. Leaving the Little River Band had been the first of many right moves Farnham had made.

One afternoon in early November, John, who hadn't yet heard the news about 'You're the Voice', was in Wheatley's South Melbourne office.

'I'll drive you home, John,' Wheatley said as his day drew to a close. On the way out to Bulleen, Wheatley called the RCA office on his car phone. He spoke briefly and signed off.

'Do you know,' he said excitedly to John, who was in the passenger seat, 'that we have the number one record? *Number one*. All across Australia. Can you believe it?'

Farnham didn't say much; he mumbled something about not being able to believe this was happening, as Wheatley continued driving. At the next red light, Wheatley looked over. John was crying – tears of joy.

12

BACK ON TOP

The 'You're the Voice' phenomenon proved to be just the start of John Farnham's remarkable second act. Its parent album was as successful as the single it spawned. Admittedly, in 21st century terms, *Whispering Jack*, with its wheezing synths and wind tunnel drums, now sounds a little dated, but in Australia in late 1986 it was exactly the type of record that Farnham and Fraser envisaged: contemporary, cutting-edge, sleek and slick, all the way from the opening whoosh of 'Pressure Down' to the closing strains of 'Let Me Out'. It was a record tailor-made for FM radio.

They'd chosen their songwriters well: Mondo Rock's Eric McCusker contributed 'No One Comes Close'; Harry Bogdanovs, an English songwriter who'd worked with Dire Straits' David Knopfler, brought 'Pressure Down' and 'Love to Shine' to the party; John himself took a rare sole credit for 'Let Me Out' and shared credit with Fraser and David Hirshfelder on 'Going, Going, Gone'. And of course there was the beautifully haunting 'A Touch of Paradise' – Ross Wilson was one of its three co-writers – which John made his very own, as he'd done with so many ballads during his recording career.

John's voice was the star of the show, wisely placed front and centre in the mix. He was strident when required, during 'You're the Voice' and 'Let Me Out'; soft and sensual on 'A Touch of Paradise'. Even lesser tracks such as 'One Step Away', a piece of lightweight fluff that could have been lifted straight from the Huey Lewis and the News songbook, were elevated by John's energetic, insistent vocal chops. There couldn't have been a better showcase for Australia's premier vocalist: *Whispering Jack* was a 40-minute reminder to the public that Jack was back.

The critical response to the album was swift and emphatic. Writing in *The Age* on 8 October, Paul Speeman heaped on the praise. '*Whispering Jack* is a brilliant album. It's not only a triumph for Farnham and his musical associates but a credit to the Australian record industry. The single, the political "You're the Voice", has been picked up by Melbourne radio remarkably quickly and deservedly so – it's destined to be a No. 1 hit if quality means anything these days.'

'Ever since *Uncovered*,' Speeman concluded, 'I have suspected that John Farnham is the best singer in Australia. *Whispering Jack* confirms it.'

It was the type of early release review that artists dream about. Finally, after 12 albums and almost 20 years, John Farnham had gained the credit – and the credibility – he'd long deserved.

Lazarus had nothing on John Farnham – and his comeback had only just begun. By February 1987, as 'Pressure Down' was readied as his next single – it'd hit number 4 – sales of *Whispering Jack* ticked way past platinum; it was fast-tracking its way to becoming the highest-selling Oz album of all time. Despite lively competition from recent releases like the Eurythmics' *Revenge* and Billy Joel's *The Bridge*, *Whispering Jack* ruled the charts and the airwaves for much of late 1986 and deep into '87. It became a staple of 'classic rock' radio pretty much from then onwards and stuck like glue to the Australian charts for an incredible 127 weeks, 25 of those spent at number 1. Its rival in the all-time bestseller stakes, Skyhooks' *Living in the 70's*, spent a mere 52 weeks on the chart, 16 of those at number 1. *Living in the 70's* sold some 200,000-plus copies, not a notch on the sales of *Whispering Jack*.

In March 1987 John ruled the inaugural ARIAs, taking home the awards for Album of the Year, Single of the Year, Best Male Artist, Highest Selling Single and Album and Best Adult Contemporary Album. A clean sweep. He thanked one and all, from top to bottom, while execs from the labels that had rejected the *Whispering Jack* demos (essentially everyone outside of RCA) wept quietly into their drinks. In one of his acceptance speeches, John even took the chance to dig up the old chestnut about saving Wheatley from drowning in the toilet bowl on his 21st. He was having a blast.

Fans expressed their love for *Whispering Jack* in the strangest ways. David Thai, a contestant on Network Ten's *Pot Luck* talent show, intended to give everything he had to his own version of John's 'Pressure Down'. Unfortunately, he gave a little too much; the faux Michael Jackson dances moves and unique interpretation of the lyrics reminded viewers why the show was called *Pot Luck*. The song was best left in John's hands. The show's hanging judge, the oh-so-arch Bernard King, had a field day.

'It's very difficult to decide if there's a future for this kind of work,' he sniffed. 'You almost gave yourself whiplash. Perhaps if you were to join a chorus, a huge chorus – say, 20 or 30,000.'

Most fans, however, expressed their love with their hard-earned cash. Wheatley's $150K outlay wasn't merely safe as houses; it now looked like a pretty fabulous investment.

Television was John's natural domain, and he and Wheatley had used it (perhaps even exploited it) very effectively since joining forces back in 1980. TV was the perfect vehicle for pushing John's golden locks shone brighter than ever before, if that was possible, when he stepped onto the set of Ray Martin's *Midday* show in July 1987. Success had done wonders for Farnham: he positively glowed.

Like Don Lane before him, Martin embraced Farnham like a long-lost son – as did his blue-rinsed audience. When introducing John, Martin mentioned that it had taken John 20 years 'to shake the tag of being the boy who sang about the cleaning lady', but as the *Midday* orchestra struck up 'The Voice' – and Martin introduced him as 'The Voice, John Farnham' – it was clear that Sadie was well and truly a thing of the past.

John was in a bubbly mood, talking about his family, both his son, Robbie – 'I love him,' John gushed, 'he's great' – and his yet unborn child (Jillian was pregnant with their second child, James, due in January).

Then Martin asked the far-reaching question: 'What happened between the King of Pop and *Whispering Jack*?'

'I did all sorts of different things,' John replied. '[But] I got to the stage, just before I joined The Wheatley Organisation... where I wasn't being stimulated by what I was doing. I was still trading on "Sadie" and "Raindrops", things I'd done 10 years before. It wasn't particularly stimulating for the audience I had at the time – all nine of them.'

The crowd broke into nervous laughter, but John put them straight. It was the truth. 'Seriously. I remember going back to do a show in Dandenong, where I lived as a kid, and my whole family came along. That was it. No-one from school. I was mortified.'

So what about overseas? Martin asked. John had just returned from one of many European trips promoting *Whispering Jack* and 'You're the Voice', and the single was fast becoming as big a hit on the continent as it was in Australia. The album would achieve similar success in Sweden (number one), Switzerland (number three), Austria (number three), Germany (Top 10) and Norway (Top 20). Surely this type of success tempted him to chase global domination a bit more enthusiastically, no?

John made it very clear, despite the constant chirping of people like Molly Meldrum, that Australia was his home, had always been his home and would remain his home. Offshore success was great, but the notion of pursuing pop's pot of gold with the same single-mindedness as Olivia Newton-John, Helen Reddy, Peter Allen and Rick Springfield was not for him.

'This is not to make light of what's happened to me in the rest of the world of late,' John said, turning serious after a quick flurry of mother-in-law jokes, 'but this success hasn't been the most important thing in my life. What's happened here, the fact I've been able to work, is absolutely fantastic. Ian Meldrum used to give me hell, saying "You've got to crack overseas, why haven't you done it?" It seemed more important to other people than to me. I was happy with what happened here. I live here.'

This would become something of a Farnham mantra over the next few years.

Still, there were international highlights for John, such as an outdoors show in Munich in July 1987, where he shared the bill with Tina Turner, the Eurythmics, bluesman Robert Cray – who Farnham particularly liked – and Joe Cocker. They drew a crowd of 110,000 people, a sea of people. John was stunned when virtually the entire crowd shouted the words of 'The Voice' back at him. 'It was just fantastic.'

But the demands of building a new audience could be overbearing, especially with a young family. Farnham recalled one occasion around that time when he returned from a holiday and even before he'd unpacked, Wheatley called.

'You better leave some clothes in your suitcase, John,' he said. He'd booked him on a midnight flight to London, for an appearance on *Top of the Pops*. His performance would go out to 90 million people. Now that was an audience!

'I was still shaking the sand out of my shoes,' said John, who went on to say that he instantly forgot all the words to the song when he learnt the exact size of the show's audience. It wasn't the first time for the sometimes forgetful Farnham.

Regardless, 'The Voice' eventually reached number 6 in the UK and the Farnham resurgence rolled on.

Events the night prior to his Ray Martin appearance meant more to Farnham than all his European success combined. *Countdown*, the ABC show that John had helped launch, had finally run its course, broadcasting its 563rd and final episode on 19 July 1987. John, after his period in the wilderness, had again become the show's artist du jour. He had a curious history with the show: he'd appeared on the first episode in late '74, then the first colour episode a few months later – and now its swan song. Three big episodes, despite long gaps in between.

The last *Countdown* awards, staged at the Sydney Entertainment Centre, took place immediately after that final episode aired. John swept the pool, collecting gongs for Best Album, Best Single and Best Performance in a Rock Video. No wonder the oilskin-clad Farnham looked so chuffed when he strode onto the stage for the fourth time, having just been announced winner of the Most Outstanding Achievement award, and squeezed host Molly Meldrum in a bear hug. He struggled to be heard above the screams of the crowd; John Farnham had become a sex symbol all over again.

'I have had 20 of the most enjoyable, terrifying, annoying, fun years anyone could wish to have,' he shouted over the din. 'All through my time I've been supported by people, very strongly. I'd like to say thank you to the industry for letting me stay around, but most importantly to those who supported me and bought the records and listened to them and [have] been there when I needed you. Thank you very much indeed.'

With that, Meldrum took over the mic and gave a shout-out to Jillian Farnham, 'the strongest support of my mate here'. The overwhelmingly good vibes spilled onto the stage, and Wheatley picked up the bass and stood in on 'The Voice', the song that had firmly re-established his number-one client and dear friend as the man of the moment, the hour, the year – perhaps even the latter half of the decade. As John whipped the Ent Cent crowd into a frenzy, he walked over and put his arm around Wheatley; both were sporting million-dollar smiles. All the drama and hardship of the past eight years was swept aside.

Then the bagpipers, positioned on the first level of the big concrete bunker, exploded into sound, and the place erupted.

John, backed by guitarist Brett Garsed, now a permanent fixture in Farnhamland, bassist Greg Macainsh, keyboarder David Hirschfelder and drummer Angus Burchall, along with backing vocalists Lindsay Field and Venetta Fields, also Farnham regulars, hit the road for the Jack's Back tour, beginning in Adelaide on 2 December 1987. John was a bit disappointed: he had hatched a grand plan for veteran actor Frank Thring to open the shows, addressing the audience in his trademark arch tones while seated on a throne. John may have been the king of pop, but Thring was the king, period. But on the same day Farnham met Thring to discuss the idea, the actor suffered a heart attack; he survived but was out of action, unable to tour. Still, the show went on, now featuring a video message from the recovering thespian.

Initially planned as an 11-date run – Wheatley's expectations modest due to competing tours from Michael Jackson and Billy Joel – public response was so feverish that eight more Farnham shows were added, at significantly larger venues. Eventually spanning two months, Jack's Back became the highest-grossing national tour to feature an Australian act, a huge achievement. Over the course of the tour, John played to 120,000 people and it seemed as though every one of them had nothing but love for the man on stage. It was the type of fervent fan response rarely seen – or heard – this side of the Beatles' legendary campaign of 1964. John was breaking hearts, and records, all over again.

John was clearly loving his time on stage. He'd drop into long, funny monologues between songs, covering such pressing issues as the 'spit catchment' in front of the stage – 'my mouth gets very moist' – and the perils of where to put his hands while performing ('Never in your pockets,' Jillian had instructed him; he duly obliged), all the while responding to the ongoing shrieks of 'We love you, John!' with his usual humble charm: 'Thank you very much indeed. I love you, too, and I can't even see you.'

'If you know the words to the following song,' John would announce before 'Comic Conversation', which he performed as a two-hander with Hirschfelder, 'don't join in, 'cause you're going to ruin the bloody thing. Several thousand people singing out of tune ...' He'd then grin, close his eyes and shake his flowing mane, as if the very thought was too much to comprehend. It was great theatre, good fun, a mix of music and stand-up.

John and band played three nights at the 12,000-capacity Sydney Entertainment Centre, a venue that from then onwards would prove to be a very happy hunting ground. Mind you, John almost missed the first of those Sydney shows. Wheatley always insisted on collecting his star and driving him to the gig; it was something of a ritual for the two of them. But in the car on the way to the Entertainment

Centre, with Wheatley at the wheel, John was a little confused by the sights that swiftly flashed by his window: why could he see Luna Park? Wasn't that North Sydney in the distance? Weren't they on the wrong side of the Harbour Bridge? Farnham pointed this out to Wheatley, whose navigational skills seemed as sketchy as John's ability to remember his song lyrics. Shoot, Farnham was right.

'Erm, John,' Wheatley said sheepishly, easing the car off the bridge, trying to throw a U-turn. 'I don't have any coins for the toll.'

'Neither do I,' John realised. He joked about not carrying money because 'the band picks my pockets'; tonight it was a big problem.

They rolled up to the tollbooth, debating their next move, when a female fan pulled up next to them. She immediately recognised John. Who wouldn't?

'Hey, love, can you do us a favour?' Farnham asked.

Toll paid, fan duly thrilled, star and manager reached the venue just before showtime.

During this Sydney run, in the twilight zone between sound check and the start of the concert – when he did make a gig on time – John delighted in cold-calling his fans from the Ent Cent's backstage area. He'd received a hefty amount of fan mail, sent directly to the venue, some with phone numbers. So to kill the time, and shock his fans, he'd start dialling. 'Hi, this is John Farnham...'

'Some people didn't believe it was me,' he laughed, 'so I would sing a song to them and I got passed around the room to talk to the whole family a bit. And there were screams and tears. I loved it.'

In the moment just before the house lights went down and the show began, John and the band, along with the crew and Wheatley, who rarely missed a Farnham gig, would gather. A bottle of 'fighting brandy' – cheap, bottom-shelf plonk – would be produced and a toast proposed. Drinks downed, bond reinforced, they would hit the stage, ready for anything. (This proved to be an effective warm-up technique; when John was about to face a global audience of four billion at the 2000 Olympic Games opening ceremony, his preparation amounted to getting 'absolutely drunk'.)

Every night John and the band worked through a hits-heavy set, which included *Whispering Jack* in entirety, as well as songs from his Little River Band days – 'When the War Is Over', 'Playing to Win' and 'Down on the Border' – along with 'Help!'. He and Fields joined voices on a mighty, gospel-ly 'Amazing Grace'. In Sydney, the 60-piece Sydney University Choir helped out on 'The Voice', as did the now obligatory piper – several pipers, in fact. It was a powerhouse set of quality pop. And there wasn't a 'Sadie' to be heard.

'Well, I guess you could say it's keeping me busy,' John laughed wryly when asked about this new wave of Farnham mania. 'But I'm always as busy as a blue-arsed fly anyway.' As usual, he was using his deeply ingrained sense of humour, his regular-bloke-iness, to avoid getting too serious about all the madness. If he'd stopped to consider how fast he'd risen – again – it might have been too much to contemplate.

'A lot of people at the shows don't seem to be regular concert-goers,' noted silver-haired bassist Macainsh, who'd tasted a little of this craziness during Skyhooks' mid-1970s peak, 'but they do love the idea of John Farnham coming out of the wilderness to be a star again. It's a bit like being on a campaign trail for the silent majority.'

John's upward mobility wasn't lost on the media.

'It's not unheard of for a local artist to move from 300-400 crowd'em-in-a-pub lounge to a 2000 seater theatre and thence to an audience of 12,000 at the cavernous Entertainment Centre,' noted the *Sydney Morning Herald*'s Anthony O'Grady. 'But no one has been so upwardly mobile so quickly. John Farnham's second rise to the top has been faster that his first.'

Nothing said success mid-1980s-style more than a TV/radio simulcast. The *Jack's Back* special, a ratings winner when it was screened on Channel 7 soon after the completion of the tour, was essentially a concert doco, with snippets of backstage and downtime footage thrown in to add that personal touch. And it was revealing in an inoffensive, tailor-made-for-middle-Australia kind of way. John met fans, threw himself into lively water-pistol fights with the band, blazed on stage – and in quieter moments reflected on his all-conquering second coming. Much of the doco's key interview was conducted while John was seated in a tinnie, his second home, on the water at Lake Eildon, Victoria, a favourite spot of his since he was a teenager.

'I've had a good piece of news about this project every day since the day I gave it to Wheatley,' he said from his boat. 'All that positivity has been unbelievable. I'm enjoying success now more than I ever have in the past because I'm able to understand it more – I feel a bit more credible within myself.'

John's success was reflected by his appearance: he even looked good in fishing gear, a flannel shirt and red fluoro life jacket, the wind tousling his mane. As ever, he played everything down, even joking about his bald spot.

Jack's Back began with John ready to hit the stage, in red stormtrooper jacket – a look Jillian had suggested to him – cuffs rolled, tearing into 'Reasons'. Stage lights flashed in all directions, the excitement level was massive. The rich voices of Field and Fields chimed in beautifully with Farnham, who owned the stage – and the super-responsive crowd loved him. He was theirs.

Elsewhere, Molly Meldrum spoke on camera, as did Wheatley, producer Ross Fraser, much of John's band, and the man himself. Vocalist Venetta Fields casually, coolly, rattled off her highly impressive CV: she'd sung with Ike and Tina Turner, Diana Ross, Steely Dan, Pink Floyd, the Rolling Stones, Neil Diamond… and now John Farnham, whom she rated as highly as the others. John revealed how Sam See told him he'd never write a good song, 'because I was too bloody happy'. John shrugged; See was right. But being happy was hardly a crime.

A Coke spot, featuring John, 'You're the Voice' and his band prominently, appeared during every ad break, the first time a major sponsorship deal had been inked between the soft-drink giant and an Australian star like John. It was another Wheatley coup. John Farnham was officially everywhere.

There was a price to pay for all his success, John admitted during *Jack's Back*: he was losing his private life. He told the story of the first time he walked the corridors of Channel 9 as a wide-eyed kid in the 1960s. John spotted Eric Pearce (later Sir Eric), the esteemed newsreader, heading towards him. Farnham, without thinking, said, 'G'day, Eric,' despite not knowing the man. It was a bit cheeky. (Farnham later apologised.) Flash forward 20-odd years and Farnham was now in the same position as Pearce, a public figure recognised by every man, woman and child pretty much wherever he went, and they all wanted to say 'G'day'. It wasn't in John's nature to reject people, even if they got a bit pushy and demanding. He aimed to please.

American Wayne Nelson, on an LRB sabbatical to tour with John, was impressed by Farnham's calm demeanour, the way he coped with his fans' endless requests. John truly was a man of the people.

'You can't go anywhere in this country without people wanting his autograph or to talk with him,' noted Nelson.

John stressed that he had two key priorities: his family and his performance. If something got in the way of either, well, it 'had to suffer'. The problem, of course, was that as John's public profile exploded, more and more demands were placed on him: to meet kids in hospital, speak at charity events, do the right thing, raise money for good causes, and all the rest of it. He was happy to help in any way he could, unless it messed with his family time.

As for being on the road, it was a classic catch-22 situation for John: he loved touring but hated being away from his family. Jillian was pregnant, so she and Robbie stayed at home while John toured *Whispering Jack*. He missed them enormously. It all came home to him when he called Robbie during a Canberra pit stop.

'I'll be home soon, son,' John said down the line.

'Forever?' Robbie innocently asked, as his father's heart broke.

Back on stage, John was having some fun with a fan's gift, playfully examining a bouquet of flowers handed to him – 'Oh, hello, there's a phone number,' he said on closer inspection – and then providing a little man-of-the-people stage patter, graciously accepting more gifts and offerings from his doting audience, all the while turning on some serious charm. Screams punctuated John's every comment, his every gesture. His smile, meanwhile, said that no-one should be taking all this too seriously, as thankful as he was of the recognition. To his own way of thinking, John was just a singer, a regular bloke in an irregular job, just as comfortable in a tinnie on the river as fronting the screaming masses. He didn't need his ego massaged. Well, not too much.

When John and the band finally pulled off the road in late 1987, his resurrection was complete. And the stats were astounding: *Whispering Jack* continued to sell strongly a year after its release, outstripping Crowded House's hit debut, Paul Simon's *Graceland* and U2's *The Joshua Tree*. It even made the Top 20 of the bestselling albums in 1988. (At time of writing *Whispering Jack* is inching towards sales of 2 million in Australian alone, making it the number two bestselling album of all time in Oz, just behind Meatloaf's *Bat Out of Hell*.) 'You're the Voice' was the second-bestselling Oz single of 1986 and it made John a household name throughout Europe. 'Pressure Down' was among the top-five bestselling Australian singles of 1987; 'Touch of Paradise' also hit the Top 20 on release. John collected virtually all the silverware at the 1987 *Countdown* awards and the ARIAs. He played to hundreds of thousands of punters in Oz and Europe.

And after 20 years in the biz, finally he was flush; he could now pay off all his debtors, the taxman included. John indulged himself and bought a Porsche. Second-hand, admittedly, but still a Porsche.

The Nine Network's top-rating *Hey Hey It's Saturday* pretty much gave its entire program over to John on 1 August 1987. Farnham played several songs, grinned a lot, traded lame gags with pint-sized Dickie Knee and the rest of the cast, and looked pretty damned great in a knee-length, stonewashed denim coat. It was like *The Don Lane Show* all over again; the camera loved him. He didn't even mind being upstaged by former Skyhooks' singer Shirley Strachan, who commandeered the mic for a roaring 'Women in Uniform', an old Hooks' shouter that John now often sang. The smile never left John's face as he retreated to the rear of the stage and happily joined voices with Field and Fields. Why should he worry? He was back on top.

Even more important than his lofty sales figures and bounty of awards, John had achieved what many thought impossible: he'd gained credibility. He may not have been the most serious of men, but he was a serious singer, a major talent, now rated with the world's best. Finally, some respect.

13

AUSSIE OF THE YEAR

Even in his wildest dreams, John would never have dared imagine success on the scale of *Whispering Jack*. But in early 1988 his profile would climb even higher. Already John was widely recognised as the 'Ray Martin of pop', a public figure, but he was set to enter a whole new stratosphere of popularity.

It started with a letter that hit Wheatley's desk in late 1987, from the Australia Day Council, stating that John was on their Australian of the Year shortlist. While thrilled, Wheatley knew straight away there was a potential issue – John wasn't an Aussie citizen, despite living here for the past 30 years. He put in a call to the Council's office.

'Is there any way I can find out in advance if John will win?'

He was shut down immediately; no-one, not even the PM, knew this information in advance. Wheatley revealed John's citizenship problem and was promised a call back the next day.

His phone rang early in the morning.

'Mr Farnham could very well be the next Australian of the Year.'

Wheatley reminded the Council of the possible hiccup; if John was going to be anointed, he'd need to become an Australian citizen, and fast. And this may not be a decision he'd make lightly, given that he still had family, and ties, in the Old Dart.

The next day, Wheatley's phone rang yet again; it was the same staffer at the Australia Day Council. Wheatley was immediately sworn to secrecy. Yes, he was told, John was about to be crowned the Australian of the Year. A bureaucrat was despatched from Canberra to sort out the citizenship situation.

Farnham, fortunately, was fine with the arrangement: as a dual citizen he could keep his British passport *and* become an Aussie. So on 5 January John took a day off from being a parent-in-waiting – his second child was due around Australia Day – and rolled up to Wheatley's office at EON FM in South Melbourne. A few minutes later, John walked out into the January sunshine as an official Aussie. It was a big moment for him, but he knew that an even bigger event was just around the corner.

Since its inception in 1960, an eclectic bunch had been named Australians of the Year, including comic Paul Hogan in 1985 and explorer/business-brain Dick Smith in 1986. Historically, it had been the domain of sporting greats – Dawn Fraser (1964), Evonne Goolagong Cawley (1971) and Shane Gould (1972) – and big thinkers like historian Manning Clark (1980) and author Patrick White (1973). Even business mogul Alan Bond had been crowned in 1978, well before his fall from grace. But with the exception of The Seekers in 1967, musicians had not been named Australians of the year.

The criteria for Aussie of the Year failed to mention entertainers at all. It stated that the award provided 'an insight into Australian identity, reflecting the nation's evolving relationship with the world, the role of sport in Australian culture, the impact of multiculturalism, and the special status of Australia's Indigenous people.' Not a word about big-haired singers with runaway hit albums.

But the impact of 'You're the Voice' and *Whispering Jack*, John's remarkable rebirth and his under-the-radar social conscious made him the perfect choice for the bicentennial year gong. Officially, he was anointed 'for his outstanding contribution to the Australian music industry over 20 years'. Unofficially, he'd been the people's favourite ever since 'You're the Voice' heralded his return. And if Hoges could be Aussie of the Year, why not Farnesy?

But there was the odd dissenting voice.

'I wonder what the process is for naming the Australian of the Year?' sniffed one letter writer to the Fairfax press. 'Apart from having a number one hit tune in 1987, I cannot recall anything John Farnham has done for the nation.'

Clearly the writer knew nothing of Farnham's charity links, especially his role with the Victorian Association for Deserted Children, an organisation he'd been involved with since the mid-1970s. If John had a dollar for every telethon and fundraiser he'd taken part in, he'd be an even wealthier pop star.

John, his son, Robbie, and his parents – Jillian was at home, very pregnant with their second child, James – rocked up to Kirribilli House to accept the award on a blazing hot Australia Day. TV cameras from Channel 10 took it all in, cutting between the festivities at Kirribilli and events on the harbour, as the 'tall ships' glided through

Sydney Heads – it being the bicentennial year – and were quickly swamped by spectator craft.

John looked fit and tanned, if slightly stunned.

'It's very difficult to put into words how this feels,' he managed to say. 'I'm very overawed. I sometimes sit back and wonder how I can live up to it. All I am is a singer – that's what I do best.'

'I wasn't chosen because of my political beliefs,' John continued. 'Australian music has made one hell of a contribution to me. I've been able to do what I love more than anything else in the world for the past 20-odd years.'

John paused, taking this in.

'Twenty-odd years!' he repeated, stunned by the thought. 'I'm more grateful for that than you'll ever know.'

Bob Hawke was never a man to shy away from a TV camera, and he soon joined John ('Johnny' to the grinning PM, whom Farnham addressed more formally as 'Mr Hawke') on the makeshift Channel 10 set. Hawke laughed about meeting Farnham at the recent Adelaide Grand Prix, where they had shared a cheeky ciggie, a habit John hadn't quite kicked yet. It was a cosy moment, even though John looked a bit uncomfortable when Hawke grabbed his hand. That was unexpected.

On this, his first official day of duty, John quickly learnt that the questions got a little harder, as hosts Tim Webster and Katrina Lee, both huge Farnham fans, threw some curly ones his way.

'You deal with young people all the time – what are they like out there? Are we relating to them?'

'I think we're doing a good job,' John replied, a little hesitantly, 'but even if we're doing an excellent job, we could do better.'

Hawkey then slipped into his natural role as Australia's number one spruiker, smoothly taking the load off John.

'Look at that,' he pronounced, gesturing towards the sun-splashed harbour like a proud parent. 'What other country has 16 million people, basically united, the vast spaces, the resources we've got? There's no hierarchy of class. Everyone, no matter where they come from, is an Aussie and they have as much right as anyone else.'

Hawke seemed just one breath away from his famous 'any boss who sacks anyone for not turning up today is a bum' line, which he'd declared after Australia's America's Cup win back in 1983.

'What about your children?' asked Lee, turning back to John. 'What do you want for them, growing up in Australia, over the next few years?'

'There's obvious things: health and happiness. And I travelled a lot recently, in the last few years, and I don't really think you know what you've got until you haven't got it anymore. Just flying back into this country – there's nothing like it.

'If we spoil what we have we can't just move next door, we can't find another paddock to build another house on ... Australia does deserve national pride, we are right to instil national pride in our children but please, let's make our national pride include humanity.'

'If I had one wish,' John said later in the day, 'it would be to stop people shooting each other, abusing each other and killing each other. As Australians, we also must look at the darker side of this country.'

He was right. There'd been several brutal slayings over the past few years: five family members shot to death in the Sydney suburb of Campsie by a deranged father, then seven killed during the infamous Milperra bikie massacre. Seven people also died during the 1987 Hoddle Street carnage. Eight died a few months later in Melbourne's Queen Street massacre. The death count was high and rising. The cautionary lyrics of 'You're the Voice' were taking on a whole new and confronting meaning.

John seemed more at ease when he talked through all things Australian of the Year with DJ George Moore, in front of a happy audience of invitees and radio competition winners. They discussed such pressing issues as young Robbie Farnham's career aspirations (fireman, bike rider and definitely 'not a pop star', according to his doting dad), John's childhood nickname – 'Wingnut', a nod to his jug ears – and exactly who took out the Farnham family garbage (John, whenever he was home). John was at his most animated when he spoke about a three-day break he had awaiting him.

'I'm going to put the champagne in the freezer and share it with the bride. She likes that,' John smiled. 'Can't wait.'

As for upcoming business, John mentioned a possible trip to China, which Wheatley was busy negotiating.

'Music is a universal language, doesn't matter what colour you are or language you speak, that's the bottom line.'

In between shrieks from his rapt audience, John took the moment to reflect on his remarkable recent history.

'I have had the most amazing two years of my life. I've met a lot of people and never felt so warm. It's been lovely.'

The events of Australia Day 1988 typified John's manic new life. He, Wheatley and John's parents had a standing invitation for drinks with Channel 7 owner Christopher Skase, on board his $6 million boat *Mirage III*, which Skase had sailed down from Brisbane for the occasion.

Getting to Skase's floating gin-palace proved to be a harrowing experience. First stop after Kirribilli House was their hotel at The Rocks, for a quick change of clothes. But the entrance was blocked with hundreds of fans and well-wishers, many of whom clamoured onto John's limo, yelling for his attention, screaming his name.

John was concerned for his dad, immobilised by his recent stroke. They were trapped.

'We've got to get out of here!' John barked at Wheatley, at the driver, and at anyone else who might be able to help deal with the madness. But they couldn't move for fear of running someone over.

Finally, thankfully, police on horseback trotted up to the hotel and formed an equine entryway for a flustered John and his entourage. They then required a police escort to travel the short distance to the Opera House, where they were taken out to the *Mirage III*. Once on board, John breathed deeply, perhaps for the first time all day, and got himself a drink.

But it wasn't all smooth sailing, at least for manager Wheatley. Skase was hoping to do a deal and obtain Farnham's services for his Mirage resorts and for Channel 7. He wanted exclusivity; the stakes were high, the figures huge. Wheatley also had ongoing talks with Skase about the purchase of a radio station, Brisbane's FM104, as part of his expanding broadcasting empire. Business and pleasure had a habit of merging in the world of Wheatley and Farnham.

Discussions over for the time being, drinks consumed, the next challenge for the Farnham party of four was finding a safe way back to shore. Thousands of people had lined the harbour, hoping to catch a glimpse of the newly crowned Aussie of the Year. There was nowhere for them to disembark safely. This reignited Farnham's concern for his father; suddenly all the excitement and fun had been sucked out of the day. This was crazy. Why were these people getting so worked up? he wondered. He was just a singer.

Finally they found a safe haven at the Royal Yacht Squadron, on the northern shore of the harbour; however, the stuffy Squadron members weren't impressed to have some 'commoners' roll up to their dock – and so what if one of them happened to be the Australian of the Year? And no, they couldn't use the phone. That was strictly for members. There was, however, a phone box down the street...

Wheatley, who, like his star client, was now on the brink of hysteria, was forced to use the public phone to call for an emergency ride back to the hotel. Not a great look for either Wheatley or Farnham. An hour later they finally reached their digs in The Rocks, exhausted and angry, bypassing another starstruck mob on the way inside.

John's nerves were shot.

'Come on, we're leaving,' he told his parents, who couldn't have been more relieved. They were on the next flight to Melbourne. Sydney was out of control. So much for the celebrations.

As Wheatley would write, 'It was the most awful day we could have gone through.'

Everything that had just happened was tangible proof of the new conflict in John's life. Off stage, he may have craved the everyday and the normal – 'doing the gardening in my undies,' as he would tell reporters. But that was now more difficult than ever. He was a superstar, a very public figure, with all the complications and pressures that entailed.

John, however, still had one safe haven: the studio. Being Australian of the Year was incredibly flattering, and a huge responsibility, but it was also time to make a new record. He needed to prove *Whispering Jack* was no fluke.

Johnny Farnham,
apprentice plumber turned
unlikely pop star.
Courtesy Glenn A. Baker

While plugging 1967's smash 'Sadie', no gimmick was too cheesy.
Courtesy Fairfax Media

Johnny at his 21st in 1970, held in Melbourne, with parents John Sr and Rose.
Courtesy Peter Barr, Fairfax Media

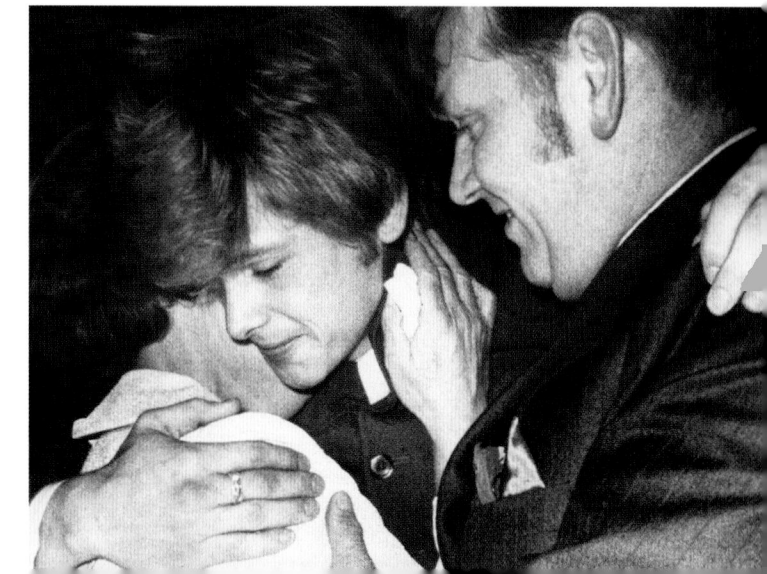

Johnny with Darryl Sambell, his first manager, mentor and true believer.
Courtesy Fairfax Media

Johnny marries Jillian Billman in 1973. The chopper was Sambell's idea.
Courtesy Fairfax Media

Johnny in 1977, having parted ways with Sambell, his career adrift.
Courtesy Glenn A. Baker

Joining the Little River Band in 1982 was meant to be a lifeline for John.
Courtesy Fairfax Media

Recording *Whispering Jack* in 1986, the album that rescued John's career.
Courtesy Glenn A. Baker

Above: With American legend Stevie Wonder, a huge influence on John.
Courtesy Glenn A. Baker

Left: John scooping the pool at the 1987 ARIAs, with wife Jillian.
Courtesy Glenn A. Baker

FOSTE
Telecom MobileNet™
HOLDEN
Nova
1.8
TWIN CAM
6
PHOENIX HOLDEN
Castrol

Opposite, top: With his mate PM Bob Hawke, after being crowned 1988's Australian of the Year.
Courtesy Glenn A. Baker

Opposite, below: John takes the wheel at the Australian Grand Prix, Adelaide 1989.
Courtesy Lyn Albury

Above: On set for the cover shoot of *The Last Time* LP, Melbourne 2002.
Courtesy David Anderson

John with Glenn Wheatley,
his friend, partner and manager.
Courtesy Steven Siewert, Fairfax Media

14

SPOKESMAN FOR THE COMMON MAN

'Age of Reason', the title track of John's new album, came with something of a backstory. It sprang from a random comment at a Dragon gig at the Palais in Melbourne. The NZ-born, Sydney-based group, having dissolved at the end of the previous decade in a haze of hard drugs and disinterest, were in the midst of an unlikely rebirth, on the strength of such hits as 'Rain' and 'Dreams of Ordinary Men' – John wasn't the only act enjoying a second coming.

Farnham and Wheatley were backstage at the Palais, checking in with Todd and Marc Hunter, the brothers who were the mainstays of Dragon, and talk turned to new songs. John was on the hunt for material for the follow-up to *Whispering Jack*, and the Hunters, along with keyboardist Alan Mansfield, a David Hirschfelder-like figure in Dragon, were fast becoming songwriters-in-demand on the strength of their recent hits.

'Why don't you write a song for me?' Farnham asked.

Todd Hunter turned to his wife, Johanna Pigott, a fellow songwriter, and whispered, 'Farnham's asked us to write a song.' In the late 1980s there was no more attractive offer for songwriters than the chance to write for John Farnham. A song on an album like *Whispering Jack* could generate serious money.

Dragon were heading out on a European tour with Tina Turner, with whom Farnham had recently shared a stage in Germany, but that didn't deter Todd Hunter. He set to work on the song, retiring to his hotel room after each show, while his fast-living bandmates were elsewhere getting blotto. Tinkering away on a Mac computer and a keyboard, he laboured over the basic musical structure for what would become 'Age of Reason'. Tour over, he returned to his home studio in Sydney's Bondi. Pigott set to work on the lyrics while heavily pregnant with their first son, Harry.

Writing bespoke music necessitated a different approach to the usual for both Hunter and Pigott; they needed to take into consideration the expectations of Farnham's audience, rather than just draw on their own experiences and emotions. The song's words needed to be more universal, less personal. But while the structure of the song took months to come together, the lyrics took only the best part of 10 minutes. The broader message of 'Age of Reason', its theme of measured optimism and global responsibility, made it the perfect sonic companion piece to 'You're the Voice'. Ross Wilson described John as a 'spokesman for the common man', and these two songs proved him right, as did later Farnham hits such as 'That's Freedom'.

Although the song was completed, it wasn't a given that John would record it, let alone make it his next single and the title of the new album. Marc Hunter had recorded a demo of 'Age of Reason' with Dragon, but struggled with one of the verses. And he didn't appear to be a big fan of the song. The demo tape was sent to Farnham and Ross Fraser, who'd signed on to produce John's new album, and the waiting game began. 'Age of Reason' was among 3000 contenders for John's record, a staggering number – more proof, if needed, of how *Whispering Jack* had changed everything. Two years back, John, Fraser and Wheatley were desperately searching for material; now, hit songs were delivered to their doorstep.

A year, perhaps more, after completing the 'Age of Reason' demo, Hunter and Pigott got a call from Fraser.

'Love the song,' the producer told them, 'we're doing it.'

On the surface it seemed an unlikely alliance: the key songwriters for Dragon, a band of legendary hedonists, writing for the darling of the Aussie mainstream. But the proof was in 'Age of Reason', the perfect track for Farnham, a song that flexed both his powerful voice and his burgeoning social conscience. The layers of keyboards and programming applied by Fraser and Hirschfelder in the studio gave it the requisite contemporary sheen; it sounded every bit as modern as anything else on the airwaves upon the single's release in July 1988. Chart-wise, in August it quickly took the poll position from fellow Oz popster Kylie Minogue and her latest hit, 'Got to Be Certain', and stayed atop the charts for three weeks – a dream return for Farnham. And 'Age of Reason' had legs, becoming a staple of John's live set for the next three decades. The royalties helped Hunter and Pigott buy a rustic country home on the NSW south coast, where they still live, write and record today. Everyone was a winner.

The *Age of Reason* LP dropped in late July, muscling aside Crowded House's *Temple of Low Men* and topping the album chart for nine weeks, quickly going platinum. Picking up on the momentum of *Whispering Jack*, the album hit the Top 10 in Sweden and Norway – Scandinavians couldn't get enough of the man with the windswept hair and the powerful voice.

There were some familiar names among the credits of *Age of Reason*. Ross Wilson wrote 'We're No Angels'; Chris Thompson, one of the co-writers on 'You're the Voice', contributed to 'The Fire' and 'Don't Tell Me It Can't Be Done'. The 'house band' consisted of Farnham regulars Hirschfelder, guitarist Garsed, drummer Angus Burchall and backing vocalists Lindsay Field, Venetta Fields and Lisa Edwards. This time around there were a few star cameos: James Morrison blew his horn on 'Some Do, Some Don't', while expat Kiwi singer Jon Stevens, from Noiseworks, helped out on 'Listen to the Wind'.

John launched *Age of Reason* with a seriously hefty splash on 25 July 1988 at the World Expo in Brisbane, ruling the Expo's River Stage in front of 25,000 fans. Unlike with *Whispering Jack*, he was now a fully fledged superstar; John confidently reminded the public that 'You're the Voice' and all that came with it was just the beginning. With the support of high-flying businessman Skase, who had finally locked John in for a series of TV specials, the Brisbane show was broadcast live and nationwide by Channel 7. Local radio station FM104, recently acquired by Wheatley, presented the show; Hoyts FM simulcast it around the country.

On Channel 7, popular radio DJ Jonathan Coleman introduced the gig as 'the concert event of the decade'; Farnham fans had been filing into the site since the morning of the show, the moment the Expo gates were opened. 'What do you think of John Farnham?'

asked Ian Rogerson, the broadcast's co-host, as he walked through the crowd, pre-gig. 'He's excellent,' gushed one devotee. 'He's gorgeous,' said another. John must have felt like he was reliving the wild days of 'Sadie', but this time with a whole new generation of fans. 'He's a good singer, a good entertainer,' observed an older member of the huge crowd. 'But he could cut his hair.' John was forced to ride a boat from his hotel to the venue; there was simply no way he could make it through the crowd to the stage. Farnham fever had reached critical mass.

'Now we're going to get into some serious rock-and-roll,' John told the huge crowd at the end of his rapturously received set. 'This is the definitive rock-and-roll song.' Never one to bypass a good laugh, John, a plectrum wedged between his teeth, then strapped on a guitar and placed a tiny practice amp next to his microphone stand. 'You may laugh,' he quipped, 'but let me put this thing on 11.' He pulled a few guitar god poses before getting down to business, he and the band tearing into 'It's A Long Way to the Top' with a ferocity rarely witnessed in anyone but AC/DC themselves. Hirschfelder replicated the song's immortal bagpipe solo on his keyboard axe as John worked the crowd and the band into a serious sweat. The applause continued long after they left the stage. This was the concert event of Expo – maybe even the decade, as Coleman had said earlier in the night. Even the ever-creative and resourceful Wheatley couldn't have planned a better album launch – a crowd of 25,000 and a TV audience of several million.

There was only false step. John thirstily slugged a Heineken after this frenetic closer, as he joked on camera with Coleman and

Rogerson, his every gulp captured by the TV crew. Unfortunately, the show's sponsor was Coke. They were on the phone to Wheatley first thing the next morning, voicing their complaints. 'No beer, John must drink Coke!' The stakes were higher now, as Wheatley – and John, by association – scaled the corporate ladder.

That faux pas aside, John had locked into a million-dollar groove: more charting singles were lifted from the album ('Two Strong Hearts', number three in September 1988, and 'We're No Angels', which brushed the Top 40 in May 1989) and it garnered a swag of ARIAs at the 1988 awards. John was declared Best Male Artist and also won gongs for Best Adult Contemporary Album and Outstanding Achievement. *Age of Reason* was the highest-selling Australian album of 1988. In a couple of years, John Farnham had transformed himself from yesterday's hero to a solid-gold, highly bankable brand.

Dapper George Hamilton, legendary Hollywood lounge lizard, provided the most unlikely of cameos in the clip for 'Two Strong Hearts', an informal, sun-and-fun and colour-drenched affair shot on the run in northern Queensland. In it, John and George shared a chilled poolside tipple like two drinking buddies catching up on old times.

The only thing missing from John's trophy cabinet was a Logie – but at the 1988 awards he collected the statuette for Most Popular Music Video for 'Age of Reason'. John, his mullet now in full bloom, wearing a smart black tux, stepped on stage to receive the award from fellow entertainment industry lifer, Bert 'Moonface' Newton.

'Thank you very much indeed,' John said, all smiles. He proceeded to thank director Robbie Wellington, who made him look good, Farnham insisted, via the use of 'mountaineer socks on the lens'. This drew hearty laughs from the crowd. He also thanked his band, 'among the finest musicians and singers you can find'. But then John paused for a beat too long; something wasn't quite right. Oh crap, he realised, he'd just talked up the wrong video. Wellington had directed the clip for 'Two Strong Hearts', not 'Age of Reason'; that was the handiwork of Stephen Priest. Ever the pro, John turned his embarrassment into a joke, borrowing Newton's glasses to check his notes.

'It's the hair,' he explained, as the crowd laughed along with him, 'it's taken all the brain food out.'

The same music critics who'd written John off as a blast from the past were now paying him long overdue respect. Mike Daly, writing in *The Age*, noted that Farnham resisted cloning *Whispering Jack*, which must have been hugely tempting. *Age of Reason* 'is a measured response,' he wrote, 'less strident than the first, with fewer obvious singles, but melodically sounder ... It's also a band album.' Daly gave credit to Hirschfelder, Garsed and producer Fraser. *Age of Reason* fared the best of the other new releases covered in Daly's 4 August column, which included Kylie Minogue's *Kylie* – 'efficient, mind-numbing machine music', according to the critic. Ouch.

John, however, still had moments when he struggled with his role as a very public commodity – Australian of the bleeding Year, thank you very much. One day, John was out with his son, Robbie, when someone approached the boy.

'What's it like having a famous dad?' he was asked.

Robbie looked confused. 'What do you mean, famous? He's my dad.'

Farnham tried hard to smile, but he really wanted to throttle the fool.

'Some people's perception,' he scoffed, 'is that you live 24 hours a day thinking how famous you might be.'

That simply wasn't the case for John Farnham, family man and pop star.

The Age of Reason tour was the next stage of John's now financially rewarding album/press/performance cycle, and it reaped huge returns. He played to almost 200,000 people during shows in December 1988 and January 1989. Having decided to mix things up, John was backed by his band during the first set, and by the Melbourne Symphony Orchestra in the second.

With the inclusion of the MSO, the tour party numbered about 150. Wheatley struck up a deal with Australian Airlines; John now had his own touring plane. (It would be years before another Australian act, the reformed Cold Chisel, were afforded the same luxury, in 2011.) Coke, having forgiven John his Heineken slip-up, stumped up more cash for a national TV campaign, for which John recorded 'It's A Long Way to the Top'. He'd come a long way since warbling about Susan Jones for TAA back in the days of Darryl Sambell.

The only genuine on-tour drama came about in late November, when John was ill, and the first of three Brisbane Entertainment Centre shows was put on hold. The plan was to postpone the show until three nights later. But then Wheatley was exposed to the mysterious inner workings of the musicians' union. The MSO had to vote on whether this extension was acceptable to the musicians; union rules stipulated seven days' notice. As Wheatley looked on, a rep asked, 'Would all non-union members please leave the room so that we can take a vote?' Silence. It took two more requests before Wheatley realised the request was directed at him. The vote, when it was finally held, was 'no'. Wheatley solved the problem by opening up more seating for the two nights on which John was able to perform.

Clearly at ease on stage, and kept at arm's length from any behind-the-scenes drama, Farnham briefly dipped into his past during the tour, dusting off 'Comic Conversation', 'Please Don't Ask Me' and 'Don't You Know It's Magic' in a smartly constructed mini-set with piano man Hirschfelder. Long-time fans at the Sydney Entertainment Centre show were insistent, chanting 'Sadie! Sadie! Sadie!' Until recently, this would have been enough to erase the ever-present smile from Farnham's face, but not tonight, not now. He laughed, revved up the orchestra and granted the full house their wish.

'Farnham's ability as an entertainer was reaffirmed,' noted *Variety*'s reviewer at the show. 'Yet again.'

Manager Wheatley's ambitions weren't just restricted to corporate empire building; he wanted to spread all things Farnham into new territories. They'd conquered Europe with *Whispering Jack* and 'You're the Voice', so now Wheatley turned his gaze to China, pop's final frontier. Brit duo Wham! had stepped beyond the Great Wall in 1985, becoming the first Western pop act to perform in China and gaining huge coverage in the process, so why not the man known (almost) universally as The Voice? Armed with a personal letter of introduction from PM Bob Hawke, a promise from Coke that they'd underwrite a tour, a few promo copies of *Whispering Jack* and photocopies of John's song lyrics, Wheatley left for China in August 1988. First stop Beijing, then Shanghai.

Showing all the dogged commitment he'd displayed when lobbying US record companies on behalf of LRB, Wheatley, who'd recently been crowned *BRW*'s Marketeer of the Year, attended banquet after banquet, eating his way, diplomat style, through the many layers of Chinese bureaucracy. Everywhere he went, party officials shadowed him.

There were matters of cultural sensitivity to tackle – every word John proposed to sing would need to be dissected by bureaucrats, just in case they led to an uprising (hence the lyric sheets). The mention of a gun in 'You're the Voice' was a big issue, as was AC/DC's 'It's A Long Way to the Top', now a staple of John's live set. It was deemed 'too rock-and-roll' for the proletariat. Both songs were out. The Chinese pencil-pushers wanted their people to hear ballads and nothing but; this 'Touch of Paradise' song was lovely, they decided.

'We want more of those. What else do you have?'

Wheatley's persistence was rewarded by a sit-down with Deng Pufang, the son of leader Deng Xiaoping.

Finally, after perhaps more argy-bargy than at any other time in his managerial career, Wheatley had a deal and John became the first Australian entertainer to be invited to perform in China. There'd be four shows in late October 1989, including one in Beijing's Great Hall, where Placido Domingo had recently performed, and another at Tiananmen Square. John had even been given a Chinese name, which roughly translated to 'Golden Hair'. The planned tour was a huge coup, both for Farnham and Wheatley – who, it must be said, was probably the more driven of the two in this particular odyssey.

It was no commercial windfall, though, as Wheatley revealed in his memoir *Paper Paradise*. 'They were talking about paying us in produce.'

'How about soy beans?' John half joked, when the subject arose.

The planned China trip turned out to be a rare failure for Team Farnham. As soon as tanks rolled into Tiananmen Square in June 1989 and all hell broke loose, Wheatley knew that the tour would never happen.

By this time, however, John had made inroads into another spot that didn't feature on the typical Farnham tour itinerary. A new openness was being enjoyed in the former Soviet Union, thanks to a reform movement known as Glasnost, introduced by leader Mikhail Gorbachev in 1988. It allowed the Soviet people more liberties, including enjoying Western-style music.

'You're the Voice' had been included on a Greenpeace album entitled *Breakthrough*, which had been compiled by Brit Ian Brooks, a friend and colleague of Wheatley. John was joined on the LP by U2 (who contributed '[Pride] In the Name of Love'), the Pretenders ('Middle of the Road'), Sting ('Love is the Seventh Wave') and Peter Gabriel ('Red Rain'). Big names.

In February 1989 Farnham and Wheatley, along with The Edge from U2, Gabriel, Annie Lennox and Chrissie Hynde, embarked on a Greenpeace-arranged globetrotting mission to promote the record and the cause, taking in London, Bremen, New York, Montreal, Toronto and, finally, Moscow.

First port of call in the USSR was the Russian Press Club. Rather than referring to himself by song or band – as in 'I'm Chrissie Hynde from the Pretenders', 'I'm The Edge from U2' – John simply said, 'I'm John Farnham and I'm from Australia.' His very grounded personality registered strongly with the press; despite being the least familiar face at the media conference, John fielded most of the questions. His easy-rolling personality broke through the language barrier.

Australian writer Glenn A. Baker reported on the mission for *The Australian* magazine. 'John Farnham, the unknown quantity and the first artist to speak [at the press conference], continued to do so throughout, impressing even the politicos with his unpretentious attempts to inject sincerity and simple humanity into the unwieldy forum.'

Basically, John won them over by being himself.

With armed guards nearby at all times, there were record signings and various meet-and-greets during their 72 hours in the capital. Muscovites queued for hours to get an autograph from Farnham and his fellow stars. Glasnost may have changed the Western notion of the USSR, but life still wasn't easy there. Farnham couldn't help but notice that the shops were empty and boarded up. Cold-eyed working girls cruised the foyer of the Cosmos Hotel, where the Greenpeace troupe stayed.

One day, when Farnham and Wheatley sat down for lunch, they were told that there was nothing to eat. A sly packet of Western cigarettes and a discretely placed $US10 dollar bill helped fix the food crisis. Vodka, however, was at all times plentiful and flowed during each and every meal.

John did have a moment of genuine concern during his time in Moscow. One night the boisterous group were out and about in Gorky Park, snapping photos and generally enjoying themselves – aided, no doubt, by a shot or two of the local brew. John was in the thick of things, the leader of the pack. Once back and settled on their bus, Farnham made a joke about a Molotov cocktail. Local soldiers boarded the bus soon after and seemed to be headed for John, who'd been the rowdiest of the bunch; maybe they'd heard and misunderstood his Molotov joke. It turned out the local *soldat* were after a UK reporter, seated near John on the bus, who'd been spotted exchanging money. But it was a sharp reminder of how dangerous life could be in the Soviet Union.

The road trip, however, paid off: the album sold several million copies and raised some big bucks for Greenpeace. Yet for John it marked the end of his time as an international star; from now on he focused almost exclusively on Australia. As the father of two small children, the idea of spending extended periods away from home had little appeal, especially after the grind of LRB. And why try and build a new audience when he had his own ready-made fan base back home? He was Australia's biggest pop star; that was enough. John also had his charity work, his family, his fishing, his close friends – all in Oz. Why leave?

'I have no intention of going to America and busting my arse for four years trying to get it to work,' John said while promoting *Age of Reason*. 'I don't know whether I necessarily want the world. I'm quite happy doing what I'm doing.'

It was around this time that John really embraced horse riding – soon a popular pastime of his. Together, he and Jillian would ride along the Yarra River, through the bush, then settle down for a lunch of cheese and wine 'and have a kiss and cuddle in the sun'. Then they'd ride home into the sunset as if they were living in some old Western. 'It was fantastic,' said John.

Over time, John would become a cutting horse devotee, a practice he described as 'a bit like riding a bucking horse – sideways. I've always been a bit of an adrenaline freak; it gives me a bit of a release.'

Jillian, as ever, was there for him. She too became a keen rider.

'Jillian is the best thing that ever happened to me,' John has said dozens of times. 'She is my anchor and I know I'm hers, too.' Some pundits, only half jokingly, referred to the Farnhams as the 'Paul and Linda McCartney' of Australia. The McCartneys also enjoyed the equine life, so maybe they were on to something.

Now, as a new decade dawned, John finally had time to reflect on how much his life had changed. At the end of the 1970s he had been washed up, as good as finished, lacking a label and ambitious management, resigned to a life of suburban club gigs and 'good ole days' package tours. But now, 10 years down the line, with Wheatley guiding him, John was king of the hill, outselling such hot acts as U2, George Michael, Crowded House and INXS in Australia. *Whispering Jack* was the highest-selling album in Australia across the entire decade, outstripping Michael Jackson's *Thriller*, Dire Straits' *Brothers in Arms* and Bruce Springsteen's *Born in the U.S.A.* Cynics were sniggering that *Age of Reason* had somehow failed by comparison to *Whispering Jack*, not having matched its runaway sales, but it was still among the Top 10 bestselling albums of 1988, and would continue to set cash registers chiming. At the time of writing it's 11 times platinum, inching towards sales of 800,000, huge numbers for an Australian-made record. Together, *Whispering Jack* and

Age of Reason clung to the Oz album charts for some 175 weeks. In a stretch from October 1986 to the end of the decade, John's albums never left the charts.

Then there were the concerts. During the Jack's Back and Age of Reason tours John had played to roughly half a million Australians; Jack's Back had broken all previous box office records for an Australian act. Farnham genuinely loved performing, the sense of communion and exhilaration that a great show could bring.

'I enjoy that,' he said, 'the sweat – you can reach out and touch [the audience].'

It had been an astonishing turnaround, the type of resurrection rarely witnessed in the local music scene, perhaps only rivalled by Billy Thorpe's transformation in the late 1960s from pop idol to hedonistic acid rocker. But Thorpey couldn't compete with Farnham's massive record sales and the manner in which he repeatedly filled the largest rooms in the country. And it was highly unlikely that the wild and crazy Thorpe would ever be a contender for Australian of the Year.

'I've been quoted as saying that if nothing good ever happens to me again, I'm okay with that, this is good enough,' John said of his rebirth, and he meant every word.

Farnham and Wheatley were reflecting on all this when John dropped a bombshell on his manager.

'Wheats,' he grinned, 'I think I might retire.'

His manager's face went deathly pale. Was he serious?

'But I don't think I can,' John continued, 'because I like it too much. Success has made me a happy man and I don't think I can ever stop doing it.'

Wheatley exhaled. Phew.

Maybe, looking back, the lyrics of John's hit 'Help!' were prescient, but not in a manner he could have ever envisaged. His life *had* changed in oh so many ways. But could he maintain the momentum?

15

BURN FOR YOU

The past decade had been a heady ride for John. And Farnham never missed the opportunity to praise Wheatley, who he rightly believed had saved his career when Wheatley took over his management in 1980. When they weren't on the road together, the Farnhams and Wheatleys would holiday together at the Skase-owned Mirage Resort in Port Douglas, where they both owned condos. They were very close friends and unreservedly loyal to each other, ever since the early days when Wheatley handed over a cheque for $50,000 to keep John afloat. Farnham never forgot the trust and belief that lay behind that gesture. But now, their roles were about to be reversed: it was Farnham who needed to believe in Wheatley.

Wheatley's drama began, as many problems do, in a nightclub – or more accurately, because of a nightclub. In 1988 he'd agreed to a business co-venture with his brother-in-law, Clinton Casey, to convert a building in Melbourne's Flinders Lane into a club, which they'd call The Ivy, after one of the Wheatleys' favourite LA eateries. The building cost $4 million, and another $2 million was required for refurbishment. The money was acquired through the Farrow Corporation, part of the Pyramid Building Society. An opening date was announced and then pushed back, as work plodded on with the rebuild and Wheatley butted heads with his contractor. First it was 22 December 1988, then 9 March 1989.

Farnham was on the road in early 1989 with the MSO, and Wheatley, as he always did, ensured he was there to see John perform. But this kept him away from The Ivy worksite. Wheatley was thinly stretched; the cost of the as-yet-uncompleted Ivy renovations kept mounting, reaching $6.5 million in early 1989, as interest rates ballooned to almost 20%. Wheatley had to use his $6-million Toorak home as collateral. John Farnham's success was now the one thing keeping Glenn Wheatley afloat.

If his life wasn't complicated enough, Wheatley was also toying with the notion of a tilt at politics, and politicians were starting to gravitate towards John. When Farnham played Canberra's Bruce Stadium in mid-November 1988, MPs Gareth Evans, Ralph Willis and Graham Richardson, plus members of the Keating and Hawke families, attended the show.

PM Hawke, who'd shared another sly ciggie with Farnham at the Adelaide Grand Prix a few days earlier – now something of a ritual between the two – hosted John, Glenn and their wives at Parliament House after the show. Wheatley, in particular, was impressed with the lifestyle. 'This was power,' he'd write of the encounter, 'and I was loving it.' John was preoccupied laughing at Hawke's post-dinner gift – a knock-off watch he'd recently bought from a street vendor in Bangkok – and generously sampling the PM's best reds. Politics wasn't his game, but this was the big time, no doubt about it.

That night, Hawke asked Wheatley if he'd consider joining the Labor Party, but Wheatley leaned more towards the right, politically speaking. After much deliberation, he decided to put a padlock on his political aspirations, having learnt from subsequent discussions how lonely Canberra life could be. He had more than enough to deal with back in Melbourne – and he was insistent that John and his career remain his number one priority. There was no logical way he could juggle both being a pollie and managing John Farnham.

Early in 1989 John got a call from Wheatley, asking him to lunch. There was nothing unusual about that, but this time their catch-up would take an unexpected twist.

'Mate,' Wheatley said, as they settled down over drinks, 'I need to borrow some money.'

'How much?' Farnham asked, as he reached for his chequebook, just as Wheatley had done for him a decade earlier.

'$300,000,' Wheatley admitted.

For the first time in their shared working career, John – or more specifically, his lawyer, Ken Starke – asked that Wheatley sign a loan agreement. Wheatley accepted that under the circumstances it was the right thing to do. But it only served to prove how tenuous his circumstances were – his friend and star client needed documentation to ensure he'd get his money back.

It was also time for John and Wheatley to renegotiate Glenn's managerial contract, which happened every two years and was usually a formality. Wheatley was about to get another surprise: Ken

Starke advised that while Glenn could continue to manage John, no formal contract would be forthcoming.

Meanwhile, The Ivy budget blowout reached some $5 million. But finally The Ivy opened to the public on 18 August 1989. John sang for his supper that night, repaying his friend for his many years of devoted service with a few songs. Wheatley named the upstairs area Jack's Bar in his honour.

But Wheatley's problems weren't over, no way, not yet. He and Farnham got the sense that something big, and potentially disastrous, was in the wind when they returned to the Mirage Resort in early December 1989. As usual, they dined with Mirage owner and Farnham supporter Skase and his wife, Pixie. But when the bill arrived, the Skases turned their eyes towards their guests; for the first time, Glenn and John had to pick up the tab. Skase was clearly in financial strife. When John and Wheatley returned to the Mirage in January 1990, the Skase condo had been stripped of furniture and belongings. They'd cleared out.

Wheatley, meanwhile, was forced to put his Toorak home on the market in early 1990 to help cover The Ivy's bills. He was dining with John at The Ivy when news came through of an offer – $6.1 million. At the same time, whispers began spreading within the financial community that the Farrow Corporation, who'd backed The Ivy, were in financial trouble – and Farrow held the title of Wheatley's house.

In late June 1990 Wheatley was in New York for a key BMG meeting; for the first time it appeared that a John Farnham LP (his newie, *Chain Reaction*) would have a simultaneous worldwide release. Even though John was at best a reluctant international artist, this was huge.

On 27 June, Wheatley's hotel room phone rang, waking him up. It was his wife, Gaynor. She read him a newspaper report.

'It says the Farrow Corporation and Pyramid have closed their doors. What does this mean for us?'

It meant the sale of their house, the offer they'd received that night while he was with John at The Ivy, wasn't going to happen, for one thing. And Wheatley's two-week-long overseas trip, his attempt to take John global, would now have to be compressed into seven days.

Coopers & Lybrand were appointed mortgagee in possession of The Ivy; Wheatley now had no control over the club he'd built. He had quickly joined Christopher Skase in dire financial straits. John's manager was now in the same situation Farnham had been in when they started working together in 1980: stone broke. Wheatley was forced into a fire sale of his assets – there'd be no more Port Douglas vacations with the Farnhams for the foreseeable future. Effectively homeless, the Wheatleys moved into a friend's house. They slept on the floor.

This financial turmoil was hardly the best backdrop to the release of John's new album, *Chain Reaction*, in late September 1990. Yet that didn't prevent it racing to number one soon after its release, and sticking to the charts for almost a year. Three singles were lifted from the album – the title track, 'That's Freedom' (a companion piece to John's other fanfares for the common man, 'You're the Voice' and 'Age of Reason') and 'Burn for You'. Each hit the Top 10, going to show beyond any doubt that John's hot commercial streak was far from over. He'd scored eight Top 10 hits in just the past four years, outstripping most other local artists. Kylie Minogue came close, with seven; INXS had five in the same period. But John ruled the charts.

Chain Reaction, while it was the third part of a hugely successful trilogy – the 'Farnham comeback' phase, if you like – was a strikingly different record to *Whispering Jack* and *Age of Reason*. It was also the most musically satisfying and enduring of the three. The first sound heard was a scrubbed acoustic guitar, rather than the whir of a keyboard, and that was true for much of the album. Though contemporary-sounding, it felt more organic, less computer-generated, which gave Farnham even more room to roam with his vocals, especially during songs like 'In Days to Come', which came with more than a hint of church. The title track, with its blazing harmonica and knee-slapping melody, was the closest John had yet come to recording a straight-up country song.

And John was much more than vocalist/interpreter here: he co-wrote nine of the dozen tracks, most with producer Fraser and band stalwart Hirschfelder. Phil Buckle, a tunesmith for hire who'd recently struck pay dirt with Southern Sons, also contributed to a number of *Chain Reaction* songs. Apart from the universal theme of a song like 'That's Freedom' and the anthemic 'See the Banners Fall', the prevailing mood of the album was more personal, closer to home. A true John Farnham album.

The new approach was typified by the ballad 'Burn for You', a real standout, a spare Farnham composition using little more than a strummed acoustic guitar and his voice. When singing this very sombre and serious ballad on stage, John would play the jester. 'Burn for You', he'd explain, was a 'sucky love song', written for Jillian while he was on yet another road trip. 'And it worked,' he'd sometimes add, with a knowing wink.

Perhaps there was an additional line or two on his face, and his golden locks had thinned ever so slightly since the time of 'You're the Voice', but John still looked great, stepping out in the video for 'That's Freedom' in what would become his new go-to look: a stylish bespoke suit, matching dark shirt buttoned to the collar. He'd finally ditched the Driza-Bone. John looked sophisticated, a man moving into a comfortable middle age. Australia now had its very own Man in Black.

Chain Reaction sold almost 200,000 copies in its first two weeks of release, and powered its way to becoming the highest-selling Australian album of 1990. Yet Wheatley's problems were never too far away. In the media's mind, Farnham and Wheatley were intertwined; any *Chain Reaction* publicity seemingly presented another chance to dig a little deeper into Wheatley's ongoing business troubles.

John dealt with Wheatley's situation in typical Farnham fashion. In late September the two were on an Australian Airlines jet to Sydney. As they settled in for the hour-long trip, the flight attendant began handing out copies of newspapers. The headline on the front page of the *Financial Review* was a shocker: 'Farnham Caught in Chain Reaction,' it screamed. The story documented Wheatley's recent financial woes, and revealed that John had loaned Wheatley money, which was true. As the plane left Tullamarine, it was clear to John that many of those on board were reading the story. Passengers were looking in their direction. Wheatley started to sink into his seat, praying for the power of invisibility.

John's innate sense of loyalty towards his troubled friend kicked in. He called over the attendant.

'Could you do me a favour?' he asked. 'Can you give me every leftover copy of the paper?'

As soon as the seatbelt sign was extinguished, John strolled down the aisle of the plane, *Financial Review*s in hand.

'Would you like to read about my embattled media-magnate manager Glenn Wheatley?' he asked, as he distributed copies of the newspaper left, right and centre. 'He's just sitting over there with me.' With that one funny gesture, John diffused a hugely awkward situation. Laughter broke out in the cabin. Wheatley breathed a hefty sigh of relief, easing himself back into an upright position.

'My embattled manager Glenn Wheatley' now became John's standard line regarding his friend. It quickly shut down any speculation about their ongoing relationship: Farnham intended to stand by his man, wherever Wheatley's problems led.

Soon after that flight, a reporter spoke with John.

'How do Glenn's financial problems affect you?' he was asked.

'I'm his mate and I'm not going anywhere,' John said very directly. 'He was there when I needed help and I'm not about to bail on him now he needs my help. I'm just evening up the score.'

John needed to escape for a while. He had been receiving mysterious, threatening notes, perhaps from someone involved with The Ivy, the same people who were making Wheatley's life hell. Someone incorrectly assumed that whatever Wheatley owed could be strongarmed from Farnham. When these notes started to appear under the windscreen wipers of the crew's rental cars on the Chain Reaction tour, it was clear that someone knew John's comings and goings a little too closely. This was scary stuff. On 6 October artist and manager left for a three-week promotional trip, ostensibly to talk up *Chain Reaction* in Europe, but also to put some space between themselves and an increasingly difficult situation in Oz.

But even in Europe there were reminders of Wheatley's problems. Old friend Christopher Skase had been in touch, inviting John and Glenn to Majorca, where the Skases were now based, as the investigation into Skase's crashed company, Qintex, continued apace back in Australia. Their stay was pleasurable, opulent even, but neither John nor Wheatley dared ask the Skases how they could still afford the jet-set lifestyle. Not long after they returned home, authorities tried to extradite Skase back to Australia to face his creditors. He was now officially the 'failed businessman' Christopher Skase, a man on the run – not a great omen for Wheatley.

John and Wheatley, wisely, downplayed their relationship with the exiled businessman. For Wheatley, especially, any public awareness of this could only further harm ongoing speculation about his financial future.

While overseas, Wheatley's former dream club, The Ivy, had been flogged for $2 million. He'd sunk $12 million into the venue. Not surprisingly, he hated the place. The good news was that the threats towards John had stopped. He went back on the road during November and December 1990, and kept touring in January 1991, as 'Burn for You' was released, the third charting single from *Chain Reaction*.

While Farnham filled the venue at Sanctuary Cove in Queensland mid-November 1990, his manager's personal effects were sold at auction, returning a fraction of their value. An Arthur Boyd painting, purchased for almost $100,000, was flogged for $15K. But Wheatley was prepared to do anything to get his creditors out of his hair, at least for a while.

John, meanwhile, sold out a staggering eight Melbourne Tennis Centre shows, between 14 and 22 December 1990. Again, he'd broken all existing box-office records – records he'd set in the first place. His set list now read like an Oz pop jukebox: 'You're the Voice', 'Playing to Win', 'Age of Reason', 'Pressure Down', 'Reasons', 'Burn for You' ... not a 'Sadie', 'Raindrops' or show tune in sight. Wheatley could take some solace in the ongoing success of his star client, now deep into the fifth year of an amazing and seemingly unstoppable run.

On that eighth night in Melbourne, John paused for his pre-gig slug of 'fighting brandy'. As he did, he grabbed Wheatley's arm. John was reeling – he'd played to some 80,000 people over the past week and a half. He could have moved into the Tennis Centre and kept playing there for the rest of his life, or so it seemed.

'Wheat,' Farnham shouted over the crowd, shaking his head, 'I can't believe it.'

Nor could Wheatley, but for different reasons. As the new year dawned, John and Wheatley's careers were polar opposites: John couldn't fly any higher, whereas his main man had bottomed out. Or so he hoped.

Anyone hungry for a little symbolism could read plenty into John's next choice: not merely content with reigning supreme over the pop charts, he was now about to return to the stage for the first time since the panto days of the early 1970s. And John wasn't playing any old role – he was set to step out as Jesus Christ. It was the perfect coda to the second coming of John Farnham.

Some wags called it typecasting. 'People often report having religious experiences while attending a Farnham concert,' snickered one reporter. 'Fans in the very back row, while squinting to see the stage, have been heard to utter to their partners, "God, is that him?" and, after looking through binoculars, they exclaim, "Jesus, there he is!"'

When first staged in Australia in 1972, *Jesus Christ Superstar*, the handiwork of West End hit-makers Tim Rice and Andrew Lloyd Webber, had helped build stellar careers for Jon English, Trevor White, Marcia Hines, former Easybeat Stevie Wright, future Air Supply-er Russell Hitchcock and comic Rory O'Donoghue, as well as Reg Livermore and John Paul Young – they'd all appeared in the show during its first run, which ended in early 1974. The production was ripe for a revival.

The show's producer, Harry M. Miller, had first approached John with the idea while at the 1989 Adelaide Grand Prix.

'Me play Jesus Christ?' John laughed. 'You're kidding, right? I'm too old to play Jesus, Harry.'

Miller insisted it was an easy gig. 'I'll make sure they light you softly,' he reassured Farnham, 'and all you have to do is pat Mary Magdalene on the bum.'

John laughed it off, but Miller was persistent. He knew the huge box-office potential of anything with the Farnham name attached to it, let alone a show as iconic as *Jesus Christ Superstar*. There was an emotional connection, too: Miller had produced the original version and this would mark his return to the theatre after an absence of almost two decades. The offer become more enticing to John when Miller's business partner, Garry Van Egmond, came up with the idea of staging *JC Superstar* as a concert – an 'arena spectacular' – in venues such as the Sydney Entertainment Centre. This had far more appeal for John: rather than a lengthy theatrical season, he could play selected gigs, much like a short tour. At least that was the plan.

Kate Ceberano had been confirmed to play the highly pinchable Mary; Jon Stevens, who'd worked on *Chain Reaction*, was tapped for the role of Judas; while Angry Anderson, Russell Morris and Jon Waters (who replaced Anthony Warlow, who was being treated for cancer) were also in the cast. David Hirschfelder would work on the arrangements and play in the house band. Now all Miller needed was his Jesus.

Wheatley required what he described as a financial 'incentive proportionate to John's drawing power' – he knew only too well that Farnham could transform this revival into an even bigger commercial draw. After lengthy negotiations, Wheatley and Miller came to an understanding, what they called a 'tiered payment structure'. For the first 10 shows, which needed to sell out in order for the production to break even, John's fee was kept relatively low. He'd receive a pay bump after those 10 shows, another at 20, and yet another after 40. Anything beyond that was renegotiation time. But given that crowds for each night in Sydney, Melbourne, Brisbane, Perth and Adelaide would be around 10,000, it seemed unlikely they'd run for more than 40 nights. That was close to half a million people; surely they couldn't expect more than that.

But when the Farnham-headed line-up was announced, with the opening show to take place in Sydney on 4 August 1992, sales went crazy. Tickets sold at the rate of 400 per minute on the opening day of sale – and this was still the pre-internet era, when a punter had to hit the phone or line up at a retail outlet to buy seats. John's Christ-like appeal seemed to know no bounds. Eight Sydney shows were sold within days, a massive response. Forty shows suddenly didn't seem so far-fetched.

Producer Miller, to his credit, was no scrooge: rehearsals, which started in late July, were held at the Sydney Showgrounds, the site of the Royal Easter Show. Miller arranged for a stage to be erected in one of the Showground's pavilions, which typified his leave-nothing-to-chance production stance. Every day of rehearsal, as their warm-up, John would lead the entire ensemble through a roof-raising 'Amazing Grace', a hangover from his recent solo shows.

During the Sydney press conference, Farnham joked about the control-freakishness of 'Mr Miller'.

'The only thing you haven't done,' he chuckled, looking over at the producer, 'is sing the songs.'

At the Sydney premiere, PM Bob Hawke – a Farnham regular – showed up, as did the cast of hit soapie *E Street* and NSW Premier John Fahey. Paparazzi clogged the street outside the Ent Cent, which, by now, just like the Melbourne Tennis Centre, could easily have been renamed the John Farnham Centre, he played there so often. It was every inch the A-list occasion, maybe even the theatrical event of the season.

On stage, John's flowing mane gave him a certain biblical presence, while his gold-trimmed jacket, by contrast, brought a little rock-and-roll pizzazz. During the show, John sang with the broody, leather-clad Stevens – they sparred like singing gladiators during

'The Last Supper' – and gypsy woman Ceberano, while his solo spots included such standouts as 'Gethsemane' and 'Poor Jerusalem', when John stood alone on stage, lit by a spare, single spot. It was lighting fit for Christ himself.

Superstar was a very different world to a John Farnham show; while far more collaborative, there was none of the natural, earthy humour that made his own concerts so easy to enjoy. *JC* was a pretty stodgy affair. Sometimes John looked as though he was dying to tell a joke, just to lighten the mood (during the show's run he make a humorous appearance on ABC's *The Late Show,* looking very happy to have a laugh). Still, it was no less fulfilling for John as a singer – and there was the added luxury of the occasional break between songs, a rare indulgence.

The Fairfax papers' review of that opening night, however, was scathing.

'*Jesus Christ Superstar,*' wrote Bruce Elder, 'still seems to need real actors, real theatrical situations, and some sense of drama to make it work effectively. In this production, all those elements have been drained away and all that is left is a number of pop stars singing songs that don't really suit their voices – songs with which they have very little empathy.' And John's Jesus? 'When he is finally crucified there is not a hint of concern or pity.' Jesus – or John – needed the thickest of skins to tolerate such a critical axe-grinding.

Proving how strong the disconnect often is between critics and audience, tickets for the show just kept on selling. By the time the troupe reached Melbourne in mid-August, a further eight gigs had sold out. That meant John's first salary bump kicked in, with the second, at 20 shows, simply a matter of time. The threshold of 40 shows was passed while they played Brisbane in September – and they still hadn't yet left the east coast. By the time the tour wound up, with a return to Brisbane in November, John had been crucified no less than 82 times. The show sold more than a million tickets.

Neither John nor Wheatley has ever publicly revealed exactly how much Farnham pocketed for his efforts in *JC*, but Wheatley did state that Farnham fared 'better even than Harry M. Miller'. In short, with almost one million tickets sold at $40 a throw, John made a motza. And he somehow found the time on tour to give up smoking; soon after the end of the run he'd kicked a four-pack-a-day addiction. Jillian also kicked the habit. *Superstar* had proved lucrative: he'd made buckets of money *and* gotten healthier.

The cast recording was also a runaway success, spending 12 weeks atop the Oz charts and selling 350,000 copies. It was the biggest-selling Australian album of 1992, standard business now for any record featuring the Farnham name, beating out up-and-comers such as the Baby Animals and the Red Hot Chili Peppers and chart perennials Lionel Richie and Neil Diamond.

16

RIDING THE RAILS

After such a high-profile return to the stage – what could be bigger than playing Jesus Christ? – John was content to disappear into country life, as usual keeping his private life very much private. He had little, if anything, left to prove. He'd now had three smash albums in a row – four counting *Superstar*. There was more money in the bank than he'd ever known, or ever needed. His two boys were growing up – Robbie was now 12, James five – and Jillian remained by his side. Life was good.

John's new obsession was breeding pure quarter horses at the stables on his property in Goornong in rural Victoria. There was a dressage and full cutting horse arena on the property, along with the main two-storey residence and several smaller dwellings. One day, early in 1993, he startled a group of Tamworth locals when he turned up unannounced to the home of Australian country music. But John wasn't toting a banjo, ready to change his sound: instead he'd come to compete in a celebrity cutting horse event, as part of the national championships. John was up against some serious competition, including five-time Olympian and Australia's greatest-living horseman, 78-year-old Bill Roycroft. John showed real form; so much so that he was declared the best guest on horseback.

Roycroft was hugely impressed. 'John's a nice rider,' he said afterwards, 'no risk.'

'He can hold his own,' said local Joe Dwyer. 'He was a novice rider who has stuck to it.'

No-one, however, was more impressed than Farnham; for him, this unexpected win rated as highly as the ARIAs, platinum records, sold-out tours, playing JC, the lot.

'I've had some success in my life in a lot of ways,' he said as he picked up his award, 'but winning here is up with anything. I'll cherish it.'

Something John also cherished was that among fellow riders and horsemen, he was simply another competitor, some friendly bloke named John. He wasn't John Farnham, certified superstar, 'The Voice'. He was just another face in the crowd.

'Everyone is more interested in their horses than they are in me,' John laughed.

John may have been content with his life but the same couldn't be said for Glenn Wheatley, John's guru. His financial problems hadn't let up. In late 1992 he and his wife, Gaynor, had a sit-down with their creditors and eventually agreed to what is known as a 'deed of arrangement', in order to try to sort out the crippling debts brought on by the disastrous Ivy project. His next financial battle, with the ATO, became the theme of yet another news story: 'Glenn Wheatley, God and Taxes.' Yet none of this changed John's attitude towards his friend; his support and loyalty never wavered.

Buoyed by his successful contributions to *Chain Reaction*, John continued writing. By mid-1993, when he and Fraser agreed to return to the studio, John had several new songs in the works. Though not quite ready to step out as a solo songwriter – co-writes remained his preferred MO – John's contributions made his new album, *Then Again...*, another more personal collection of tunes. In the final wash-up, Farnham co-wrote eight of the album's 14 tracks, again working with Ross Wilson (for the single 'Seemed Like a Good Idea [At the Time]'), Peter Buckle and Fraser, as well as Jon Stevens and, in an interesting new twist, American Richard Marx.

John and Marx had bonded in the late 1980s, when the American, whose hair was almost as big as that of his Aussie pal, spent some time at Farnham's country hideaway. John nicknamed him 'Skid' (of course). Marx, by his own admission, was a vocal Farnham fan, ever since he'd heard 'You're the Voice', joining an ever-growing list of admirers that included everyone from Stevie Wonder to Dionne Warwick and Elton John. While on stage in Melbourne in January 1989, Marx paused and told the crowd: 'If anyone sees a guy called John Farnham around tell him that I think he has one of the best voices I've ever heard and I would love to work with him.'

'It changed my musical life,' Marx said of 'The Voice', 'I became obsessed with this guy. I think Sam Cooke is the greatest singer who ever lived. I think John Farnham is the greatest singer alive.'

It was a very relaxed John who appeared on the cover of *Then Again ...*, decked out in black jeans and a snappy leather jacket, reclining in a sort of horizontal manspread. He was cool and calm, a man at ease with the world. That look set the tone for much of the record; the intensity of 'Age of Reason' and 'You're the Voice' were toned down, making this a more mellow affair.

'If you are looking for an album that plumbs the dark depths of the human condition,' John Mangan wrote with no small amount of insight in *The Age*, 'then you are in the wrong place. Judging by John Farnham's record-breaking sales figures over the past 26 years, there are plenty of us out there keen to hear sincere upbeat ditties with positive messages.'

While there were the mandatory big ballads on *Then Again ...*, including an attention-grabbing rework of Alice Cooper's touchy-feely 'Only Women Bleed' and reflective moments like 'When All Else Fails', at its core this was a singer's album, a solid set of grown-up pop songs, just the tonic for John's baby-boomer audience. The soulful 'So Long in Love', one of John's co-writes with Richard Marx, was a highlight.

While it lacked the chart longevity of its three predecessors, *Then Again...* hit number one soon after its mid-October 1993 release, becoming John's fourth straight chart-topper, and went on to claim yet another ARIA – for Highest Selling Album of the Year. Interestingly, its closest rival was The Seekers' *Silver Jubilee Album*, a nostalgic comeback for John's 'Sadie'-era peers and harmonisers. *Then Again ...* shifted roughly 300,000 copies, which meant John had now sold in the vicinity of four million albums at home since the release of *Whispering Jack*. Amazing numbers. (*Full House*, 1991's live

LP, was closing in on 350,000 sales.) But only one of *Then Again...*'s four singles, the breezy, Motown-ish 'Seemed Like a Good Idea (At the Time)', could be called a genuine hit, reaching the Top 20 days before the album dropped.

The track inspired one of John's funnier videos, thanks to the input of his buddies from the D-Generation, stars of ABC's *The Late Show*, who turned the clip into a good-natured, cross-cultural, piss-taking romp. 'What my grandfather is saying,' the D-Gen's Santo Cilauro told John as the 'Seemed Like a Good Idea' video began, acting as interpreter, 'is that if you want to crack the international market, you should play the piano accordion.' John listened and nodded politely – and the clip got goofier from there on in, with earnest discussion of the potential of smoke machines, porn-star moustaches, monster trucks, the lambada and chainsaws.

John's commercial clout as a recording artist may have simmered down ever so slightly, but he could still pack venues from one end of Oz to the other. He drew a remarkable 350,000 paying customers to the two-month-long Talk of the Town tour, which ran from February to April 1994, yet again breaking his own records. Tickets to four Melbourne Tennis Centre shows disappeared in one day. John remained astounded by the response; he called Wheatley every hour for a sales update, genuinely shocked by the ever-increasing numbers.

'Mate, that's amazing,' he said – several times. The demand was huge.

John's great band was full of regulars – Lindsay Field, Brett Garsed, Angus Burchall – with a new face in keyboardist Chong Lim, who'd taken over from the long-serving David Hirschfelder and would become a permanent fixture in Farnhamland.

During the night of the ARIAs, John played the jester with the event's host Richard 'Stubbsy' Stubbs in a TV link-up. Farnham was on stage in Canberra, Stubbs in Sydney.

'I'm having a great time,' John told Stubbs, now that he was back out on the road for the first time as a solo act since late 1991. 'It makes me feel, oh, 40 years old,' laughed the 44-year-old. John then wheeled out his mate 'Skid' Marx, 'for, oh, about the eighth time tonight.' Marx just so happened to have Farnham's pointy ARIA statuette for *Then Again*..., which he cheerfully handed over.

'You know what I love most about this,' said Marx, all smiles, 'is that I have four songs on the record.'

After much thanking and back-patting, the dynamic duo got back to work, Marx on the piano, John closing his eyes tight and hitting the big notes on 'The Reason Why'. The crowd, of course, ate it up.

Talk of the Town was the last time John would go out on the road, at any length, until spring 1996. The only gig of note he played in 1994 was a 7 August fundraiser for the victims of the Rwanda genocide, a one-off at Flinders Park in Melbourne, which was televised on Channel 9. The show raised a whopping $3.5 million.

John and producer Ross Fraser entered into a business arrangement of their own in 1995, setting up Gotham Records, whose releases would be distributed by BMG, John's current label. Over time, Gotham would release music from Merril Bainbridge, who'd have a worldwide hit with the subtly risqué single 'Mouth' and sell 250,000 copies of her album *The Garden* in Australia. They'd also record Richard Pleasance, The Lovers and Olympic golden girl Nikki Webster and score huge success with pop twosome Bachelor

Girl. For John, a record label was a much safer bet than Backstage, the restaurant into which he had sunk so much money back in the dark days of the 1970s. He understood music.

During his King of Pop days, John – then Johnny – had once toured northern Queensland with Col Joye, travelling by train. The idea of another tour by rail had held major appeal to John ever since.

'It was just the most incredible time for me,' John recalled of that long-ago tour with Joye. 'The sense of camaraderie and fun was always something I wanted to capture again.'

Rail seemed like a relatively logical way to get to some of the more far-flung places John and his 50-plus-person crew would play on the Jack of Hearts tour, which was scheduled to begin in Toowoomba on 23 September 1996. Wheatley struck a deal with Queensland Rail, who provided six carriages, broken down into sleepers, a party room, rehearsal space and a dining car.

'It's not a cheap way to travel,' Wheatley admitted, 'but it is a lot of fun.'

John was promoting his new record, *Romeo's Heart*, which dropped on 3 June and was well on its way to quadruple platinum sales. If John's take on Alice Cooper's 'Only Women Bleed' was the unlikely surprise of *Then Again* ..., with *Romeo's Heart* it was Farnham's soulful read of English folkie John Martyn's 'May You Never'. The man had taste.

Nine days of the tour would be spent riding the Spirit of Queensland, in not unreasonable comfort – the train's dining car resembled something out of the Indian Pacific, if not quite the

Orient Express. They covered 2000 miles, with a film crew nearby capturing everything for the *Time in Paradise* TV doco. Gaynor Wheatley, Glenn's wife, narrated the journey in voiceover, and threw the occasional question John's way. John's son documented more personal moments on what the crew dubbed 'Robbie cam'.

John's train odyssey started well when he was met by hundreds of screaming locals as he boarded the rattler at Cairns. The good people of Far North Queensland were undeterred by the tropical heat; neither was the man of the hour, who took time to meet and greet.

'We love you!' a voice yelled from the crowd.

'I love you, too,' John replied, 'and I can't even see you.'

John was greeted by the same kind of happy pandemonium when he disembarked in Ingham. The local community turned out en masse and in strong voice. King John was hoisted onto a makeshift cane throne – 'The things you do for a living; I feel like such a dill!' he yelled as he was lifted upwards – and carted through the town's streets. He'd been pop royalty for so long now that it seemed the townsfolk were taking it literally. After his lap of honour, John belted out an unplugged version of 'You're the Voice' for the excited locals.

Next stop was a two-night stand in Townsville; again a madly enthusiastic crowd, this time with a brass band in tow, greeted his train. Many hands were shook and autographs scrawled. By now the trip had all the trappings of a political campaign – if John had been running for office, he would have been a landslide victor. The people simply loved him.

Then he headed south, to Mackay, for an outdoor gig at the wonderfully named Leprechaun Park. Even a threatening tropical storm didn't slow them down.

'We play rain or shine,' Wheatley assured John, as the crew set up the stage, one eye on the darkening sky.

Nine hours down the tracks they reached Emerald, something of a country music hotspot. Another day, another train ride, another impromptu public gathering for Farnham and his crew. 'I'm signing Paul Hogan, just in case,' John joked with the Emerald locals, as he scribbled one autograph after another. Wheatley hovered on the edge of the mob scene, an eye on his watch.

'The big question is when to pull him out,' he said, nodding towards John and his true believers. 'Leave him and he could be there all day.'

A nearby busker rocked 'It's A Long Way to the Top', as John, RSI kicking in, ducked into the Emerald pub for a beer. It was thirsty work being king.

A more traditional city tour followed, another 30 big shows in all, but the country rail trip remained the peak of the Jack of Hearts tour, certainly for Farnham and his crew. The only dampener was the news that his mother-in-law, Phylis Billman, had died on 14 October. John dedicated the tour, which played to more than 200,000 people and grossed somewhere in the vicinity of $8 million, to her memory.

17

FACING FIFTY

Marc Hunter's death from throat cancer in July 1998 reminded John that no-one was invincible. In February John had joined an A-list ensemble – Paul Kelly, Renée Geyer, Tex Perkins of The Cruel Sea, Colin Hay from Men at Work – at a show staged at the Palais in Melbourne entitled 'The Night of the Hunter', to raise money for Marc's treatment. John, his band and the other performers sang 'April Sun in Cuba', a rousing finale.

John was reminded of his own mortality every time he looked in the mirror – his face was now a little craggier, his hair a bit thinner, his waistline fuller. He would turn 50 next year. Fifty! John joked that he'd 'worked really hard for these wrinkles – I was a pretty boy for so long it used to drive me nuts.' He also talked about marking the event of his 50th by buying every black suit in Melbourne, but the truth was he'd been wearing form-flattering black for years. For a New York minute, John even considered a little cosmetic surgery, perhaps some work around the eyes. Then he moved on. 'Why bother?' he figured. He could live with his signs of ageing, even the bald patch, though he wouldn't mind dropping 20 pounds.

Before hitting the big 5-0, John had an equally big occasion on the horizon, a triple-headed tour with Olivia Newton-John and Anthony Warlow, called The Main Event. It was a tour made in middle-of-the-road heaven. The press couldn't resist: as soon as news got out that the trio were set to tour Oz for two months from October 1998, they dubbed them the Blando Kings.

Newton-John and Farnham had history dating back to the 1960s, when 'Livvy' was a fledgling singer from Melbourne via the UK. They were close – she'd confessed to having a crush on him in the 'Sadie' days – and had always hoped to tour together. Warlow, Australia's very own Phantom (as in 'of the Opera'), had been cast in *Jesus Christ Superstar*, alongside John, in 1992, but withdrew when he was diagnosed with cancer. He was now in remission and good to go. Well, sort of.

During a press conference called to formally announce the tour, Warlow seemed the most apprehensive of the three. Who could blame him: he was about to share a stage with Australia's favourite middle-aged son and 'Our Livvy', John's shiny female equivalent. Warlow said he was 'petrified'. Still, he was in good spirits. He mentioned that he'd rejected a proposed new nickname, 'because Farnsey and Warnsy doesn't work'. He settled on Anthony. Farnham asked to be called 'Johnny', for old times' sake.

Warlow also came clean about the planned set list: he didn't quite have the hits of Farnham or the Grammy-winning Newton-John.

John reassured him that one hit would be enough, the Phantom's 'Music of the Night'. Everybody knew that one. 'Just sing it 12 times.'

The Main Event spared neither bells nor whistles. Backed financially by SEL, the company who in 2005 would back *Grease*, another vehicle for John, the touring ensemble included Farnham's band and a 40-piece orchestra. The shows would be staged on a specially constructed diamond-shaped hydraulic set, with lights bright enough to land an airplane.

John, as ever, joked his way through the media conference. He harked back to his rough early days crossing the Nullarbor in a Kombi, squeezed in the back 'sitting on a drum kit and amplifier'. Things had changed. Nowadays, he chuckled, his biggest challenge was trying to work out how to turn off the lights in his hotel suite at night. It was a struggle; those rooms were huge. 'It takes about 20 minutes.'

Farnham was sporting a new, end-of-the-millennium haircut: not so much a comb-over as a brush-forward. Typically, he laughed about it. When asked who might stand in for John Travolta during the essential *Grease* medley, Farnham said he wasn't the guy, nor was the shiny-domed Warlow. 'Neither of us has enough hair.' (He spoke in jest: Farnham would take the Travolta part for 'You're the One That I Want'.)

The tour began in Melbourne with six sold-out shows: more than 65,000 tickets snapped up in a heartbeat. On stage at Melbourne Park, Farnham and Warlow opted for basic black, whereas the 50-year-old Newton-John dazzled first in chiffon, then red velvet and, later on, her go-to leather jacket for the *Grease* mini-set. They offered up a two-and-half-hour show, with Newton-John delivering such hits as 'Hopelessly Devoted to You' and 'If You Love Me (Let Me Know)', John dusting off 'Age of Reason' and 'That's Freedom', and Warlow wheeling out his Phantom repertoire, featuring his 'one hit', 'Music of the Night'. 'You're the Voice' closed the main set, before they were called back for encores.

In what was now a common ritual, women of a certain age rushed the stage when Farnham appeared solo, some bearing flowers, some presenting lips, others trying to drag him off the stage. John smiled, puckered up and then played on. The rest of the crowd, a seemingly unlikely mix of rusted-on fans, oldies and teenagers, lapped it up.

So did the press, who figured early on that it was impossible trying to find faults in The Main Event; its participants were just too damned nice to criticise, the production too polished and audience-friendly. And you couldn't argue with numbers: The Main Event, during its 30-concert run, would break Australian box office records – once again, those set previously by John. Around 300,000 punters attended the shows.

'It was hammy and manipulative,' noted *The Age*'s reviewer, 'yet it still worked, because the trio are so polished they carried it through.' Even when Newton-John tried out a few new songs, it was well received. 'Because she's our Livvy, nobody minded.'

'The real star of the night was Farnham,' declared the *Sunday Mail*, 'who remains the ultimate showman after three decades of performances.'

Away from the stage, the accolades and awards kept piling up. John had been given the Order of Australia in 1996 and had been proclaimed a 'National Treasure' in 1998. This last honour gave him pause: it sounded like a tribute reserved for stately buildings or famous racehorses, not ageing singers. Wheatley, meanwhile, had tried and failed to get John's mug on a postage stamp, only to be told that John had to die first. That particular honour would have to wait – for a long time, he and John hoped.

Whispering Jack was now ARIA's all-time top-selling Australian album, its sales topping one million copies.

And Wheatley knew they couldn't let an event such as Farnham's looming 50th slip by unnoticed. Surely, his wily manager figured, they could build a new tour around the occasion. When Wheatley overheard Farnham discussing plans for his birthday, he asked cheekily, 'Can I sell tickets?'

John consented to Wheatley's idea to pin a tour to the celebrations, but he also had his own plans. His son Robbie, now aged 17 and sporting blue dreadlocks, had formed a band, a hard-rocking metal outfit called Nana-Zhami.

'If I go on tour,' John asked Robbie, 'would you like to open for me?'

Robbie was in. A few songs from N-Z were bound to zap a few volts of life into John's middle-aged audience. Other acts were brought on board for the 'I Can't Believe He's 50' tour: Gotham artist Merril Bainbridge, former Wheatley client James Reyne, 'Touch of Paradise' composer Ross Wilson and harmonisers Human Nature, who'd had a huge hit with John in 1997 called 'Everytime You Cry'. The song was a feature of John's recent best-of, *Anthology 1*, the first of a three-disc set chronicling his career to date. Farnham clearly enjoyed the vocal band's company; during the filming of the song's video, he stood off camera, pants-less, trying his best to distract them as they did their all-singing, all-dancing thing. 'Those kids can really sing,' John gushed – even when a half-naked 'National Treasure' was trying to put them off, it seemed.

Each artist was given the challenge of first singing with the man himself and then taking a Farnham song and reinventing it as their own: Wilson put his own cool spin on 'Age of Reason'; Kate Ceberano gave 'Help!' the kitchen sink; Reyne claimed the chestnut 'Comic Conversation' as his own; Bainbridge and Jack Jones reimagined 'Raindrops', beautifully, as a spare guitar-and-voice ballad.

On John's actual birthday, 1 July, Melbourne Lord Mayor Peter Costigan presented him with the keys to the city. 'John Farnham is a great Australian,' the lord mayor told the press at a Town Hall event. No-one was likely to question that statement. Thirty-five years earlier, The Beatles had stood on the Town Hall's balcony as 200,000 Melburnians greeted the hottest foursome on the planet, screaming their lungs raw. John planned a little street party of his own after the ceremony.

To be honest, the party to mark John's 50th was the main event; the tour was a pleasant, pocket-filling first course. That party, held at the end of the tour, was staged at Melbourne's Regent Theatre. Wheatley mapped out the 300-strong guest list, including such notables as Newton-John (the album of their recent tour, *The Main Event*, was currently high in the charts). Hip-swiveller Tom Jones, too, was on the invite list.

Candelabras were laid out on every table; French champers flowed. It was a stylish, classy, black tie affair.

John was genuinely chuffed as he unwrapped his gift from his record company: a hand-made American saddle, a dream present for a keen horseman. (John had recently gifted BMG staffers a $20,000 coffee machine, as thanks for keeping him king of the hill.) In place of other, regular birthday gifts, John quietly requested that attendees donate their hard-earned to the Children's Welfare Association of Victoria.

During the night, Kate Ceberano, whose bum Harry M. Miller had suggested John pinch during *Jesus Christ Superstar*, approached the mic, a mischievous grin on her face. Slipping into Marilyn Monroe guise, she cooed 'Happy birthday, Mr President', as Marilyn had once famously sung for JFK, while John's face blazed a bright red. An even bigger surprise followed: a tutu-and-cowboy-hat-clad Molly Meldrum burst out of John's birthday cake, waving a feather boa like a flag. Wheatley had talked Meldrum into this startling cameo, every bit as awkward for John as their infamous bathtub incident from England in the early 1970s.

'That was exciting, wasn't it?' John deadpanned, the look on his face somewhere between horrified and amused. 'And a bit scary.'

He then looked around the gathering as he collected his thoughts. He was surrounded by family, friends, peers and colleagues – and a middle-aged urban cowboy in a ballerina's outfit. As 50th birthdays went, this had been huge.

'Every one of you in this room I know and love,' John said, his eyes getting a little watery. 'I'm grateful that you're here. I'm grateful that I can spend the time with you, and you with me.' Then he paused, just for a beat. 'And I'm 50!'

Imagine that.

Outside the Regent, several thousand Farnham fans had gathered. John couldn't let them down, so he stepped out into the winter chill and serenaded the gathering with a few songs. Then, finally, at around 4 a.m., back inside the Regent, as the guests slowly drifted away, John sat his father down in a chair and sang him 'Burn for You'. There wasn't a dry eye in the place.

John figured it was finally time to head home.

'What's your birthday wish?' a straggler asked him as he left.

'To have another,' John laughed.

As for the tour, which ran from 11 June to 8 July, it sold almost 200,000 tickets, grossing somewhere in the vicinity of $13 million. John had shared his birthday with a solid chunk of the entire country. He had a history of sharing his big occasions: a TV camera had captured his 21st at Melbourne's Talk of the Town, when he'd quaffed Great Western with such admirers as Johnny O'Keefe. His 1973 marriage to Jillian had been a paparazzi field day. Why should his 50th be any different?

It seemed as though the entire country was raising a toast to Farnham's 50th, with everyone keen to share anecdotes. A man named Simon Collins wrote to the *Herald Sun*, relating an event from late 1996, when he first arrived in the country. He recalled sharing a drink in a Sydney hotel with a stranger 'who told me he was in the music business'. Collins tried to get his barfly friend to say more, 'but he seemed reluctant to do so'. Drinks consumed, the stranger wished Collins all the very best in Oz. 'When we said goodnight, I tried to charge his beers to my room, but he insisted on shouting me instead.' The next morning Collins switched on his TV set and discovered exactly with whom he'd shared a friendly beer: John Farnham, Aussie superstar. He was gobsmacked.

Writing in *The Advertiser*, Geoff Roach took a stab at explaining exactly why John was so immensely popular. 'In an industry that thrives on controversy and is riddled with jealousy, spite and rancour, not a speck of mud has settled anywhere near Farnham. He has always been a devoted husband and father, a committed supporter of countless charity causes and charities, a loyal mate to associates in trouble and an irrepressible lifter of people's spirits.'

In short, not just a great singer, but also a thoroughly decent bloke.

'I don't think of myself as a 50-year-old pop star,' insisted John. 'Hopefully, I am a 50-year-old grown-up.'

In an interview with *The Australian Women's Weekly*, Farnham also took the time to discuss his relationship with Wheatley, a relationship that was surviving despite his manager's recent troubles.

'Glenn is really my motivation. He motivates me to do things, because I'm a lazy bugger – I truly, truly am. But our partnership goes way beyond business. We are truly good friends. In fact, he is like a brother to me. He's supported me through some difficult times and I've supported him too. Sure, we have our disagreements, and when it comes to the crunch, he can take his mate's hat off and so can I, and we'll get down to it, but above all we're friends and that's the most important thing.

'I'm very fortunate. I'm 50 years old and I can count the number of truly close friends on one hand, with a few fingers left over. I have lots and lots of friends, but my close friends are few and far between. Glenn and his wife, Gaynor, are two of my dearest friends. I consider ours a lifetime friendship. This man is in charge of my universe. I really have no idea where I'd be if it weren't for Glenn.'

As public an event as his 50th had been, John still seemed more than happy to disappear from the spotlight for extended periods of time, if not quite retire. It now took a very special opportunity to lure John away from his family and his horses and back onto the stage. Whatever he did had to mean something for him; otherwise why bother? He didn't need the money or the acclaim.

But there was one other offer John chose not to refuse during his 50th year, the chance to entertain Australian troops operating in Dili, the capital of the newly independent East Timor, troops three months' deep in their mission to help with liberation of the country. Doc Neeson, singer of the Angels and a former Vietnam-era digger, called Wheatley, whose company Talentworks helped put the project together. In November 1999, Farnham and Wheatley undertook a 'reccie' trip to figure out what was required to stage a brief tour a month later.

'We're going into a third-world country, a war zone,' reported a very sombre Wheatley on his return. 'There's no infrastructure, we have to bring everything with us: generators, roofing, flooring. They have nothing.' Meanwhile, John and the rest of the Tour of Duty troupe – Kylie Minogue, James Blundell, the Living End, Neeson, hosts HG Nelson and Roy Slaven – prepared to board their military transport and head for East Timor.

This type of morale-boosting tour has a long history: Farnham's former mentors, Johnny O'Keefe and Col Joye, had rocked the troops in Vietnam in the 1960s, along with Little Patti, Rick Springfield and many others. Entertaining the troops had become a rite of passage for Australian singers, from Vietnam to Iraq and now East Timor.

Thousands of screaming troops and the occasional local – some perched in the nearby trees – packed the Dili Stadium on 21 December. Despite the tropical heat and ever-present rain, the mood was overwhelmingly positive. John got into a good-natured tete-a-tete with the huge crowd, who chanted 'Sadie!' as if it were game day at the MCG. Farnham had no option but to submit.

'I'll do whatever you say,' he said, raising his hands in submission. 'After all, you're armed.'

Even Nelson and Slaven couldn't resist, joining John on stage and demanding that the audience spell out the song they wanted to hear. 'Gimme an "S"!' HG yelled, and the crowd erupted.

John complied, sort of, mumbling a quick grab of 'Sadie' before he and the band burst into an inspired, roof-raising 'That's Freedom', a way more suitable song for the occasion. 'Sadie' jokes peppered his brief set of songs – and he did eventually sing it in full, but only after a ripping take on 'Chain Reaction' and an urgent 'Playing to Win'. During the latter John was almost pulled into the crowd as he slapped hands with eager punters down the front.

Then John, keeping his cool in blue shirt and matching tie, shades firmly in place, and Doc Neeson, rocked an Easybeats' medley of 'She's So Fine' and 'Sorry'. The band, horn section roaring, sounded tight.

Then, finally, it was a group rip-and-tear through 'You're the Voice', John's very own anthem, as the Timor rain fell almost horizontally, drenching everyone and everything. 'The Voice' mightn't have won over the Chinese officials, back when Wheatley almost stage-managed a tour behind the Great Wall, but it struck a powerful chord with the thousands of saturated Aussies in Dili. Seemingly every single arm in the stadium was raised and waving in time with John, whose smile couldn't have been any broader. It was a huge moment.

John then shouted himself hoarse for 'It's A Long Way to the Top' as the crowd simply refused to leave. Wheatley joined everyone on stage for the closing 'Take a Long Line'. John, shaking a tambourine, happily took a backseat to the scarf-waving Neeson, in full 'wild Doc' mode. Dili was well and truly rocked – and the rain just kept falling.

As you'd expect, a TV crew documented everything. 'There was something good happening in East Timor today,' announced the report when it was screened back home. 'Australian entertainers Kylie Minogue and John Farnham were in town, leading the troupe and getting a jubilant reception at their first stopover.'

'These people are real, they're resilient and they've come back from the most awful trauma,' John said. He was soaked to the skin.

Off camera, John was speechless as he was driven through the streets of Dili in an armoured vehicle, his security guards, soldiers 'bristling with arms', by his side. He spotted young children 'who'd been in this horrendous situation'. As reality checks went, they didn't come any more real than a trip through a war zone.

When they played smaller, unplugged shows in Suai and Balibo, John and his fellow entertainers were mobbed as often by locals as by Aussies. 'It's unbelievable, fantastic,' John gushed as yet another wave of people rushed forward to get close to him and Kylie Minogue.

On one of the Aussie bases, John even tracked down a soldier who shared his surname, happily posing for a photo. 'We're the Farnham brothers,' he proclaimed. 'And I'm the oldest.'

'It was the concert of a lifetime,' Farnham told a reporter on his return.

For his first studio project in five years, John decided not to work in a studio at all, or at least not in a conventional, digital-age facility. Instead, during the early months of 2000, he and his regular crew – producer Fraser, bandmates Lim, Edwards, Field, Burchall and the rest of Team Farnham – spent six weeks holed up in a (barely) converted Richmond warehouse, getting back to basics. The control room, such as it was, was in a truck parked inside the factory. Fraser and his team needed to turn sideways and try not to breathe too deeply in order to work together. There were none of the usual studio indulgences: no spa, no pool, no bar. The only escape was a nearby back alley. There was barely a functional bathroom – during one of the first days of recording, John walked in on Field, who was scraping the crusty sink clean with paper towels.

John was taken aback; he had a flashback to old days on the road.

'This is just like being back in LRB,' he joked. Sort of.

There was a method to this madness, because John was fulfilling a long-held dream to cut a selection of soul and R&B standards – 'black music', in pre-PC vernacular. The philosophy was simple and classic: he and the team would rehearse each song, get it right and then record it pretty much live. A bare-boned inner-city factory lent the right amount of grit to such a project, as did a red-hot three-man brass section brought in for the sessions, comprising Steve Williams, Bob Coassin and Lex Tier. Alabama's legendary Muscle Shoals, the studio where many of these types of songs were born, was hardly a five-star joint, so a backstreet Richmond warehouse felt right. And perhaps lightning could strike twice: after all, John and Fraser cut much of *Whispering Jack* in an equally gritty garage.

This wasn't the crowd-pleasing jukebox soul of Jimmy Barnes and his bestselling *Soul Deep* records. John might have cut 'When Something Is Wrong with My Baby' with Barnesy back in 1991, but he wanted to dig deeper. Now he dusted off such R&B/soul greats as 'I've Been Lonely for So Long', a 1972 hit for American Frederick Knight, released by the renowned Stax records, soul music's label of choice. He also covered 'You Don't Know Like I Know', which had been recorded by Sam and Dave, of 'Soul Man' legend, and co-written by Isaac 'Shaft' Hayes. As for 'That Driving Beat', it had been cut by US bandleader Willie Mitchell, while Otis Clay had grazed the charts with 'Trying to Live My Life Without You' in 1972, a song that had since been covered by working-class hero Bob Seger. John particularly related to the lyric about the lengths a scorned lover was willing to go to in order to win back his lady – he, too, had been smoking close to 'five packs of cigarettes a day' back when he and Jillian shared their chronic addiction to durries.

These songs weren't obvious choices; they were interesting, challenging soul nuggets, songs that would push John as a singer and also stretch the band and producer Fraser. The Farnham crew would be the first to admit they'd locked into a comfortable groove over the past few hit records and it was now time to push themselves. The sound John wanted was pure, not pretty. Soulful.

'It's been amazing,' John said of the entire process, as the album slowly came together. 'I've always loved brass, big band, swing – I get a lot of joy out of this stuff.'

The word 'organic' came up time and time again as the best way to describe the entire exercise. All the players praised the organic nature of the record, its rootsiness, the fact that it was another example of John's willingness to mess with the formula just a little. This was no pop record. If anything, it was retro, a flashback to the 1960s and '70s, the golden age of 'black music'. It was clear that Farnham loved the material and felt connected to it, even if he struggled with some of the slightly raunchier material. John may have had soul in spades, but he was no lover man.

Even John's wardrobe, if you could call it that, reflected how at ease he felt: most days he'd enter the makeshift studio decked out in a checked plaid shirt and jeans, mountain man clobber, ideally suited to his increasingly heavy build. He looked as though he'd come straight from his beloved country hideaway. There was probably a little horse manure on his boots.

The mood, as always, was good. One day, John was sent a gift from a fan – a talking toy bear, operated by simply inserting one's finger up its furry, beary backside. John briefly thought about regifting it to his buddies in Human Nature, but considered it weird enough to keep. It became a surrogate studio mascot.

John's soulful makeover was not left unnoticed by critics on the release of $33 \frac{1}{3}$ in July 2000.

'It worked for Phil Collins almost two decades ago,' noted Fairfax music writer Bernard Zuel in an astute review. '[And] it mostly worked for Jimmy Barnes a decade ago (sales wise, anyway; musically, he murdered the songs). It always works for whichever teen pop band needs a quick injection of easily recognised brilliance. So why shouldn't John Farnham give it a go?

'Happily, unlike the majority of those who turn to the wellspring of Stax/Motown/Chess/Atlantic, Farnham hasn't gone for the standards, the "Mustang Sallys" and "Midnight Hours" you can hear any day on classic-hits radio. Don't worry, Farnham fans, while there are great-but-unknown-to-most-Australians songwriters such as Little Milton Campbell, he hasn't gone completely obscure – we are still talking material from the likes of Isaac Hayes and David Porter and Norman Whitfield and Barrett Strong.'

John found himself in an unlikely sparring match upon the album's release. Jimmy Barnes had again taken the more predictable route with his 'new' tribute record, *Soul Deeper*, and the two Aussie icons were competing for airtime and sales with a similar concept. It was no contest. John's album debuted at number one, Barnes's at number three, a reflection of the superior quality and judgement that went into John's LP. Barnesy was merely recycling; John was reinventing himself, just a little.

But neither act could persuade commercial radio to get on board, a problem John really hadn't encountered since the dark days of the late 1970s. The first single was 'Trying to Live My Life Without You', a punchy cover of a great song, but programmers either passed, preferred to play John's 'old' material – from the *Whispering Jack* era, that is – or reached for the new single from Bardot, Killing Heidi or Madison Avenue. It was more a reflection of the risk-averse mindset of Australian radio programming than a comment on the quality of 'Trying to Live My Life' and *33 1/3*.

'I actually get a lot of play on radio, but it's not mainstream radio,' a slightly disgruntled Farnham told a Fairfax reporter. 'But that's always been the case. When we released *Whispering Jack*, we had enormous problems getting it played. It was the highest-selling record in Australia's history and we had to put that out on a label that didn't have a name on it so people could get past my past image.'

Nowadays, that public image could be a bit of a problem, at least when it came to the cooler customers. John understood this. Joked about it, even. 'You're not allowed to say publicly that you own a Farnham album,' he admitted. 'You've got a Farnham record in your hand and you'll be like, "Yeah, I found it on the bus."'

As for those who did embrace his music – and would even admit to doing so in a public place – was he concerned how they'd react to *33 1/3*? After all, it was quite a departure from what had come before.

'I worry every time I make an album,' John admitted. 'Yeah, of course I was worried people wouldn't accept this, but I also didn't want to make *Romeo's Heart Part 2*. I thought this is something I want to do; it gives me somewhere else to go. I thought maybe I needed to take a different approach, to not be so predictable.'

The unspoken truth was that John also needed to shake things up; after five albums of grown-up contemporary pop music, he needed a creative left-turn such as *33 1/3* to keep him engaged and interested. He also needed to remind his fans that he was more than a song-and-dance man with a good line in mother-in-law jokes: he was a seriously good song interpreter. Barely two years later, Rod Stewart would undergo a similar reinvention with the *Great American Songbook*, which sold close to four million copies globally. *Australian Idol* winner Guy Sebastian followed suit in 2007 with *The Memphis Album*.

In order to gain traction for the record, Wheatley drew on his early source of inspiration: Stan Cornyn's article 'The Day Radio Died'. If radio wasn't interested, Wheatley figured, then he'd book

John on TV and also get him back out on the road. The 20-show Man of the Hour tour ran through October and continued in December 2000, packing the big venues that his peer Barnesy could only dream of filling: five nights at the Melbourne Tennis Centre, four at the Sydney Entertainment Centre, with equally full houses in all the capitals. John and band added staples 'You're the Voice', 'Two Strong Hearts', 'Chain Reaction' and 'That's Freedom' to the smattering of 'new' songs from $33^{1}/_{3}$.

Channel 9 broadcast the obligatory TV special, also entitled *Man of the Hour*. Wheatley allowed himself a told-you-so chuckle and took solace in a job very well done. $33^{1}/_{3}$ sold around 100,000 copies domestically, topping the charts for five straight weeks. Even without mainstream radio support, John could still shift some units and pack venues; he also picked up a staggering 14th Mo award in 2000, for Arena Performer of the Year. John had few, if any rivals.

John had received so much media exposure over the past 15 years that news outlets started spreading a wider net for their definitive Farnham story. Prior to his Man of the Hour shows at Melbourne Park, *The Age* managed to track down the joint presidents of the John Farnham Fan Club, 43-year-olds Maree Illingworth and Sue Smith. The very notion that an old-school fan club still existed in the age of the internet – there were currently 1200 members, down from a late 1980s peak of 5000, but still good numbers – said plenty about John's rusted-on audience.

Illingworth and Smith were like walking, talking Farnham time capsules; they'd seen it all. They'd been outside the Glenroy church in 1973, in tears, when John and Jillian tied the knot; they were among the few at his poorly attended 1970s gigs – they'd even seen Johnny croon 'Sadie' at the Chadstone Shopping Centre way, way back. *Don Lane Show*s, 'comeback' *Whispering Jack*-era concerts: they'd witnessed the lot. Their scrapbooks bulged with Farnham clippings and memorabilia; their walls were lined with photos and posters. They were the truest of true believers, who, like so many Farnham diehards, would now organise work holidays around his touring schedule, flying from city to city, show to show. Some attended eight, 10, even a dozen shows in one run. They could not get enough of the man.

'He's not aloof, like many of them,' Illingworth said, when asked to explain Farnham's enduring appeal. 'When he speaks to you, even if it's only for five minutes, it's like you're his best friend. And he could move down the line and talk with 28 people, and they would all react the same way.'

Just before setting out on the I Can't Believe He's 50 tour, John was asked about being overexposed: had he passed his use-by date?

'I was a bit apprehensive,' he admitted at the time. 'How was everybody going to take the news that I am going out … again? I don't want to bore people to death. There's nothing worse for any performer than to be met with indifference.'

A similar question came up again in 2000, but this time the 'R' word was used: when was he going to retire? Was it even a possibility?

'That's going to happen one day – I don't want to finish playing to half-houses or quarter-houses,' he accepted. 'But we just pretty much sold out this tour. Why would I consider retirement when everything is going so well? I'm having the greatest time and doing it in the best circumstances. I don't have to drive over the Nullarbor Plain or drive for 500 miles after the show. I get up the next day and get on a plane, get taken to a hotel and I'm a happy daddy.'

It was a good response, but this became something John considered more and more over the ensuing years. When was he going to quit? And could it be done with a little dignity?

18

HOW MANY LAST TIMES?

If Farnham and Wheatley made one mistake during their remarkable union it was that they never clearly stated if and when John intended to retire. But by calling a tour The Last Time, as they did in 2002, if John kept touring he risked being viewed as the man who didn't quite know when or how to say goodbye, stuck with tags such as 'The Dame Nellie Melba of Pop'. There was also the risk of alienating punters who'd bought tickets to shows in the belief they'd never see Farnham perform again. And as history would prove, The Last Time was anything but.

Wheatley conceded that they'd 'created confusion in the marketplace,' as he'd write in his second memoir, *Facing the Music*. 'While we'd been very careful not to say that John was retiring, of course that's exactly what many people thought. [But] retiring was the last thing on our minds.'

As usual, Farnham and Wheatley turned to the small screen to build anticipation for the tour, which was set to kick off on

6 November at Melbourne's Rod Laver Arena and continue until the end of the year. John's latest TV special, *An Audience with John Farnham*, was a very polite, seated-and-greeted kind of event, pitched somewhere between a celebrity roast and an episode of *This Is Your Life*. Farnham and the band played, and John took some questions between songs. The studio audience was stacked with friendly and familiar faces – Wheatley was in the front row and Farnham's fishing buddy Rex Hunt was prominently positioned, as was his sometimes touring companion Olivia Newton-John, fellow performers Christine Anu, Marcia Hines and Col Joye, and such acquaintances as race car driver Peter Brock and former boxing champ Johnny Famechon (who called Farnham 'one of my absolute heroes'). Jillian and Robbie were quietly seated a few rows back from the stage.

'Thank you and welcome to my nightmare,' laughed Farnham, as he walked onto the set and dropped into some RSL-club-friendly patter. After a song or two, his old buddy 'Livvy' – who as always absolutely glowed – posed the first question. It was one Farnham was starting to hear with some regularity.

'John, when are you retiring?'

'I'm not retiring,' smiled Farnham, 'but I'm feeling huge pressure to fill these big venues.'

(Wheatley backed this up, writing that he was concerned they could no longer fill arenas year in, year out. 'It would be impossible to keep doing that sort of business.')

And what about The Main Event, the 1998 triple-headed bill he'd shared with Newton-John and Anthony Warlow, which had filled one entertainment centre after another. Did that rate as a career high?

'That was an absolute joy,' beamed Farnham, smiling at Newton-John, who beamed right back at him.

After The Main Event, Farnham and Newton-John had teamed up for the 2000 Olympic Games opening ceremony, holding hands and smiling broadly while singing 'Dare to Dream' to some four billion viewers. Their smiles belied what had just transpired: uncharacteristically John had given a hefty serve to event producer Ric Birch just before the opening. John was upset that more locals weren't being given the chance to appear. 'There's not an artist in the country, or a marching girl or boy or marching band or dancer or entertainer of any kind that wouldn't love to be there on that day,' John roared. 'Whether they be high-profile, or brand-new kids doing stuff, is immaterial. How dare this fool deprive, or even consider depriving, our kids of the opportunity of being at that venue, at that ceremony, at that event.'

Back at John's celebrity roast, the subject of musical influences was brought up. Eyebrows were raised when Farnham mentioned Eminem. It seemed as though he had been listening to more of his sons' music than just Nana-Zhami.

And his life influences, someone asked – who would they be? Well, that had to be Jillian, of course. The perfect response.

John talked about life away from the stage and his many passions: skiing, scuba diving, horse riding, angling, and being a father and husband. He had plenty going on. In fact, he wasn't sure how he fit everything in. He'd just taken up welding, thanks to a recent birthday gift from Jillian and the boys. Not the sexiest of hobbies, but another way to occupy himself during downtime.

Talk inevitably turned to his relationship with Wheatley, the man who'd rebuilt his career and become his best friend in the process. They'd even started appearing together in a lucrative series of TV ads for Telstra MobileNet, yet another coup for John's highly proactive manager. They plugged it ever-so-subtly during the show, cheesily posing with their Telstra-provided handsets. (During The Last Time tour, fans were encouraged to send text messages to win prizes, the ultimate being a meet-and-greet with John after the show.)

'I have a brotherly relationship with Wheatley,' Farnham said. But he admitted they sometimes fought 'like sisters'.

'So,' piped up Marcia Hines, once the laughter subsided, 'are you comfortable being a sex symbol?'

The blush said it all: no, not really. Instead, Farnham talked about the cabbie in 1973 and the advice he'd given John the day before he married Jillian – to always fall asleep in each other's arms.

'And I always do what I'm told,' Farnham grinned.

Farnham didn't even consider himself a clotheshorse, let alone a sex symbol. And as for that haircut ...

'My band call it a world-class mullet,' he said, casting a glance over his shoulder at a grinning Garsed, Burchall and co.

Ross Wilson was another familiar face in the crowd. He spoke about the trilogy of songs – 'You're the Voice', 'Age of Reason' and 'That's Freedom' – that positioned Farnham as a 'spokesman for the common man'. Farnham said that was one tag he was comfortable with; he even delivered a very serious diatribe on the horrors of life post-9/11, describing the Twin Towers disaster as 'flat out murder'. (Days before the first official Last Time show, John had played a fundraiser for victims of the 2002 Bali bombing. His social conscience was as engaged as ever.)

But this was a rare moment of seriousness. In the main, like the man himself, *An Audience with John Farnham* was rock-solid, family-friendly entertainment. The songs were impeccably played and beautifully sung. Everything was polished, polite and well rehearsed, even down to the bespoke closing song, a take on the Rolling Stones' 'The Last Time'. Ironically, 'The Last Time' had marked the beginning for the Stones; it was the first original Jagger/Richards song to become a worldwide hit, way back in 1965. But for John it was intended to be a farewell, of sorts.

Checking in at a concise 38 minutes, *The Last Time* LP carried very little baggage. Production-wise, John didn't waver too far from his usual team; it was essentially his band – Chong Lim, Burchall, Edwards, Field, bassist Stuart Fraser – plus a few additional players, with the Victorian Philharmonic bringing the strings. This time around, there were no Farnham co-writes; instead, he cherry-picked songs from a broad range of writers. John brought some vocal muscle to the melodic pop of 'No Ordinary World', which Joe Cocker had covered in 1999. He also tackled the soulful ballad 'Lonely Man', the handiwork of Brit hit-maker Wayne Hector, who'd written for Britney Spears and Wheatley's other star client, Delta Goodrem.

John's spin on the Stones' 'The Last Time' led the album, with some arresting electronic touches and a nagging guitar riff that Keith Richards wouldn't kick out of the studio. It was a curious mingling of the old and the new, with a lively chanted chorus tossed in for good measure. This typified *The Last Time*; it was perhaps the most modern-sounding, digital-era recording John had ever made, in much the same way *Whispering Jack* had clearly been an album of the mid-1980s. John was never going to kid anyone that he was a cutting-edge artist, but he sounded pretty comfortable amid the programming, sequencing and sonic layers of *The Last Time*.

The album debuted at number one on its release on 7 October 2002, and went on to sell 200,000 copies. John also picked up another ARIA, this time for Best Adult Contemporary Album.

The Last Time became a real fan favourite, reflected in glowing online reviews. 'John is truly one of Australia's great musical talents,' wrote a fan on Amazon. '*The Last Time*, the remake by John, is great, vibrant and catchy all the way.' 'It is a great CD,' stated another. 'John Farnham is Australia's greatest singer – anything John Farnham puts out will always be worth listening to.'

What was especially interesting about *The Last Time* was its lack of real pathos; there were no grand statements contained within if this was to be John's studio swan song. In hindsight, of course, the song 'One More Try' could have been prophetic – John wasn't quite done with the studio yet.

Before heading out on a more substantial tour, John launched *The Last Time* on 6 October in a highly unlikely venue: Melbourne's legendary Espy Hotel, the sticky-carpeted site of SBS's *RocKwiz* and the home of everything alternative. Hipsters and taste-makers were regulars at the Espy – it was fair to say they weren't the typical Farnham audience. But John figured that if he was stepping back into the spotlight, he might as well mix things up, make the event different and interesting.

There'd been some lively byplay in the days leading to up the invite-only gig. The Espy placed an ad in the street press, which read: 'John, if you are to do the Espy, you've got to play "Sadie" – and you've got to send us a demo.' Basically, the same rules that applied to novice acts applied to John Farnham.

John took it in the right spirit. He thought the ad was 'fantastic'.

And was it a career goal to play the Espy?

'I've only really wanted to play here since about last Tuesday, actually,' John laughed. 'But I'm looking forward to it, it's a fun place.'

About 100 Farnham diehards gathered on the Espy steps well before the doors were flung open. Among them were fans travelling from interstate to get a close-up glimpse of their idol, along with winners of an online contest. One of these fans, a woman named Sue Williams, admitted to having been a Farnesy fan 'since I was 12 – but I'm not going to tell you how old I am now.' Ms Williams did reveal she'd seen every Farnham tour since 1986. 'At the moment we have eight tickets – one for every single [Victorian] concert,' she said before heading inside and making her way down the front. John's fans were nothing if not dedicated.

John was insistent that this tour was his last on such a large scale. *Seriously*. He'd continue touring, but in smaller venues, and on shorter runs.

'I'm not looking forward to the end – or even to the end of each night's performance,' he said after the Espy showcase went down a storm. 'I think it'll be a pretty emotional thing.'

The Last Time roadshow began with the now requisite city-by-city run: an astounding nine Tennis Centre shows in Melbourne during November, then another half a dozen in Sydney. While Farnham was in the Harbour City, Premier Bob Carr presented the man of the moment with a plaque honouring the opening of the John Farnham Room at the Entertainment Centre. Six more full houses followed in Brisbane.

Prior to the city run, there'd been a one-off concert in rural Cohuna, on 12 October, a gig that was especially poignant for John. There were huge signs lining the streets, reading 'Thanks Jack' and 'Jack is Back', which sent a conflicting message: was he retiring or simply returning? No-one seemed quite sure. John's albums and posters filled the windows of every shop in the township while his music blared from loudspeakers; it was Farnham-mania. Five thousand fans gathered for the mid-afternoon show: a pretty impressive turnout, considering the town's population was only 2300.

Cohuna, of course, was where John had first encountered Darryl Sambell in the local Memorial Hall back in 1967, when Sambell had asked, 'You're not the drummer are you?' This chance meeting had changed John's life forever; Sambell laid the groundwork for John – Johnny, back then – to become the superstar he was today. The Cohuna gig was even more poignant as Sambell had died from lung cancer on 19 September 2001, at the age of 56.

After his divorce from John in the mid-1970s, Sambell had left the management biz and spent many years back in New Zealand. In later years, Sambell moved back to Australia, settling on the Gold Coast, where he died. He was buried in Adelaide, his hometown.

They may have become estranged, but it was fair to say that without Sambell's wonderful way with hype and his fervent belief in John's talent, Farnham would probably have become a tradie on a building site, living a very different life. Sambell had told Rose

Farnham that he could make her son a star; he'd proved true to his word. He'd cut Johnny's hair, ironed his clothes, chosen his songs, mapped out his future, interfered in his love life. The impact he had on John's life, for better or worse, was huge, undeniable.

'Why did I spend nine years and three months with Johnny?' Sambell said at the end of their relationship. 'Because he had the voice.' Now, John *was* The Voice.

The Cohuna show may have been a one-off, but for much of 2003 John took his show to places way off the regular tour map. This lengthy, exhaustive and unique country run was called The Last Time: Under the Big Top. It kicked off in Kalgoorlie on 31 January 2003.

The intention of the tour echoed those of tours by folks like Slim Dusty: get out to the more remote parts of the country, set up a big top, and give the locals a fair old night out. The tour rolled on for five months, with 58 shows in 27 locations, all under the enormous 45 by 60 metre 'event tent', which had a capacity of 4000. This was the first time a tour of this scope had ever been undertaken in Australia. Thirty trucks and 50 support staff were required; there were two separate big tops, one always in transit to the next gig.

But The Big Top tour did not begin promisingly: anything but. Ticket sales in Kalgoorie were slow. A camera crew, filming the obligatory TV special, captured John as he stepped off the bus in the former mining town.

'We've got half a house, maybe,' he said. Mind you, John had a plan to boost the box office. 'We're going down to the hospital and [we'll] beg people to come. Then we're going to the old people's homes and [we'll] tell them they've got to come.'

John was convinced he knew the problem. A little research revealed to him that Kalgoorlie had been the site of Australia's first brothel, back during its goldrush-era heyday, and out here in the wild west, sex continued to take precedence over other forms of entertainment. 'Hooker, Farnham, hooker, Farnham,' John said, weighing up the options, when he uncovered the town's lively reputation. 'What are you going to take?' In downtown Kalgoorlie, a joint named Skimpies was doing lively business. However, interest in John's concert eventually picked up – so much so that a second show went ahead on 1 February.

After Kalgoorlie, the roadshow headed to Geraldton and Bunbury, then made its way through Whyalla, Broken Hill, Griffith, Wagga Wagga, Bendigo, Wollongong, Lismore and Caloundra and several other rural spots that rarely, if ever, witnessed events of this size, before returning to Melbourne Park on 15 June, a venue where John had now sold more than one million tickets over the years.

The offstage mood, as ever, was lighthearted – loud shirts were now all the rage among band and crew. Not for Wheatley, however: as always, he was the definitive businessman, looking smart in crisp, collared numbers, checking tickets, counting receipts, ensuring that Farnham Inc. ran smoothly. During soundcheck, John would mess with his songs, turning 'Please Don't Ask Me' into the most tragic country and western heartbreaker you'd ever heard. When boredom set in, he'd vacuum the stage.

On stage, John took the 'Big Top' idea to its natural conclusion, producing a hoop and directing the more obliging band members to jump through it. Circus Oz – John Farnham Band–style!

Facilities were not quite the five-star standard Farnham and co. had grown accustomed to over the years: one venue didn't even have a box office. Sometimes there were no dressing rooms or there was very little in the way of basic necessities. In a few motels the troupe installed their own high-pressure shower roses on the sly – John and his team felt as though they were living out their own version of the *Seinfeld* episode 'The Shower Head'.

Some nights it rained buckets. After a few soggy gigs, John earned himself a new nickname from the band and crew: he was now the Rain God.

'It's like any camping trip,' Farnham figured, 'it's bound to rain. Want to go for a swim; it's going to get cold. Shit happens.'

Typically, John led the lusty, boozy singalongs after most shows, usually while holding up the bar. 'Does Your Chewing Gum Lose Its Flavour (On the Bedpost Overnight)' – a novelty song to rival 'Sadie' or 'Underneath the Arches' – was a particular favourite.

'That's it, it's over, go home,' John told the ever-present camera as the tour finally drew to a close. 'I want to go out with my reputation intact, at the top of my profession. I don't want to end up playing to the crickets and the cleaners.'

But was it really the end?

19

WARM UNDIES AND SHAMELESS NOSTALGIA

An exhausted John spent much of the remainder of 2003 kicking back and collecting new trophies: he was inducted into the ARIA Hall of Fame on 21 October and was named Victoria's Number One Living Treasure in a radio poll during early December. He'd been King of Pop, Australian of the Year, received an Order of Australia – and now he was a Living Treasure again (he'd won a similar award in 1998). A bronze statue of John was erected in Melbourne's Docklands. He claimed two more ARIAs in 2003, making a remarkable 20 in all. He'd already received awards from the Brisbane and Sydney Entertainment Centres for being their highest grossing artist of all time. If Australia ever got around to becoming a republic, John was a shoe-in for president.

John marked all this pomp and ceremony by doing what came naturally: he played a series of late-year shows at the Twin Towns club on the far north coast of New South Wales and at Penrith Panthers, a huge outer-Sydney pokie palace. Wheatley, meanwhile, was putting together the final pieces of a highly lucrative new recording deal with BMG; John would commit to another five albums over the next 10 years. So much for The Last Time.

Unlike virtually all his peers, John's popularity wasn't fading. If anything, he was becoming even bigger as the years rolled on.

In the background of all this activity, however, the situation wasn't so rosy. Glenn Wheatley's business woes were far from over. In the mid-1990s, he'd set up a new company, Talentworks, wholly owned by John, since as part of his ongoing deed of arrangement Wheatley was not allowed to be a director of a company. Much of 1996 had been spent building the company. John had played at the Formula 1 Australian Grand Prix at an event staged by Talentworks. The huge Jack of Hearts tour followed. It had seemed that Wheatley was back on his feet: at least debt-free, if not completely flush.

When his deed ended, on 31 December 1996, the Wheatleys were holidaying with the Farnhams, this time in Whistler, Canada – ski country. John had insisted on being with 'Wheat' when his 'sentence' ended. On New Year's morning the pair awoke at dawn, well before their wives or children. They were the first people out on the mountain; it was solitary, beautiful in its isolation. They scaled right to the peak and proceeded to ski downhill, not knowing quite where they were heading.

At one point, Wheatley stopped and surveyed the slope.

'I'm not sure if I can do this,' he said to Farnham.

John knew better.

'Come on, Wheat,' John insisted, 'of course you can.'

He was right: from there, they both virtually sailed to the bottom of the mountain. Of course he could do it.

Yet despite Farnham's ongoing support and friendship, a big dark cloud was zeroing in on Wheatley. After 1993's hugely successful Talk of the Town tour, Wheatley had been introduced to Philip Egglishaw, principal of the bank Strachans, based in the Jersey Isles, a tax haven. Egglishaw outlined an arrangement: in order to avoid being slugged with a full 47% tax in Oz, Wheatley would move his money to a Swiss bank account and bring it back into the country as a loan. All he'd have to pay was 15% withholding tax in Switzerland. Wheatley transferred $256,000, unaware that Egglishaw was taking that 15% as a fee; the withholding tax wasn't paid. It didn't really matter anyway, because although Wheatley said he wasn't aware of it, the entire set-up was illegal.

In 2004, with Talentworks now in full swing, Wheatley did the same with $400,000 he earned promoting a boxing title fight featuring Aussie hero Kostya Tszyu. He would write of the venture, 'I justified it at the time by the fact I was paying a lot of tax [in Australia] and I was aware that a lot of companies and individuals were doing the same thing.'

On 9 June 2005 Wheatley's home and office were raided by officers from the federal police, the tax office, even Australian Customs. It was part of a sting known as Project Wickenby, set up to pursue prominent Australians who were alleged tax cheats – Paul Hogan and his manager, John Cornell, among them. Wheatley said he had no idea what the raid was about: perhaps, due to his involvement with the music biz, it had something to do with drugs? He could only speculate.

That wasn't even close. Philip Egglishaw's scheme had been exposed and Wheatley was one of several names found on the banker's laptop, hence the raids, which consumed something like eight hours at his office and home. Throughout investigations, Wheatley maintained that he had been naive, rather than deliberately deceptive, and in mid-December 2005 he was given assurance that if he agreed to help with the investigation he'd be given a non-custodial sentence. He signed an agreement to that effect. Unfortunately, that deal was revoked a month later. His future was very much uncertain.

As for John, he'd gotten back out on the road, yet again. He had agreed to a double-headed tour with ageless sex-symbol Tom Jones, another high-profile fan of John's, in February 2005, playing shows in John's regular happy hunting grounds (and two outdoor shows in Sydney, at the Domain).

The pair talked up their tour on Channel 9's *Hey Hey It's Saturday*. This time Jones was the man in black – pulling off an unlikely duet on the terribly earnest 'My Yiddishe Momme'. Their relationship had its roots way back in 1993, when they teamed up at the Logies, growling and swaggering their way through 'It's a Long Way to the Top'. They looked and sounded great together, two middle-aged troopers oozing sex appeal, with voices that could fit pretty much any repertoire. 'Long Way' went over so well that the normally staid Logies audience dragged them back for a reprise.

Their vocal dexterity proved handy, because when they hit the road in 2005, Tom and John tackled a set list that comprised their hits (Jones's 'It's Not Unusual' and 'Delilah', John's 'Playing to

Win' and 'You're the Voice'), along with soul greats like 'Hold On, I'm Coming', 'Try a Little Tenderness', even Randy Newman via Three-Dog Night's 'Mama Told Me Not to Come'. The show was designed along the lines of a heavyweight bout, both taking the stage after a warning announcement: 'Let's get ready to rumble!' They also knew when to get out of each other's way, John giving Jones space to belt out standards like 'Green Green Grass of Home'; Jones repaying the favour for some *Whispering Jack*-era numbers. In the end, though, it was a vocal love match. (Farnham would go on to take part in other double-header tours: with Lionel Richie in 2014, and then Olivia Newton-John in 2015. The format worked for him.)

'Fellow fans of live music, take note: this is not what you might call a regular audience, or a regular gig,' noted Fairfax's George Palathingal of the 12 February Sydney show. '[Farnham and Jones] are, in fact, a lot more fun than many. It's ... an evening of shameless nostalgia, Vegas-cheesy entertainment and sometimes terribly dated music, yes. But it's also a refreshingly unpretentious, enjoyable one.'

During their Domain show, a roving camera caught a middle-aged fan down the front, in a summery dress, standing atop her chair. Slowly, she bent forward, wriggled out of her undies and hurled them in the direction of the stage. In Melbourne, during the bump and grind of 'You Can Leave Your Hat On', several pairs of knickers were hurled at John and Tom. John's fans could be evangelical, even lusty sometimes, but you didn't usually find a lot of warm undies on stage at a Farnham gig.

With Wheatley knee-deep in legal hassles, John had some dramas of his own, but on two vastly different fronts. Just prior to transforming himself into Teen Angel for the 2005 Australian *Grease* tour, John found himself entangled in an awkward spot of Trans-Tasman politics. John had responded positively to a request to perform at the Gallipoli dawn service for the 90th anniversary of the ANZAC landing, in April 2005, along with New Zealanders the Finn brothers. On paper, it appeared to be a perfectly reasonable prospect: Australia's favourite entertainer performing at a site of great historical significance to Australia.

John had the backing of Bill Crews, the national president of the RSL. 'It's not a rock concert,' Crews emphasised. 'John Farnham was very mindful of that and choosing things that were appropriate to the occasion.' Farnham also had the support of army chief Peter Cosgrove, who he'd met in Timor back in '99, and Prime Minister John Howard – in fact, the original request for Farnham to sing had come via government channels.

In mid-February New Zealand PM Helen Clark and Howard discussed the 'Farnham situation' at the Beehive in Wellington, as part of Howard's goodwill mission to New Zealand. It was their first point of discussion in their meeting. Clark, who opposed the idea, dug in, and the proposal was shut down.

'I think the bottom line,' Clark told reporters, 'is what we, as the descendants of the Anzac tradition, do there will be dignified, will be appropriate.'

Apparently a performance from John Farnham wasn't deemed appropriate, or dignified. The Voice would be silenced, at least as far as Gallipoli 2005 was concerned.

Wheatley relayed the bad news to Farnham.

'It is a very important day in our calendar and the emotion of what this was going to be, being a 90th anniversary, I think, was going to be extraordinary,' Wheatley told the ABC's *World Today* program. 'We would have treated it as an honour, treated the show with respect, in the way that it should be.'

John's next challenge was rather different. In the wake of his successful double act with Tom Jones, he had agreed to another bill-sharing tour, this time with American Stevie Nicks, which was set for February 2006. The plan in place with promoter Andrew McManus seemed relatively straightforward: six gigs in Australia and New Zealand. The shows were double bills – that is, Farnham and Nicks split everything down the middle, from onstage time to publicity and billing. It wouldn't be a shared set, as John had done with Tom Jones; they would each have 75 minutes on stage with their own bands.

All seemed fair and reasonable, even if it was immediately apparent the vibe was a bit strange. In a pre-tour interview, Nicks said she felt that she might have met John before, 'but I can't bet on that absolutely. He's an Aussie, right?' She'd know his name well enough by the end of the tour.

On the afternoon of their first gig, John and band arrived to do their sound check, as usual. But Nicks was nowhere to be seen. Her band came in and sound checked without her. That's a bit odd, John thought, looking on. At the airport, Nicks's private jet awaited her, while John and his band had tickets to travel commercially. The gulf between the Californian diva and the grounded Aussie belter was quickly becoming obvious.

John agreed to play first on the opening night at Boondall, just outside of Brisbane. But he didn't know that Nicks was coming off an eventful day, having changed hotel three times, her hefty entourage in tow. She wasn't feeling settled. John did his 75 minutes, the crowd loved it – of course – and then Nicks went on. And on. And on. By the time her set finally wrapped up, some of the crowd had left. She'd played for almost two hours. Nicks had a new album to promote and hits to revisit and had no intention of letting an agreement get in the way of that.

The next morning, the American diva met with the promoter.

'Why didn't you tell me I was coming on after the Frank Sinatra of Australia?'

She was livid. Nicks wasn't sure the crowd was there for her; they'd made far more noise for John.

Then the review came in of the previous night's show. Oh dear. The headline said it all: 'Farnesy: A Hard Act for Stevie to Follow'. It went on to question why Nicks had agreed to share a bill with Australia's favourite son, given that his following was so feverish, his fans so devoted – and vocal. Farnham had ruled the stage in Brisbane.

John woke Wheatley and showed him the paper. They knew that Nicks wasn't going to take this well. A hasty sit-down was arranged.

An agreement was reached: there was just no way Stevie Nicks was going to follow John Farnham on stage, at least not for the remaining Australian shows. They'd swap places in New Zealand, where Nicks believed, with some justification, that she was the bigger name.

Next stop Perth. Nicks, now opening the show, didn't follow orders and shorten her 100-minute set. This meant there was no way John could do his 75 minutes without the promoter taking a $100,000 hit on the curfew. John reacted to Nicks's arrogance in the best way he knew how; he went out and put on a killer show, curfew be damned. As Wheatley put it, 'The effect on him was just to try that extra bit harder. He was clearly the star of the show.'

By the time the two parties crossed the ditch, the strain was showing on everyone. When it rained in Auckland, promoter McManus hoped it would lead to cancellation of the show; anything to spare him more turmoil. He wasn't so lucky – the clouds dispersed, the rain subsided and the gig proceeded.

To the disappointment of his Kiwi fans, John had now trimmed his set to an hour. 'Words cannot express how angry and disappointed I am that John was forced to leave out so much and do only a one hour set,' a follower named Matt wrote online. 'It was also disappointing that John had very little to say to the crowd on account of the time limitation put on him so he spent most of his time singing.'

As he played, Wheatley received a backstage request from Camp Nicks: John had to cut his set even more, to 45 minutes – he was running too long. If John went beyond 45 minutes, he was fired. But Wheatley didn't budge. They'd already made enough compromises. They had to take a stand. Wheatley let John's set run for an hour, as originally planned. The crowd lapped it up.

McManus tapped Wheatley on the shoulder during John's set.

'Stevie just fired me,' he said. She was threatening to leave the tour.

At their next stop, New Plymouth, John let his music do the talking by playing a powerhouse set. An *hour-long* powerhouse set. To hell with the consequences. Thankfully it was the end of the tour.

John may have stood his ground, admirably, but the entire Nicks experience left a bitter taste.

Glenn Wheatley's day of reckoning arrived on 19 July 2007, when judgement was handed down on his charge of tax avoidance. He'd pleaded guilty, and 'Wheats' still hoped he might be able to elude a jail sentence; he'd even joked to his wife, Gaynor, that he'd be home for lunch. He had fair reason to feel optimistic: he'd told the truth, paid his ($400,000) tax bill and hadn't hidden behind a team of lawyers. But the ATO had backed out of their original deal; Wheatley had no guarantee that the judge would rule out jail time. The charge of tax evasion carried a possible sentence of up to 16 years. That was no joke.

Wheatley came prepared. John had written a glowing character reference for him, as had Bert Newton, Sydney Swans' chairman Richard Colless and army general Peter Cosgrove. All were used as supporting material.

'I'm ashamed of what I've done,' Wheatley admitted as his sentence was about to be handed down. 'I'm ashamed of what I've brought on my family, who have had to suffer a lot.'

'I sentence you to 30 months' jail,' judge Tim Wood told Wheatley, 'with 15 months minimum. You will spend a minimum of 15 months in jail and shall be released on the 18th of October 2008. Take the prisoner away.'

Wheatley was led to a cell, where, in his own words, he suffered the 'anxiety attack from hell'.

It would be almost two very long and painful years before one of the most successful partnerships in Australian entertainment history, John Farnham and Glenn Wheatley – 'Farnesy' and 'Wheats' – would be back on course.

20

GOOD DEEDS AND CLOSE TIES

In 2009 a golden opportunity arose for Farnham: the chance to open the Lyric Theatre, in Sydney's Star Casino, during September. Sinatra and his Rat Pack had made the casino strip in Las Vegas their home back in the day – why shouldn't John find a home at the Star? It was a different scenario from all his previous tours and 'comebacks': no big tops, no outback train odysseys, no one-star motels with dodgy showers. He'd begin a new tour at the Star and this time the people would come to him.

John hadn't played a show since Wheatley's 2007 imprisonment; he hadn't toured since the Stevie Nicks debacle. He popped his head up occasionally – he sang for (and with) newlyweds Bec and Lleyton Hewitt; he'd also been named a Goodwill Ambassador for Dairy Farmers, helping to raise money for drought-affected Aussie farmers. There'd also been a 20th anniversary edition of *Whispering Jack*, packaged with a second disc containing a live recording. But John didn't tour to promote the album, at least not on its release.

At the 2009 APRAs John had presented the Ted Albert Award for Outstanding Services to Australian Music to Sony chief and industry survivor Denis Handlin. Yet he hadn't cut an album of original material since 2002's *The Last Time*. Seven years was an eternity in the world of pop music. Maybe John really had retired.

It was a very sombre Glenn Wheatley who opened proceedings on the morning of 27 May at the Star, addressing the press to announce John's upcoming shows. Wheatley wasn't that long out of Beechworth Detention Centre and his ensuing period of home detention, and was understandably media-wary.

'I can't tell you what a privilege it is to be in front of you today,' he said by way of an introduction.

Wheatley was no doubt thinking of his prison term, when his life had been stripped back to the essentials: a small cell, basic meals, a work routine, monotonous walks around the exercise yard and wary looks over his shoulder all day long. There was the occasional 'contact' visit with his wife and kids – but that was pretty much it.

John, true to form, had visited 'Wheats' in Beechworth as often as he could, although from the start he had understood there'd be fallout as soon as Wheatley's fellow prisoners got wind of his visits. John had to tread, and visit, warily. He needed to stay under the radar, for Wheatley's sake.

It didn't work out that way, of course.

John's first visit came soon after Wheatley's incarceration began in the winter of 2007. They hadn't seen each other in months. One of the prison officers, a Mr Jones, turned out to be a big Farnham fan and tried his best to keep John's visit low-key. Wheatley had spotted press outside the prison when he was first brought into

Beechworth. So what if it was illegal to photograph a prisoner on the inside? This was a hot story.

'It is daunting for anyone to visit a prison,' Wheatley wrote of Farnham's visit, 'and I think John felt very uncomfortable, as he did get the whole prison talking and trying to get a glimpse of him.'

'Hey, Wheats,' an inmate shouted at Glenn one day, 'you're the most famous crim I know.' Several others would burst into 'Pressure Down' when they spotted Wheatley in the yard. It became something of a Beechworth anthem during Wheatley's 10-month stay inside.

That was passably funny, but Wheatley also copped the downside: he was leaned on for money, favours and influence. It didn't matter that his personal finances remained thinly stretched. His fellow inmates firmly believed that Wheatley was a powerful man: after all, John Farnham didn't rock up to visit just anyone. There was little use in Wheatley trying to explain otherwise.

John visited more than once, despite his discomfort. And he spoke out about Wheatley's case, but only when it was safe – for Glenn, that is, his probation over – to do so. Wheatley was no tax fraud, John insisted; he'd simply made a big mistake, which he'd admitted to. He'd paid his hefty tax bill and was still put behind bars, while real tax-avoiders walked free. That sucked.

'He was shafted,' John said. 'He was offered a deal to come clean, which is what he did, and the deal was reneged upon. Where's the justice in that?

'He made a mistake and, quite frankly, he paid a higher price than Gary and Joan or Peter and Mary. He's scarred from it – so are we all.'

On the day of Wheatley's release from prison in mid-May 2008, John was the first person to call. It was 5 a.m.

'I've been doing a lot of fishing, Wheats,' John told him, breaking the ice. 'But more importantly, are you okay?'

They agreed that John shouldn't visit Glenn during his period of home detention; there were just too many paparazzi camped outside.

'I think that would be flaming the fire,' Wheatley's wife, Gaynor, told the press. 'He won't visit until everybody goes away.'

She joked that Farnham was the only person happy with her husband's incarceration – it meant he didn't have to work.

This had been the longest, toughest period of Wheatley's life, which perhaps explained the effusive way Wheatley spoke this May morning at the Star: he was relieved to finally be *free*.

'It's also a great honour to announce that my friend John Farnham is going to come back to the concert stage later this year, for a series of shows that I think are going to be exceptional,' Wheatley continued, his mind back on the job at hand.

Farnham joined the press conference and got straight down to it, revealing that Star City management had invited him down a few months earlier to 'do a reccie' of the Lyric Theatre. 'And I instantly fell in love with it.'

'I'll never tour on the scale we did in the past, those huge venues,' he explained, circumventing the inevitable questions about his uncertain retirement. 'That was then, this is now. But to work in an amazing venue like this, it's incredible, it sounds amazing. I'm thrilled. And I've been able to put the band back together. None of them died in the interim, which is good.'

Had anything changed during *his* downtime?

'My hair's gotten a little thinner – I haven't, but that's okay. I've been riding my horses and doing some fishing. I think half the fish in the Coral Sea have my fingerprints on them, but it's time to give them a break.'

A question was raised about one of his unlikely recent appearances: he had briefly fronted British band Coldplay at the Sound Relief concert in March 2009, a fundraiser for victims of the Black Saturday Victorian bushfires, a very special one-off. Wheatley, still lying low at the time, reluctantly picked up the home phone one night, praying it wasn't another reporter hot for another 'life on the inside' exclusive.

'Hello, is this Glenn?' an unmistakably English voice asked. 'This is Chris Martin.'

Chris Martin – really? Lead singer of one of the planet's biggest bands, partner of Hollywood starlet Gwyneth Paltrow, Martin was a superstar. He'd called with a tantalising offer – would John be willing to sing 'You're the Voice' with Coldplay at Sound Relief?

Wheatley gave Martin John's number, a conversation ensued and a meeting was arranged – in the John Farnham Room at the Rod Laver Arena, no less. Not that Martin needed reminding how big a star Farnham was; he'd toured Australia enough to know that they didn't come any bigger than 'Farnesy'.

'I think I said yes straight away – I didn't "umm" very long,' said John. 'I said to the guys [in Coldplay], "How do we break this up? Which part will I sing? Which part will you sing?" And they said no, we'll play it, you sing it.'

On show day, an understandably nervous John readied himself in the wings as Martin, already on stage with Coldplay, stepped to the mic. Fifty thousand punters looked on. They had no idea what was about to take place.

'What do you do,' Martin said, looking out over the crowd, 'to impress everyone from Row 1 to Row 5000? Well, you do something different. Ladies and gentleman, here to sing Australia's national anthem, please welcome John Farnham.'

'You're the Voice' was a song that never failed to rouse an audience, whether at one of John's full-house gigs or the 2006 Commonwealth Games closing ceremony. Wherever and whenever John chose to dust off his signature tune – the Spirit of the North post-cyclone fundraiser at Cairns in June 2006 or 2005's Tsunami Benefit concert at the Melbourne Music Festival – the reaction was always the same: mass euphoria.

But the audience feedback at Sound Relief was perhaps the most rousing of all: 50,000 voices joined as one, chanting every single word back at John and the band. A sea of waving arms stretched from one end of the SCG to the other; the staid old ground, bathed in sunshine, was fit to burst. It was epic – great theatre, a truly inspiring few minutes of music. Many of the crowd hadn't even been born when 'You're the Voice' became a monumental hit, yet their mad-for-it response said multitudes – the song transcended age and audience. As its end neared, John put a friendly arm around Martin's shoulders; this was rock-and-roll nirvana.

'To have the reaction was just ... unbelievable,' said Farnham. 'Amazing. Absolutely amazing. It was one of the highlights of my life – when I walked off stage I was two feet taller.'

Sound Relief raised $5 million for bushfire victims. And 'You're the Voice' returned to the singles list, doing some healthy business on the iTunes download chart.

Sound Relief also inspired John; he buttonholed Wheatley immediately afterwards.

'I know we called the tour The Last Time,' he shouted above the din of the still-cheering crowd, 'but that was great. I really want to tour again.' He'd erased all the horrors of Dame Stevie Nicks in 2006.

Wheatley couldn't have been more pleased. The Farnham by Demand / Star City tour soon started taking shape.

Back at the Star press conference, discussion returned to the new room at Star City: what did it have going for it?

'It's nice to be able to see people, to eyeball them,' John figured. 'There's not a bad seat in the house here. To be able to come out and get close to the people who've supported me for 40 years is fantastic. Music affects people, and to be able to look into their eyes, you can affect them that little bit more. I'm looking forward to it very much.'

So is *this* the end, one reporter asked?

John wouldn't commit: he knew how tricky things could get when you gave the impression you're retiring.

'I'm not dead yet,' he chuckled.

He was asked about his time out of the limelight; did he have any secret methods to keep his voice in shape?

'At about 5.30 every night I gargle with a glass of red wine, which makes my voice feel good – ' here John paused, a punchline imminent. 'So then I gargle with another one.'

After a quick hint at a new album, a joke about Wheatley's time away ('he's been on tax rehab') and a chuckle about his legendary mullet – 'I couldn't grow it back if I tried!' – John got to his feet, ready to go.

'Thank you for your patience, thank you for your questions and with any luck I'll see you out there. Thank you very much indeed.'

Jack was back. Again.

Judging by the result, with *Jack*, John's 20th studio LP, released in October 2010, he was hell-bent on having the best possible time in the studio. There was a lot of the vibe of *33 1/3* spilling over into this record, as John and the band raised some dust during such big moments as takes on Percy Sledge's '247365' and 'Hit the Road Jack' – of course! – which bled into a red-blooded read of Peggy Lee's 'Fever'. 'Nobody Gets Me Like You' also locked into a good-natured groove. Just as he had with *33 1/3*, John dusted off his vinyl collection, covering songs made famous by Ray Charles and Curtis Mayfield. True soul, with more than a little swing. Seven new tracks rounded out the album.

John wasn't averse to a moment or two of reflection; the big strings and heavy emotions of 'Nobody Gets Me Like You' harked back to the show tunes of his very early records, such as 1972's *Johnny Farnham Sings the Shows*. But that's where the comparison ended: John was now singing with all the hard-won wisdom and insight of a guy who's done more than a few laps of the block. The same hand-on-heart emotion ran through 'Today'. Perhaps, judging by this and the big closer, 'Sunshine', Stevie Nicks was right – John really was the Frank Sinatra of Australia.

Jack didn't quite hit number one; instead it peaked at a paltry number two, held off by neo-metal upstarts Linkin Park. No matter; *Jack* was a strong record, and if it was indeed his studio farewell, there was plenty for his fans to savour.

John did a few 'Live by Demand' shows in support of *Jack*, but it was when he went back on the road during the latter months of 2011, under the banner 'Whispering Jack 25 Years On' that things went large again. A batch of songs recorded at Melbourne venue The Chapel, entitled *The Acoustic Chapel Sessions*, emerged just before the tour began. He'd also cut a different type of covers album in 2005, entitled *I Remember When I Was Young*, where he tackled the Oz pop/rock songbook – everything from Daddy Cool's 'Come Back Again' to Cold Chisel's 'Forever Now', Oz Crawl's 'Reckless' to Men at Work's 'Overkill'.

This was a 25th anniversary worth celebrating; it had been a hell of a ride. In the mid-1980s, John had been on a fast track to suburban club hell. Then he and Fraser (and Hirschfelder, whose contribution shouldn't be overlooked) found some magic in a suburban garage, Wheatley stumped up the cash and the rest became Australian pop history. John then built on *Whispering Jack*'s overwhelming success, becoming a homegrown superstar all over again. Sure, he'd been a bit fickle when it came to retirement, flustering some fans, but audiences still clamoured to see him.

Again, the *Whispering Jack* anniversary tour was a Wheatley idea. Farnham, by his own admission, was a bit reluctant.

'I don't know, Glenn, would anyone want to be involved in that?' he asked. 'Would anyone want to see that?'

John knew that he'd been lucky; he'd filled rooms for nearly all of the post-*Whispering Jack* era. He didn't want to mess with his success.

'I don't want to play to half-full houses, beating a horse to death,' he told Wheatley.

His fears were unfounded, of course. John and the band packed venues across the country during October and November 2011, playing 27 shows in all. Throughout the tour John was in typically chatty mood on stage, especially when eager fans rushed down the front and started handing over gifts, flowers and trinkets. He responded, Elvis style, with a kiss and a smile. Sometimes he gave a lucky fan a sweaty handkerchief.

'I'll tell you a story,' he announced at one of the early shows, as he handed over a hanky. 'I've got about 70 dollars worth of product in my hair, 30 of which is in my eyes. What I put on the handkerchief is not perspiration, it's gel. If you run that through your hair, it'll be stiff for a week.'

Then a pause, followed by one of Farnham's patented cheeky grins.

'I wish I hadn't said that.'

Just like John, the crowd couldn't help themselves; they burst into laughter. They couldn't get enough of The Voice.

EPILOGUE

Jack's Back

Sydney Entertainment Centre
16 December 2015

John Farnham owned this stage. Greats such as Dire Straits and Elton John may have performed many shows here, but the Sydney Entertainment Centre – now officially the Qantas Credit Union Arena – belonged to Farnham. As of 16 December 2015, Farnham had played 77 concerts at the Ent Cent. Staggering. *Guinness Book of Records* stuff.

Certainly some things had changed since Farnham first trod the Entertainment Centre's boards in 1983. His once-golden mane was now close-cropped, showing more scalp than hair, while several inches and a number of clothes sizes had been added amidships. The 1980s-era full-length coat had long been relegated to the back of the wardrobe, along with the leather strides, replaced by a dapper black dinner jacket, sans tie. His look was more gracefully ageing Vegas crooner than middle-aged pop star. Yet John seemed totally cool with the changes that Father Time, and the good life, had wrought upon him. He was comfortable in his own skin – not something that could always be said of him in the past.

EPILOGUE

What hadn't changed one bit was his voice. If anything, he seemed to be singing better than ever, taking songs to places they'd rarely been before, sparring vocally on stage with his four-member mini-choir. John riffed and ad-libbed, twisting lyrics and playing with his inflections, seeing where each song, every note, would lead him. It was remarkable to watch: a master going about his craft. As much as he admired the 'Human Natures' – as he referred to them with a chuckle during the intro to 'Everytime You Cry' – who needed them when you had this band?

The diehard Farnham fan base, which with the passing of time had proved more stable than the Rock of Gibraltar, loved every single minute of it. The audience was a sea of mobile phones, cries of love and wild applause from the moment John strode on stage and launched into 'Age of Reason'. A Farnham concert circa 2015 was pitched somewhere between a Hillsong meeting – but with far better songs – and Elvis in Vegas in the early 1970s. Farnham was singing the soundtrack to the lives of these 12,000 fans – and the millions of other dedicated Farnham lovers – and they responded with the kind of mad love usually reserved for pennant-winning footy teams.

Surprisingly, there were also a lot of under-30s in his audience now, blowing up just as wildly as the over-60 set when he launched into 'You're the Voice' and 'Pressure Down'. Maybe they'd commandeered their parents' music collections: who knows? But it seemed that the words 'Farnham' and 'uncool' had drifted apart over recent years. Even the critics and naysayers had finally come around.

Farnham still had his onstage patter perfected, a willingness to share his inner dag with his devoted fans. He never missed.

EPILOGUE

Miraculously, in a blink he could shift emotional gears seamlessly between a deeply heartfelt ballad such as 'Burn for You' and the kind of aw-shucks, funny-old-world repartee for which he was renowned.

'John is just an amazing singer, completely intuitive,' Lindsay Field once said of his boss and friend. 'He's one of the only guys I know who can be singing from his heart, turn around and crack a joke, and then go straight back into it.' Tonight that gift was on ample display.

Chatting to the audience of 12,000 people as if he'd just bumped into them down the shops, Farnham casually mentioned a significant moment that had occurred before the show: he had been officially handed the hefty sign from the Farnham Room, the Entertainment Centre's Green Room.

'Jilly looked at me and at the sign,' he said, laughing, 'as if to say, "Where are you going to put *that*?"'

He made it seem as though being presented with a chunk of the Sydney Entertainment Centre was a perfectly ordinary occurrence. John not only owned the stage – now he owned a slice of the building.

Even at 66, Farnham could still talk the talk of everyday Australia. He bantered a bit more about the missus, joked about his age ('The band's aggregate doesn't even reach mine') and took cheap shots at his manager; at one point he chastised him for not juicing up his water bottle. ('Bloody Wheatley,' he smirked, as he chugged his H_2O, hoping for something a little stronger.)

And while his set was now peppered with material from *Whispering Jack* and beyond – the standing-ovation-ready closing bracket included 'You're the Voice', 'That's Freedom' and 'Pressure

Down' – he didn't completely disregard his beginnings. His set was barely 15 minutes old when he responded to the first yelled request for 'Sadie'.

'Bugger it,' he laughed, 'you asked for it.'

Then he stopped himself. Something needed to be said.

'You know, I don't hate this song, not at all,' explained John, dispelling a popular myth. 'Sadie's the reason I'm standing here tonight.' Then, after a beat, 'It's just not the best song I've ever recorded.'

With another laugh he began reminiscing in song about the woman with 'red detergent hands', the crowd up and singing along with him.

All of this was evidence, if it was still required, that Farnham's popularity was constant, regardless of his many, many farewells and Last Times. And the lure of performing was too strong. So here he was in 2015, still every inch the singer's singer, a regular guy who took simple pleasure in the thrill that hit him when he opened his mouth and let rip. He'd been doing this now for 50 years; why give up when he was loved with so much fervour, when there was so much goodwill in the air – and when the houses remained very, very full? His audience wasn't going anywhere. Nor was he.

John Farnham was and would always be The Voice.

DISCOGRAPHY

For a comprehensive discography, see www.johnfarnham.info.

ALBUMS

Sadie (1968)
Friday Kind of Monday / Are You Havin' Any Fun? / Turn Around / Painting a Shadow / Pay the Waiter / There's Got to Be a Word / Sadie (The Cleaning Lady) / Woman, Woman / The Old Bazaar in Cairo / Miss Elaine E.S. Jones / Otherwise It's Been a Perfect Day

Everybody Oughta Sing a Song (1968)
Everybody Oughta Sing a Song / Jamie / There Is No Season to My Love / Two-Bit Manchild / The Last Thing on My Mind / Strollin' / Scratchin' Ma Head / I Don't Want to Love You / Confidentially / Rose Coloured Glasses / Grand Unspeakable Passion / Sunday Will Never Be The Same / You Can Write a Song

Looking Through a Tear (1970)
One / I've Been Rained On / Mirror of My Mind / The World Goes Round and Round / All Night Girl / You're Breaking Me Up / Two / Raindrops Keep Fallin' on My Head / Looking Through a Tear / Visions of Sugarplums / What Can I Do / In a Moment of Madness / Ain't Society Great / 1432 Franklin Pike Circle Hero

Christmas Is ... Johnny Farnham (1970)
Santa Claus Is Coming to Town / Christmas Is / The Ringing Reindeer / Little Drummer Boy / Jingle Bells / Good Time Christmas / Everything Is Beautiful / White Christmas / The First Noel / Silent Night / There's No Place Like Home / Little Boy Dear / It Must Be Getting Close to Christmas / Christmas Happy

Johnny (1971)
For Once in My Life / Band of Gold / Stick of Incense / Knock Three Times / Rag Mamma Rag / Take Me to the Pilot / Your Song / Ma Cherie Amour / Something / Summertime / Rose Garden / This Must Be the End

The Best of Johnny Farnham (1971)
I've Been Rained On / Everybody Oughta Sing a Song / Jamie / I Don't Want to Love You / Painting a Shadow / Sadie (The Cleaning Lady) / Raindrops / One / Two / Friday Kind of Monday / The Last Thing on My Mind / Rose Coloured Glasses

Together (with Allison Durbin) (1971)
Baby Without You / The Green Green Grass Is Dying / You're

Alright with Me / Stay Awhile / I Don't Mind the Rain / Singing Our Song / That's Old Fashioned / Come on Round to My Place / Ain't Nothing Like the Real Thing / Nobody Knows / Better Put Your Love Away / Get Together

Johnny Farnham Sings the Shows (1972)
Charlie Girl / With a Little Bit of Luck / Gonna Build a Mountain / I Whistle a Happy Tune / Who Can I Turn To / Hair / Day by Day / My Favourite Occupation / You'll Never Walk Alone / Where Is Love / On The Street Where You Live / Consider Yourself / Hello Dolly / Jubilation T. Cornpone

Hits Magic & Rock 'N Roll (1973)
Everything Is Out of Season / Nobody's Fool / It's Up to You / If You Would Stay / Sweet Cherry Wine / Don't You Know It's Magic / Rock Me Baby / Lucille / Blueberry Hill / Johnny 'B' Goode / Diana / Memphis Tennessee

Johnny Farnham Sings the Big Hits of '73 Live (1973)
I Knew Jesus (Before He Was a Star) / Where Is the Love / Baby Don't Get Hooked on Me / Gilbert O'Sullivan Medley: Alone Again (Naturally) / You Are the Sunshine of My Life / Nothing Rhymed / Tie a Yellow Ribbon / The Morning After / And I Love You So / Free Electric Band

Johnny Farnham Sings Hits from the Movies (1974)
Cabaret / Speak Softly Love / Everybody's Talkin' / The Summer Knows / Carnival / Hi-Lili, Hi-Lo / Raindrops Keep Fallin' on My

Head / The Rain in Spain / Singing in the Rain / Theme From *Love Story* / Where's the Birdie / The First Time Ever I Saw Your Face / Mrs Robinson

J.P. Farnham Sings (1975)
Some People Sing / I Must Stay / Don't Rock the Boat / Till Time Brings Change / Saturday Dance / Most People I Know / Show Me the Way / Running to the Sea / Things to Do / I Can't Fly / To Be or Not to Be / So Many Years

Johnny Farnham's Greatest Hits (1976)
Sadie (The Cleaning Lady) / Underneath the Arches / Friday Kind of Monday / I Don't Want to Love You / Jamie / Rose Coloured Glasses / One / Raindrops Keep Fallin' on My Head / Comic Conversation / Rock Me Baby / Don't You Know It's Magic / Everything Is Out of Season / I Can't Dance to Your Music / Corner of the Sky

Uncovered (1980)
Matilda / She Says to Me / Jillie's Song / Infatuation / On My Own / Back to the Backwoods / I Never Did Get Through / Please Don't Ask Me / She's Everywhere / Help!

The Best of John Farnham (1980)
Raindrops Keep Fallin' on My Head / Comic Conversation / Rock Me Baby / Don't You Know It's Magic / Everything Is Out of Season / I Can't Dance to Your Music / I Saw Mummy Kissing Santa Claus / Things To Do / One / Jamie / Rose Coloured Glasses / Sadie (The Cleaning Lady) / Underneath the Arches / Friday Kind

of Monday / Walking the Floor on My Hands / Acapulco Sun / One Minute Every Hour

The Net (with the Little River Band) (1983)
You're Driving Me out of My Mind / We Two / No More Tears / Mr Socialite / Down on the Border / The Danger Sign / Falling / Sleepless Nights / Easy Money / The Net / One Day

Playing to Win (with the Little River Band) (1985)
Playing to Win / Reappear / Blind Eyes / Through Her Eyes / When Cathedrals Were White / Relentless / Piece of the Dream / Don't Blame Me / One Shot in the Dark / Count Me In

No Reins (with the Little River Band) (1986)
Face in the Crowd / It's Just a Matter of Time / Time for Us / No Reins on Me / When the War Is Over / Thin Ice / How Many Nights / Forever Blue / Paper Paradise / It Was the Night

Whispering Jack (1986)
Pressure Down / You're the Voice / One Step Away / Reasons / Going, Going, Gone / No One Comes Close / Love to Shine / Trouble / A Touch of Paradise / Let Me Out

Age of Reason (1988)
Age of Reason / Blow by Blow / Listen to the Wind / Two Strong Hearts / Burn Down the Night / Beyond the Call / We're No Angels / Don't Tell Me It Can't Be Done / The Fire / Some Do, Some Don't / When The War Is Over / It's A Long Way to the Top

DISCOGRAPHY

Chain Reaction (1990)
That's Freedom / In Days To Come / Burn for You / See The Banners Fall / I Can Do Anything / All Our Sons And Daughters / Chain Reaction / In Your Hands / New Day / The Time Has Come / The First Step / Time and Money

Full House (1991)
When The War Is Over / Age of Reason / Don't You Know It's Magic / Two Strong Hearts / Comic Conversation / Help / Chain Reaction / Burn For You / Reasons / You're the voice / A Touch of Paradise / That's Freedom / One / Playing to Win / Pressure Down / Please Don't Ask Me

Then Again … (1993)
Angels / Seemed Like a Good Idea / Only Women Bleed / Talent for Fame / When All Else Fails / What You Don't Know / Treated This Way / Always The Same / The Reason Why / So Long in Love / It All Comes Back to You / Diamonds / Rolling Home / Talk of the Town

The Classic Gold Collection (1995)
Sadie (The Cleaning Lady) / Underneath the Arches / Friday Kind of Monday / Jamie / Rose Coloured Glasses / One / Raindrops Keep Fallin' on My Head / Comic Conversation / Acapulco Sun / As Long as Life Goes On / Baby Without You / Walking the Floor on My Hands / Rock Me Baby / Don't You Know It's Magic / Everything Is Out of Season / I Can't Dance to Your Music / Shake a Hand / One Minute Every Hour / Things to Do / Please Don't Ask Me / Down on the Border / The Other Guy / Playing to Win

DISCOGRAPHY

Memories of Christmas (1995)
Santa Claus Is Coming to Town / Christmas Is / The Ringing Reindeer / Little Drummer Boy / Jingle Bells / Good Time Christmas / Christmas Happy / White Christmas / The First Noel / Silent Night / There's No Place Like Home / Little Boy Dear / It Must Be Getting Close to Christmas / Everything Is Beautiful

Romeo's Heart (1996)
Have A Little Faith (In Us) / Little Piece of My Heart / A Simple Life / All Kinds of People / Romeo's Heart / Don't Let It End / Hearts on Fire / Hard Promises to Keep / Over My Head / May You Never / Second Skin

Anthology 1: Greatest Hits 1986 – 1997 (1997)
You're the Voice / Pressure Down / A Touch of Paradise / Reasons / Two Strong Hearts / Age of Reason / That's Freedom / Chain Reaction / Burn for You / Seemed Like a Good Idea (At the Time) / Talk of the Town / Angels / Have a Little Faith / A Simple Life / Heart's on Fire / When Something is Wrong with My Baby / Everytime You Cry

Anthology 2: Classic Hits 1967 – 1985 (1997)
Sadie (The Cleaning Lady) / One / Looking Through a Tear / Raindrops Keep Falling on My Head / Comic Conversation / Don't You Know It's Magic / Everything Is Out of Season / Help! / Matilda / Infatuation / That's No Way to Love Someone / Please Don't Ask Me / Playing to Win / Justice for One / When the War Is Over / And I Love Her

Anthology 3: Rarities (1997)
I Feel Fine / Susan Jones / Birthday / Legs / Black Dog / Dream People / Good Company / Take You Back / Love's in Need / You're the Voice / Little Piece of My Heart / Break the Ice / Running for Love / Burn for You / Cool Water / Don't Let It End

Highlights from The Main Event (1998)
Overture / Age of Reason / Phantom of the Opera / Little More Love / Age of Reason / This Is the Moment / Hopelessly Devoted to You / Everytime You Cry / Please Don't Ask Me / You're The One That I Want / Long and Winding Road / Take Me Home, Country Roads / I Honestly Love You / Love Is a Gift / That's Life/ Bad Habits / Granada / You've Lost That Lovin' Feelin' / Summer Nights / If Not for You / Let Me Be There / Raindrops Keep Falling on My Head / Jolene / Hearts on Fire / Don't You Know It's Magic / You're the Voice

Live at the Regent Theatre – 1st July 1999 (1999)
Reasons (Farnham) / One (Farnham) / Everything's Alright (Farnham with Kate Ceberano) / Help! (Kate Ceberano) / A Touch of Paradise (Farnham with Ross Wilson) / Age of Reason (Ross Wilson) / Burn for You (Farnham with Merril Bainbridge) / Raindrops Keep Falling on My Head (Merril Bainbridge) / Chain Reaction (Farnham) / Infatuation (Nana-Zhami) / Don't You Know It's Magic (Farnham with James Reyne) / Comic Conversation (James Reyne) / Who's Lovin' You (Farnham with Human Nature) / Everytime You Cry (Farnham with Human Nature) / That's Freedom (Farnham) / Playing to Win (Farnham) / I Wish (All) / You're the Voice (All)

DISCOGRAPHY

33 1/3 (2000)

That Driving Beat / Trying to Live My Life Without You / You Don't Know Like I Know / Everything Is Gonna Be Alright / Man of the Hour / I've Been Lonely for So Long / That's What Love Will Make You Do / I Can't Get Next to You / You're the Only One / I Thank You / Soul Reason / The Way / Walk Away

The Last Time (2002)

The Last Time / No Ordinary World / Lonely Man / When I Can't Have You / Undeniably Real / Keep Talking / Sometimes / One More Try / Even After All This Time / Eternally

One Voice: The Greatest Hits (2003)

Disc 1: We Will Rock You / That's Freedom / Age of Reason / Pressure Down / Don't You Know It's Magic / A Touch of Paradise / Help! / When Something Is Wrong With My Baby / Chain Reaction / Raindrops Keep Falling on My Head / Sadie (The Cleaning Lady) / A Simple Life / Burn for You / The Last Time

Disc 2: You're the Voice / Two Strong Hearts / Everything's Alright / One / Seemed like a Good Idea (At the Time) / Talk of the Town / Angels / Have A Little Faith (In Us) / Hearts on Fire / Everytime You Cry / Reasons / No Ordinary World / Man of the Hour

John Farnham & Tom Jones Together in Concert (2005)

Mama Told Me Not to Come / 200 Pounds of Heavenly Joy / Man of The Hour / What Am I Living For / It's Not Unusual / Burn for You / Playing to Win / My Yiddishe Momme / You're the Voice /

That Driving Beat / Hold on, I'm Coming / Try A Little Tenderness / What'd I Say / Sweet Soul Music / It's a Long Way to the Top

I Remember When I Was Young (2005)
Come Back Again / Heading in the Right Direction / One Perfect Day / I Remember When I Was Young / Downhearted / Even When I'm Sleeping / Green Limousine / Girls On The Avenue / Forever Now / Reckless / Come Said the Boy / No Aphrodisiac / Overkill

Jack (2010)
Love Chooses You / You Took My Love / Hit The Road Jack – Fever / 247365 / Nobody Gets Me Like You / You Don't Know Me / Love Me Like You Do / Today / I'm the One Who Loves You / Love Comes Knockin' / Sunshine

The Acoustic Chapel Sessions (2011)
CD: Pressure Down / Reasons / Chain Reaction / Playing to Win / You're the Voice / That's Freedom / Two Strong Hearts / Age of Reason / Talk of the Town / A Simple Life / Hearts on Fire

DVD: Talk of the Town / Chain Reaction / Two Strong Hearts / Pressure Down / Hearts on Fire / A Simple Life / Age of Reason / Playing to Win

Two Strong Hearts Live with Olivia Newton-John (2015)
Overture / Two Strong Hearts / Let Me be There / Xanadu / I Honestly Love You / Tenterfield Saddler / No One Comes Close / Love to Shine / Suddenly / Dare to Dream / Somewhere Over the

DISCOGRAPHY

Rainbow / Burn for You / Hit the Road Jack – Fever / You're the One That I Want / Summer Nights / Hearts on Fire / If Not for You / Everytime You Cry / Physical / You're the Voice / It's A Long Way to the Top

ACKNOWLEDGEMENTS

I'll come clean: the idea of documenting the life of John Farnham hadn't truly registered with me until it was proposed by Jeanne Ryckmans at Nero and my agent, Jo Butler, at Cameron Creswell. I have to thank them both enormously, because this led me to discover that John 'Johnny' Farnham, 'Farnesy', the Voice – whatever you choose to call him – is an infinitely more intriguing character than I ever imagined. Essentially, John's is the story of three key relationships: the first with his original manager and relentless booster, the late Darryl Sambell; the second with his wife of 40-and-a-bit years, Jillian, who to this day remains his rock; the third with his manager and close friend, Glenn Wheatley, the man who got John's life and career back on track, and was then repaid a hundredfold. All played key roles in forming the man that, miraculously, is even more popular in 2016, 50 years into his career, than when he first walked off a Melbourne building site singing a valentine to dear old Sadie. You can't say that about any of John's peers; he's a music industry phenomenon.

ACKNOWLEDGEMENTS

John is a not a man known for public reflection; he prefers to let his music and his achievements speak for themselves. (A Farnham memoir is not very likely. Fair enough, too.) So this became the type of project I truly love, one of deep research and informed writing: an attempt to tell this man's story as intimately and truthfully – and engagingly – as possible, despite not having access to John himself. For helping me dig deep, I have to thank Simon Drake at the National Film and Sound Archive, an ever-reliable source of advice and assistance, among many others. Just as important for my research was my memory – it's amazing what I've been able to store away from my own Farnham-watching, both as punter and music chronicler, over the past six decades. It really says something about the man's ubiquity. Find me a born-and-bred Australian who doesn't recognise the name John Farnham and you'd best check their passport.

Even more crucial to the book was the guidance and support provided by Lyn Albury at the excellent Jack's Place website (www.johnfarnhaminfo.com) and John's manager, Glenn Wheatley, who helped enormously with the manuscript. I'd highly recommend Glenn's two memoirs, *Paper Paradise* and *Facing the Music*; they're sometimes funny, always insightful and occasionally heartbreaking stories of a life immersed in the Australian music scene. Someone should make a movie, documentary or mini-series about the man; he's been there and back.

Other incredibly helpful guides were Clark Forbes' book *Whispering Jack*, Noel McGrath's *Australian Encyclopedia of Rock*, Ian McFarlane's *The Encyclopedia of Australian Rock and Pop* and David Kent's *Australian Chart Book 1970–1992*. I trust I've kept those eagle-eyed Farnham spotters satisfied with the reliability of

ACKNOWLEDGEMENTS

my facts and figures. Even more crucially, I hope I've retold John's story with all the energy, drama and humour that it warrants. That, to me, is the key.

I'd also like to thank Jo Rosenberg, Kirstie Innes-Will, Kelly Fagan and Siân Scott-Clash at Black Inc.; this book just wouldn't be the same without the help and support of each and every one of you. I hope it's the beginning of a great relationship. Glenn A. Baker and David Anderson were also very helpful.

Closer to home, a hefty shout-out goes to my children, Christian and Elizabeth, my wife, Diana, and especially my mother, Jean, who frequently reminds me that I'm a lucky man living a fortunate life.

BIBLIOGRAPHY

PRINT

'At Last, Excellent Australian Variety', *The Age*, 25 July 1974.

'Bubble and Fizz Before Work', *The Age*, 25 October 1973.

'Farnham Rings Glenn Wheatley on Home Detention', *Daily Telegraph*, 19 May 2008.

'Farnham Looks at Dark Side', *The Age*, 27 January 1988.

'Farnham Storms St Kilda's Espy', *The Age*, 7 October 2002.

'John Farnham: My Turning Point', *New Idea*, July 1999.

'Murky Melbourne's Own Sherlock', *The Age*, 25 July 1975.

'Muscovites Have Whale of a Time', *Financial Times* (London), 7 March 1989.

'Rhythms: A Guide to Rock, Jazz, Folk, Country and Acoustic Gigs This Week', *The Age*, 31 October 1986.

'Sadie, Gold Record Lady', *Sydney Morning Herald*, 11 February 1968.

'Singer asks for $30,000', *The Age*, 12 June 1969.

Cameron Adams, 'Australia's Favourite Voice John Farnham Returns ... Again', *Herald Sun*, 15 January 2015.

Jeff Apter, *Chasing the Dragon: The Life and Death of Marc Hunter*, Hardie Grant, 2010.

Jeff Apter, *Shirl: The Life of Legendary Larrikin Graeme 'Shirley' Strachan*, Hardie Grant, 2012.

Jeff Apter, *Tragedy: The Sad Ballad of the Gibb Brothers*, Five Mile Press, 2015.

Jeff Apter, *Up from Down Under: How Australian Music Changed the World*, Five Mile Press, 2013.

Thomas K. Arnold, 'Talent in Action', *Billboard*, 22 June 1985.

Anushka Asthana, 'Dagenham's Heyday: "It Was All Just One Big Happy Family Then"', *The Guardian*, 21 March 2010.

Glenn A Baker, *The Australian Magazine*, 15 – 16 April 1989.

Fred Bokelmann, 'I Want To Be Able To Go Into My Garden Wearing Nothing But My Underwear', *BILD-Zeitung*, 10 August 1998.

Ross Brundrett, 'Trio Set for Main Event', *Herald Sun*, 22 October 1998.

Michelle Burke, 'I Can't Believe He's 50 – Whispering Jack's Private Bash', *Woman's Day*, 19 July 1999.

Peter Cochrane, 'Harry M Put his Faith in Farnham', *Sydney Morning Herald*, 6 October 1992.

Max Cooper, 'TV Legend Don Lane Dead', *Sydney Morning Herald*, 22 October 2009.

Frank Crook, 'Johnny Says I'm Sorry', *TV Week*, 7 March 1970.

Frank Crook, Show Business: Australian Style, *TV Week*, undated.

Wayne Croskell, 'Johnny Farnham Show Dragged', *The Age*, 16 April 1969.

Mike Daly, 'New Notes', *The Sydney Morning Herald*, 18 September 1980.

BIBLIOGRAPHY

Mike Daly, 'New Notes', *The Age*, 4 August 1988

Peter Dean, 'John Farnham Takes New Directions', *The Australian Women's Weekly*, 15 October 1980.

Madeleine d'Haeye, 'On The Record', *Sydney Morning Herald*, 17 August 1980.

Bruce Elder, 'Nonsensical Nostalgia', *Sydney Morning Herald*, 5 August 1992.

Christie Eliezer, 'BMG's John Farnham Enjoys Status Down Under', *Billboard*, 28 September 1996.

Darrin Farrant, 'The Main Event – There's No Room for Egos on This Stage', *The Age*, 29 October 1998.

Michelle Finkle, 'The Voice Mellows', *The Australian Women's Weekly*, June 1999.

Clark Forbes, *Whispering Jack: The John Farnham Story*, Hutchinson Australia, 1989.

Robert Forster, 'Scream – The Glory and the Madness of Being a 60s and 70s Australian Pop Singer', *The Monthly*, December 2010.

Jane Freeman, 'Toothsome Threesome Put Best Foot Forward', *Sydney Morning Herald*, 16 October 1998.

Lee Glendinning, 'You're the Voice and We Understand It', *Sydney Morning Herald*, 4 December 2002.

Peter Groves, 'Farnham Rocks and Rolls Like Thunder', *Sydney Morning Herald*, 3 March 1981.

Peter Hackett, 'The Voice Still Roars at 50', *The Advertiser*, 3 July 1999.

Helen Hawks, 'The Gospel According to John', *Sun-Herald*, 6 April 1996.

Sarah Hudson, 'Review', *Herald Sun*, 15 June 1999.

David Kent, *Australian Chart Book 1970–1992*, Australian Chart Book, 1992.

Paula Kruger, 'Farnham Pulled from ANZAC Commemorations', ABC Online, 17 February 2005.

Bert Lillye, 'Down the Line', *Sydney Morning Herald*, 24 August 1975.

Ross MacDowell, *Inside Story: 20 Famous Australians tell their Story*, Hobson Dell, 2001.

Fergus Maguire, Farnham Hits the Big 50, Still Rockin' After All These Years', *The Age*, 14 June 1999.

John Mangan, 'John Farnham Takes a Walk on the Mild Side', *The Age*, 20 October 1993.

Patrick McDonald, 'Perfect Harmony in the Main Event', *The Advertiser*, 3 December 1998.

Ian McFarlane, *The Encyclopedia of Australian Rock and Pop*, Allen & Unwin, 1999.

Noel McGrath, *Australian Encyclopedia of Rock*, Outback Press, 1978.

George Moore, 'Moore on Pop', *The Australian Women's Weekly*, 22 September 1982.

Phil Moore, 'Move Over Roy Rogers: Farnsie Feels a Bit Horse', *People*, 1993.

Shaunagh O'Connor, 'Hopelessly Devoted ...', *Herald Sun*, 29 October 1998.

Anthony O'Grady, 'The Resurrection of John Farnham', *Sydney Morning Herald*, 20 February 1987.

Kay O'Sullivan, 'Farnham Hits High Notes with Key to the City', *Herald Sun*, 15 June 1999.

Michael Owen, 'Review: The Main Event', *The Sunday Mail*, 30 November 1998.

BIBLIOGRAPHY

George Palathingal, 'Tom Jones and John Farnham Review', *Sydney Morning Herald*, 14 February 2005.

Dale Plummer, 'New TV Series for Farnham', *Sydney Morning Herald*, 27 June 1976.

Geoff Roach, 'Why We Love You, John', *The Advertiser*, 3 July 1999.

Jim Schembri, 'The Rise and Rise of John "Voice" Farnham', *The Age*, 11 March 1994.

Larry Schwartz, '10 Things You Didn't Know about John Farnham', *The Age*, 16 October 1993.

Iain Shedden, 'Voice Raised in Anger at Games March Boss', *The Australian*, 24 June 1999.

Garry Shelley, 'John Farnham Veteran at 31', *Sydney Morning Herald*, 3 March 1980.

Aneela Simone, 'Reunited with Denmark after 10 Years', *SE & HOR* (Denmark), undated.

David Sly, 'John Parties, with a Little Help from His Friends', *The Advertiser*, 12 June 1999.

Margaret Smith, 'They've Trodden the Boards for 50 Years', *Sydney Morning Herald*, 1 September 1974.

Katrina Strickland, 'Farnham at 50 … He's Mollyfied', *Herald Sun*, 14 April 1999.

Andrew Taylor, 'Farnham on ASIO's Radar for Tent Embassy Support', *Sydney Morning Herald*, 18 March 2012.

Carolyn Webb, 'A Mouthpiece for The Voice', *The Age*, 15 November 2000.

Lana Wells, 'John Farnham: What's He Really Like?' *The Australian Women's Weekly*, 28 February 1979.

Glenn Wheatley, *Paper Paradise: Confessions of a Rock and Roll Survivor*, Bantam 1999.

Glenn Wheatley, *Facing the Music*, Hardie Grant, 2010.

Richard Wilkins, 'John Farnham Talks about Fame, Fortune, Fatherhood and the Big Five O', *TV Week*, 17 July 1999.

Kim Wilson and Simon Plant, 'Singers Tune up for Knockout Main Event', *Herald Sun*, 24 October 1998.

Bernard Zuel, 'The Battle for a Nation's Soul', *Sydney Morning Herald*, 30 November 2000.

TV

ABC TV, 'The Making of a Pop Star', *Four Corners*, 1968.

Channel 9, *Jacks' Back*, TV special, 1987.

WEB

'John Farnham Hits at Tax Probe on Glenn Wheatley', news.com.au, 19 June 2011.

Greg Jennett, 'John Howard Embarks on Goodwill Mission to New Zealand', ABC Online, 21 February 2005.

Kathy McCabe, 'John Farnham Reveals He Prank Called Fans', news.com.au, 27 November 2015.

Farnham comments on his Little River Band days: www.youtube.com/watch?v=f25a24u7UFA

Farnham with Little River Band: www.graehamgoble.com/clips-farnham

Hans Poulsen: www.milesago.com/artists/poulsen.htm

Hair: The American Tribal Love-Rock: www.milesago.com/stage/hair.htm.

BIBLIOGRAPHY

Jack's Place: www.johnfarnhaminfo.com.

The Last Time Tour documentary: www.youtube.com/watch?v=deFMqi17PbU.

Little River Band shows: www.graehamgoble.com/shows-lrb

Little River Band clips: www.graehamgoble.com/clips-lrb

Live by Demand media conference 2009: www.youtube.com/watch?v=oEoMdK725rM